The Health For Life

TRAINING ADVISOR

Edited by
Andrew T. Shields, M.D.

Also by Health For Life:

- **Legendary Abs II**

- **Beyond Legendary Abs**
  A synergistic performance guide to Legendary Abs II and SynerAbs

- **Power ForeArms!**

- **T.N.T.—Total Neck & Traps**

- **Maximum Calves**

- **The Human Fuel Handbook**
  Nutrition for Peak Athletic Performance

- **SynerShape:** A Scientific Weight Loss Guide

- **SynerStretch:** For Whole Body Flexibility

- **Minimizing Reflex and Reaction Time**

- **Amino Acids and other Ergogenic Aids**

- **Secrets of Advanced Bodybuilders**
  A manual of synergistic weight training for the whole body

- **Secrets of Advanced Bodybuilders:** *Supplement #1*

ISBN 0-944831-22-2
Library of Congress Catalog Card Number: 90-80312

Health For Life
8033 Sunset Blvd., Suite 483 — Los Angeles, CA 90046 — (213) 306-0777

9 8 7 6 5 4 3 2 1

CONTENTS

TABLE OF CONTENTS

INTRODUCTION

In recent years, scientists have generated enormous amounts of new data vital to the serious athlete— information that can significantly improve both your training and performance. Unfortunately, most of this information gets no further than the sports science journals, where it often sits unread, unused, and unapplied.

Did you know, for instance, that a single 20-second rep of isometric stretching is just as effective as the usually recommended 6 reps, which take over 2 minutes? Or that most so-called ergogenic aids are completely useless—except for one which produces immediate and significant improvements for a wide variety of athletes? Or that using knee braces during contact sports such as football increases your risk of knee injury?

These and hundreds of similar findings lie buried in the stacks of the bio-med libraries. *The problem: how to get this information off the shelves and into the gyms.*

The solution: **The Health For Life Training Advisor.**

The Training Advisor bridges the gap between the theoretical and the practical; it puts you directly in touch with the latest in sports science research. In an era where "the edge" may be a matter of millimeters or milliseconds, **The Training Advisor** gives you that edge!

The Training Advisor contains eight chapters that serve as broad headings under which to organize the research from recent years: *Training, Physiology, Health, Injury, Nutrition, Drugs, Supplements,* and *Equipment.*

Each chapter contains a series of highly specific articles, each reporting the results of one or more studies on a particular topic (such as the best speed for repetitions during strength training, or how long to hold PNF stretches for maximum benefit).

Articles are self-contained—you don't need to read them in any particular order to understand them. We recommend you browse through the book to familiarize yourself with what's in it. Then, when a question comes up during training, refer to the relevant articles for specific advice on applicable techniques.

No matter what your sport or experience, this easy-access reference to the latest sports science research will greatly enhance your technical knowledge and above all, sharpen your competitive edge!

❖ ❖ ❖

TRAINING

Our understanding of the relationship between training and performance has increased dramatically in recent decades. This chapter reports on a number of investigations into training techniques that affect strength, reaction time, flexibility, aerobic fitness, and many other factors contributing to optimum performance.

DETERMINING YOUR AEROBIC FITNESS

Aerobic fitness can be measured. The results can be used to evaluate an athlete's current level of fitness, the improvement over time, and the effectiveness of an athletic program.

The best measure of aerobic fitness and cardiovascular endurance is **VO₂ max.** VO₂ max indicates how quickly your muscles use oxygen at peak exertion. The greater your fitness, the more oxygen your muscles can use, and the higher your VO₂ max.

Determining VO₂ max usually requires a treadmill, respiratory hoses, and expensive analytical equipment. However, investigators at the U.S. Army Research Institute of Environmental Medicine have recently developed a way of determining VO₂ max with only one piece of equipment: a stopwatch.

The method involves some simple calculations, based on times for an all-out two mile run. The equations:

Men: Predicted VO_2 max = 110.9 - (2.79 x 2mi time) - (0.25 x wt)

Women: Predicted VO_2 max = 72.9 - (1.77 x 2 mi time)

Two mile run time (2 mi time) must be in fractional minutes, and weight must be in kilograms (see box on next page for converting to fractional minutes and kilograms). The units on VO_2 max are ml/kg/min (milliliters of oxygen consumed per kilogram of body weight per minute).

The researchers measured physical variables such as height, weight, and percentage body fat to see if including these factors might improve the predictive power of the equations. The incorporation of weight improved the predictive power of the equation in men, but not in women. None of the other factors made a significant difference.

There are some limitations to these equations. The equations were derived using data from men aged 20 to 51, and women aged 20 to 39. About a third of the participants were sedentary, the rest were recreational joggers. The equations are therefore most applicable to athletes most like those studied, and probably less applicable to more elite athletes.

AVERAGE MAXIMAL OXYGEN UPTAKES (VO₂ MAX*) OF TEAM NATIONAL ATHLETES

EVENT	MEN	WOMEN
Cross-Country Skiing	82	63
Running 3000 meters (appr. 2 mi.)	79	—
Speed Skating	78	54
Orienteering	77	59
Running 800-1500 meters	75	—
Bicycling	74	—
Biathlon	73	—
Walking	71	—
Canoeing	70	—
Downhill Skiing	68	51
Running 400 meters	67	56
Swimming	66	57
Ski Jumping	62	—
Rowing	62	—
Gymnastics	60	—
Table Tennis	58	44
Fencing	58	43
Wrestling	56	—
Weight Lifting	55	—
Archery	—	40
Untrained	43	39

*ml/kg/min

Maximal Oxygen Uptake in Athletes
B. Saltin & P. Astrand
Journal of Applied Physiology
V 23 # 3: 353-358, Sept 1967

Furthermore, this test has a built-in bias toward runners. An experienced swimmer may be just as fit as an experienced runner, but the runner would probably turn in a much better time in the two mile run. Turning in a better time will make

CALCULATING
TOTAL OXYGEN CONSUMPTION

Let's say a 165 pound man runs an all-out 2 mile run in 13:42 (13 minutes, 42 seconds).

To be entered into the equation, his weight must be in kilograms and his time must be in minutes (not minutes and seconds). Using conversion formulae (see below), we get the following values:

- weight (in kilograms): 75 kg
- all-out 2 mile run time: 13.7 minutes

Remember, the equation is...

Predicted VO$_2$ max = 110.9 - (2.79 x 2 mile run time) - (0.25 x weight)

Plugging in his weight and time values, we get...

Predicted VO2 max = 110.9 - (2.79 x 13.7) - (0.25 x 75)
= 110.9 - (38.2) - (18.8)
*= **53.9 ml/kg/min***

Comparing this value to the chart on page 5, he has a VO$_2$ max similar to that of Team National Weightlifters.

CONVERSION FORMULAE

To convert from pounds to kilograms, divide by 2.2.

Example: *To convert 165 pound to kilograms: 165 lbs / 2.2 = **75 kg.***

To convert from minutes and seconds to fractional minutes, divide number of seconds by 60.

Example: *To convert 13 minutes, 42 seconds into fractional minutes:*
Divide number of seconds by 60: 42 sec. / 60 = 0.70 minutes
*13 min. 42 sec. = **13.70 minutes***

the runner *appear* to be more fit, even though there is no difference in fitness. However, this criticism is not limited to this study. VO2 max determined with a treadmill, respiratory hoses, and expensive analytical equipment shows the same bias toward runners. (If done with cycling machines, it would show a similar bias toward cyclists.)

Nonetheless, these equations are a simple, reasonably accurate way of determining VO2 max. By tracking your VO2 max, you can follow your aerobic fitness and fine-tune your workout for peak performance. ❑

Relationship Between a Two Mile Run For Time and Maximal Oxygen Uptake
R. Mello, M. Murphy, and J. Vogel
Journal of Applied Sport Science Research
V 2 # 1:9-12, Feb 1988

WARM-UP TECHNIQUE FOR EXERCISE AND COMPETITION

The warm-up occupies a time-honored position in the workout of most athletes. Few athletes would consider going for a personal best, or even starting their daily workout, without spending at least a few minutes in physical preparation immediately beforehand.

Although few studies have looked into the benefits of warming up, most coaches, athletes, and sports medicine professionals are of the opinion that warming up improves performance while decreasing risk of injury.

The primary goal of warming up is literally *warming up*—increasing body temperature. This is best done gradually, and involves a progressive stimulation of the cardiovascular system and the target muscles. Stimulating the cardiovascular system increases blood flow to the muscles. Working the target muscles produces heat from friction in the sliding muscle filaments; this heat is what ultimately raises body temperature.

The muscles should be warmed up gradually; the heart should be warmed up gradually, too. In one study, two groups of athletes ran on a treadmill at moderate intensity. One group warmed up with two minutes of easy jogging; the other group didn't warm up at all. In the group that didn't warm up, 30% of the subjects showed abnormal heart tracings at the end of the run. In the group that did warm up, heart tracing abnormalities were eliminated or reduced. This suggests that the heart needs warming up, and that warming up the heart can be accomplished fairly easily.

Appropriate warm-up involves more than just a few toe-touches before an event. A proper warm-up is divided into three phases:

- general warm-up
- flexibility
- sport-specific activities

General Warm-up

The general warm-up should raise the athlete's core body temperature by one to two degrees Celcius (1.4 to 2.8°F). This is the temperature rise necessary to bring on a light to moderate sweat. Examples of good activities for the general warm-up are light jogging, calesthenics, and bicycling—or any activity that involves use of large muscle groups. Other "warm up" methods of raising the body temperature, such as heating pads, massage, and sauna, are not nearly as effective as light physical activity.

As athletes improve their physical shape, their thermo-regulatory systems become more efficient. Therefore, well-conditioned athletes need longer and more intense general warm-ups to raise their body temperatures to appropriate levels.

Flexibility

Once the general warm-up has been completed, the muscles are warmer and more elastic. Consequently, after the general warm-up should come the flexibility work.

Athletes who stretch seem to suffer fewer injuries. In one study, a researcher was able to predict with 93% accuracy who in a group of elite swimmers would suffer shoulder injuries. He made his predictions based on shoulder flexibility, with a strong correlation between lack of flexibility and soft-tissue shoulder injury. Other researchers have noted decreased injuries among professional basketball players who began flexibility programs, and decreased muscle soreness among other athletes who stretch.

Most athletes realize the importance of stretching, but few actually take the time to stretch properly. Often, if an athlete is late to a workout or otherwise pressed for time, he or she skips stretching in favor of other practice activities. Even among those who claim they consistently stretch, few actually do. In one study of varsity tennis players, only 30% of men and 58% of women stretched before a workout. Many of those who did stretch neglected some important areas, and many who stretched before a workout did not stretch after.

There are three kinds of stretching: **static, ballistic,** and **proprioceptive neuromuscular facilitation (PNF).** Regardless of which kind is used, the athlete should do some general warm-up first. Stretching should include all major muscle groups, but you should pay particular attention to the areas that will be undergoing the greatest stress.

Static stretching refers to stretching done by slowly and steadily bending at a joint to put tension on a muscle group. An example might be slowly bending over to touch your toes. Static stretching should be the first kind of stretching done during the flexibility section of the warm-up, because it produces less tension and resistance in the soft tissues than the other forms of stretching. As a result, static stretching is least likely to cause injury.

Static stretching should be done as a slow, controlled movement, producing tension but not pain. The muscles being stretched should be relaxed. Some controversy surrounds how long a stretch should be held. Some researchers say 30-60 seconds; more recent research on the hamstrings indicates that 15 seconds may be sufficient. Whether the 15 seconds that may be sufficient for the hamstrings is also sufficient for other muscle groups is unclear. The effects of stretching may last for up to three hours, as long as the body temperature stays elevated through other forms of exercise.

Ballistic stretching refers to stretching done by quickly bending at a joint, relying on the limitations of muscle, joint, and ligament flexibility to stop the stretch. An example of ballistic stretching is bending over to touch your toes, repeatedly bouncing to put tension on the hamstrings. Another common ballistic stretch is the side twist, in which a wooden pole is held behind the neck and the torso is rotated sharply from one side to the other.

Although ballistic stretches are more likely to cause injury than static stretches, they can have a place in the flexibility phase of the warm-up. When done as the first flexibility activity, ballistic stretching can cause overstretching, resulting in damage to muscles and tendons. Therefore, ballistic stretches should not be done as the first flexibility activity. Once you've warmed up with static stretches, however, carefully done ballistic stretches can be done safely.

Why do ballistic stretches at all? As it turns out, most sports activities are a series of ballistic movements. Carefully warming up with some ballistic stretches can help prepare those muscles that will be undergoing ballistic stretches once the warm-up is over and the game begins.

Proprioceptive neuromuscular facilitation (PNF) is the most effective form of flexibility work. PNF refers to any of several stretching techniques in which a muscle group is passively stretched, then contracts against resistance while in the stretched position. The most common PNF techniques are the **hold-relax**, the **antagonist-contraction-relax**, and the **slow-reversal-hold-relax** techniques.

For example, a PNF hold-relax stretch for the hamstrings could be done as follows. With you standing, a partner passively raises your right leg as high as is comfortable for you and holds it, stretching your right hamstring. You then try to bring your right leg back down again, but your partner holds it up in the stretched position. Thus you are contracting the muscle in a stretched position. After 3 to 6 seconds of contracting, you relax the right hamstring, and your partner passively stretches it a bit more.

PNF stretching can result in dramatic increases in flexibility in a short period of time. It is a worthwhile technique for all athletes, but especially for those requiring extreme flexibility, such as martial artists, gymnasts, figure skaters, high jumpers, dancers, and so on.

The disadvantage of PNF stretching is that it requires a partner familiar with the technique. Done properly, it has little risk of injury; done improperly, it has a greater risk of injury than the other stretching techniques.

Stretching should be done not only before a workout, but after as well. Muscle tightness commonly follows athletic activity, and can last for two to three days. Stretching after a workout can eliminate this tightness.

The final phase of the warm-up involves rehearsing specific movements that the athlete will be using during the practice or the event, but at reduced intensity. Sport-specific activities improve coordination, balance, strength, and response time, and may reduce risk of injury.

Some researchers recommend a ten-minute rest period at the end of the warm-up, during which the athlete may do some visualization exercises and get psyched up.

Warming up seems to have not only physical but psychological benefits as well. Athletes who have not warmed up but have been hypnotized into thinking they have perform better than when they are not warmed up and have not been hypnotized. Conversely, athletes who have been hypnotized into forgetting they had warmed up do no better. This suggests there are strong psychological benefits that go beyond the physical benefits, perhaps involving anxiety reduction.

Warming up can do more than just loosen stiff muscles; it can actually improve performance. Athletes familiar with all the benefits of warming up are probably more likely to take the time to warm up properly. ❑

Sport-specific Activities

Warm-Up Techniques and their Place in Patient Education
R. Stalker MD
Canadian Family Physician
V 34: 177-181, Jan 1988

Hundred-yard dash, long jump, pole vault—these and many other athletic events involve repeated bouts of maximal or near-maximal exertion separated by rests. One result of the exertion is the production of **lactic acid**, a by-product of muscle metabolism that interferes with energy production and muscle performance. Lactic acid is probably what makes your muscles "burn" after a heavy muscular effort.

Since lactic acid interferes with optimum performance, rapid removal of lactic acid between events may enhance performance of the next event. What is the best way to recover (eliminate lactic acid) between events?

To obtain an answer, six subjects, five male and one female, were each run on a treadmill to voluntary exhaustion on three separate occasions. After running, on one of those occasions, each subject lay down with legs slightly elevated for twenty minutes. On another occasion, each subject sat upright for twenty minutes. On a third occasion, each subject stayed on the treadmill for an additional twenty minutes but at a lowered intensity.

Each subject's heart rate, V0$_2$ uptake (rate of oxygen consumption, a measure of aerobic exertion), and lactic acid level were monitored during exercise and recovery periods.

Results showed that twenty minutes of sitting or lying promoted almost identical levels of recovery. However, twenty minutes of light running resulted in a significant improvement in recovery over the other two methods.

This suggests that light "warm down" exercise immediately following maximal exertion is a better way of clearing lactic acid from the blood than complete rest. This is particularly important if you are doing a series of events. So when the coach said, "Walk it off," she was right! ❑

Supine Rest and Lactic Acid Removal Following Maximal Exercise
Ronald Bulbulian et al.
Journal of Sports Medicine
V 27: 151-156, June 1987

CLEARING LACTIC ACID FOLLOWING EXERCISE

OVERTRAINING

Athletic improvement requires more than just routine training. It requires progressive *increases* in training, or **overloading.** If an athlete fails to overload, he or she stops making gains.

For example, running at the same intensity and duration three times a week for three months produces an increase in maximum aerobic capacity of about 10% to 20%. At that point, you reach a plateau: unless there is an increase in training stimulus, no further gains will result. However, running at a steadily *increasing* workout intensity and duration produces an increase in maximum aerobic capacity of 44% over the same three months. After that, continued workout increases result in continued gains, with no plateau.

Overloading is probably necessary for peak performance in elite athletes. However, it can also lead to **overtraining** (also called **staleness, overfatigue**, or **overstrain**).

Overtraining refers to a state in which the athlete is unable to perform or train at previous levels. It is poorly understood, but appears to be associated with emotional, behavioral, physical, biochemical, and performance changes. Symptoms include chronic fatigue, appetite disorders, insomnia, weight loss or gain, muscle soreness, anemia, depression, and worsened athletic performance.

Overtraining is a direct consequence of overloading. Overloading turns to overtraining when workout intensity, duration, or frequency is excessive, and the athlete is unable to recover from one workout before doing the next one. When the physical stress and fatigue of insufficient recovery occurs repeatedly, chronic fatigue sets in, and performance and training intensity suffer.

Overtraining is common: 64% of elite female runners and 66% of elite male runners report having experienced overtraining at some point in their athletic careers.

The best treatment for overtraining is rest, or at least a sharp reduction in training. However, it is much better to prevent overtraining to begin with.

Is it possible to receive the performance-improving benefits of overloading, while preventing the performance-robbing effects of overtraining? There is increasing evidence that this may indeed be possible, but it depends on being able to identify when the athlete is beginning to overtrain. Several indicators have been found which help to identify overtraining.

The best-known indicator of overtraining is an increase in resting heart rate. Trained aerobic athletes characteristically have resting heart rates well below average. This is generally thought to reflect their better-than-average cardiovascular fitness. Elite endurance runners, for instance, often have resting heart rates below 50 beats per minute—so-called **athletic bradycardia.**

When a long-distance runner overtrains, morning heart rate increases. Why this happens is not known, but it may be due, in part, to intrinsic myocardial fatigue (fatigue of the heart muscle itself).

In a study of 12 long-distance runners who doubled their training mileage overnight (presumably leaving insufficient time for recovery), morning heart rates increased by an average of 10 beats per minute after two-and-a-half weeks. However, morning heart rates *decreased* for the first week. Thus, although the increased morning heart rate did reflect their overtraining, it did so rather late in the game. Two other signs of overtraining—persistent muscle soreness and an increase in serum creatine kinase—also developed in these runners, but much earlier than the elevated heart rate.

Morning heart rate has been studied as an indicator of overtraining for long-distance running, but really has not been well-studied for other sports (although anecdotal evidence exists). Many athletes in sports other than distance running monitor their morning heart rates anyway. This practice is probably more applicable to athletes in other aerobic events, such as distance swimming and cycling, than to athletes in anaerobic strength events, such as weightlifting. Definitive evidence for morning heart rate as a means of identifying overtraining in other sports is still pending.

In some overtrained athletes, heart rate recovery is slowed. Instead of returning to baseline after a few minutes, heart rate recovery might take up to two hours.

Other physical changes, such as temperature and blood pressure, are not reliably associated with overtraining.

Resting Heart Rate

There is some evidence to suggest that overtraining causes a shift in blood levels of certain hormones. For example, overtrained athletes have been shown to have elevated cortisol levels (cortisol is a stress-related hormone released by the adrenal glands).

Hormonal Changes

Overtraining also causes a shift in hormonal responses. Overtrained athletes show impaired growth hormone, adrenocorticotropic hormone, cortisol, and prolactin responses to insulin. This suggests that overtraining alters hypothalamic function and possibly pituitary function as well.

Some researchers have recommended that monitoring hormone responses might be a way of diagnosing overtraining and following recovery.

Enzymatic Changes

Creatine kinase (CK) is a muscle tissue enzyme. Serum levels are usually low, but if muscle tissue is damaged, large amounts of CK can be released into the bloodstream from the damaged tissue. Exercise can damage muscle tissue, and this damage is reflected in serum CK levels. For example, after a marathon serum CK levels can reach 20 times normal.

Long-distance runners routinely have serum CK levels above normal, reflecting the repeated tissue damage they subject their muscles to.

The long-distance runners who doubled their training load overnight showed CK levels four times higher than their usual high levels. CK returned to baseline after two days of rest but rose again when the doubled training regimen was resumed.

This suggests that substantially elevated serum CK levels, especially if combined with muscle soreness, might be a fairly sensitive indicator of overtraining.

Psychological Changes

Another way of diagnosing overtraining involves following psychological changes in the athlete.

Researchers at the Sport Psychology Laboratory of the University of Wisconsin-Madison have been following psychological data on athletes for ten years. These investigators pooled data from studies on about 400 men and women, all of whom were college-level competitive swimmers.

Each swimmer was given a standardized Profile of Mood States (POMS) several times during the season. The POMS is a test containing 65 items, and gives a measure of six psychological factors: tension, depression, anger, vigor, fatigue, and confusion. Scores on each of these six factors are combined to give an index score, reflecting the athlete's overall psychological state.

For these swimmers, training intensity varied through the course of a season, typically ranging from a low of about 3,000 yards/day at the beginning of the season (September) to a peak of about 11,000 yards/day nearing the end of the season (January). Intensity was tapered to about 5,000 yards/day just prior to conference championships (February).

The greatest degree of mood disturbances, as reflected in POMS scores, occurred in January following the most intense period of training. Swimmers trained twice a day during this period, and upwards of 10% experienced overtraining.

Those showing signs of overtraining were referred for psychiatric and psychologic evaluation and counseling, and about 80% were found to be suffering from clinically significant depression. Symptoms included physiologic and psychomotor retardation, chronic fatigue, depressed appetite, weight loss, insomnia, decreased libido, muscle soreness, and elevated depression and tension.

When training load was dropped slightly for the women's team one December in preparation for a dual meet, both mood states and performances improved. Thus mood states and performances respond even to slight changes in training load.

These mood state disturbances are not attributable to other college stressors (academic, financial, or social). A group of non-athletes was given the POMS, and their scores remained constant throughout the semester. Interestingly, the athletes showed better mood states than the non-athletes at the beginning of the semester, comparable mood states at the middle of the semester, and significantly worse mood states near the end of the semester when training was at its most intense.

Nor is the relationship between psychological state and overtraining peculiar to swimming. Forty members of the University of Wisconsin-Madison Wrestling Team were given the POMS evaluation several times over the course of a season. Results paralleled that of the swimmers: psychological state showed greatest disturbance during the most intense training period, and improved as training intensity tapered toward the end of the season.

The Iceberg Profile

The six factors addressed in the POMS consist of five negative factors (tension, depression, anger, fatigue, confusion) and one positive factor (vigor). Elite athletes and other

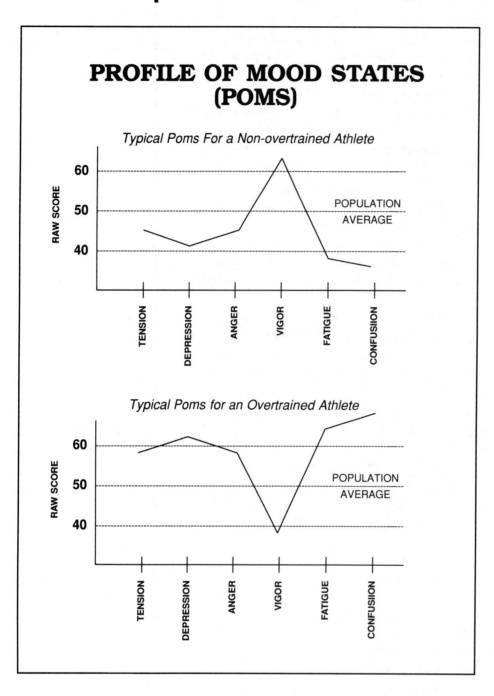

PROFILE OF MOOD STATES (POMS)

Typical Poms For a Non-overtrained Athlete

RAW SCORE

60

50 — POPULATION
AVERAGE

40

TENSION DEPRESSION ANGER VIGOR FATIGUE CONFUSIION

Typical Poms for an Overtrained Athlete

RAW SCORE

60

50 — POPULATION
AVERAGE

40

TENSION DEPRESSION ANGER VIGOR FATIGUE CONFUSIION

active people generally score below average on the negative factors, and above average on the positive factor. In other words, their scores reflect below average tension, depression, anger, fatigue, and confusion, and above average vigor. A graph of these findings produces a picture that looks a bit like an iceberg (top figure on previous page).

If overtraining sets in, however, the picture changes: athletes typically report *above* average tension, depression, anger, fatigue, and confusion, and *below* average vigor. The result looks like an inverted iceberg (bottom figure on previous page).

There is probably a point, just as the athlete begins to overtrain, when the iceberg begins to invert. If that point can be caught and workouts modified, overtraining might be prevented.

It must be noted that there is considerable individual variation in mood states. Some athletes readily lapse into overtraining; others seem to be resistant. Psychological profiles such as the Profile of Mood States can help to identify susceptible athletes.

If an athlete does experience overtraining, ideally his or her workout should be individually tailored to provide a gradual taper over several weeks. Unfortunately, an athletic season usually doesn't permit the luxury of several weeks of tapering.

If overtraining is not too severe, workout frequency can be dropped to twice a week at high intensity, and fitness can be maintained. Once-a-week training will slow down losses, but it cannot prevent them. In some cases, a short period of complete rest may be most effective.

Severe overtraining may require a complete layoff. The longer the layoff, of course, the greater the losses. Maximal work output can drop 7% in 12 days. After four weeks, glycogen content can fall 39%, and muscle respiratory capacity can drop by half.

This is not to say that with a complete layoff all is lost. In the study of University of Wisconsin-Madison wrestlers mentioned above, 10% of the wrestlers (four subjects) experienced overtraining during the season. One of the four decided to quit wrestling altogether. The other three rested either one or two weeks, with one wrestler undergoing psychotherapy as well. All three showed improved performances when they returned to wrestling; two went on to achieve national ranking at the end of the season.

Once training is resumed after a layoff, fitness returns gradually, at about the same rate as the initial gains. Gains

What to Do About It?

may *seem* to come more easily and more quickly, because the athlete is familiar with the workout, is not afraid to push, and is aware of the levels of fitness that can be attained.

Overtraining is a common and serious problem for the dedicated athlete. While indicators, such as resting heart rate, are a good place to start, each has its drawbacks and none is truly diagnostic. Since overtraining affects the athlete's emotional, behavioral, physical, biochemical, and performance status, the best diagnostic tool for overtraining may simply be close, continued observation of the athlete by the coach or team physician. Individual attention to each athlete, with individually tailored workouts, probably remains the best way to keep performance-improving overloading from turning into performance-robbing overtraining. ❑

Psychological Monitoring of Overtraining and Staleness
W. P. Morgan EdD et al.
British Journal of Sportsmedicine
V 21 # 3: 107-114, Sept 1987

Increased Morning Heart Rate in Runners:
A Valid Sign of Overtraining?
R. Dressendorfer PhD et al.
The Physician and Sportsmedicine
V 13 # 8: 77-86, Aug 1985

Hypothalamic Dysfunction in Overtrained
Athletes
J. Barron et al.
J. of Clinical Endocrinology and Metabolism
V 60: 803-806, 1985

Avoiding and Recovering From Overtraining
B. Stamford PhD
The Physician and Sportsmedicine
V 11 # 10: 180, Oct 1983

The Muscular Overuse Syndrome in
Long-Distance Runners
R. Dressendorfer PhD et al.
The Physician and Sportsmedicine
V 11 # 11: 116-130, Nov 1983

Overtraining of Athletes: A Round Table
The Physician and Sportsmedicine
V 11 # 6: 93-110, June 1983

EFFECTS OF REDUCED TRAINING ON FITNESS

Most serious athletes share a fear of getting out of shape if they back off from their regular training schedules. That fear is not totally unwarranted. Studies have reported significant decreases in aerobic capacity and local muscular endurance following a complete layoff of as little as one to four weeks.

But what are the effects of a *decrease* in exercise intensity, as opposed to total inactivity? This study attempted to determine whether workouts of reduced length, severity, and frequency can maintain aerobic capacity, strength, and power.

Twenty-four male collegiate swimmers, all of whom had completed five months of intense training (averaging 9,000 yards per day, six days per week) participated. Following the final competition at a championship meet, the swimmers were divided into three groups. Group 1 reduced training to 3,000 yards per day, three days per week. Group 2 reduced training to 3,000 yards per day, one day per week. Group 3 stopped swimming entirely.

All swimmers were subjected to a number of tests at the end of the five-month competition training period (just before the study began), and then again during the study at the end of weeks one, two, and four. Tests included measuring the swimmers' strength in performing swimming motions (measured on dry land using a special resistance machine), swimming power (the ability to apply force during swimming; measured in the water using a different machine), and maximum aerobic capacity.

Strength

Over the four weeks of reduced training, none of the three groups showed significant decreases in strength while performing swimming motions.

Aerobic Capacity

Over the course of the five-month training period, aerobic capacity for all athletes increased significantly. During the subsequent reduced-training period, Group 1 maintained their increased aerobic capacity, despite the fact they were only swimming one-third of the yards (3,000) per workout and only doing half as many workouts (three per week) as before. However, for Group 2, who swam only one day per week, aerobic capacity dropped until it was no longer significantly higher than the untrained level before the five months of training.

Power

Swimming power decreased in all swimmers, but there were no significant differences between groups in how much the power decreased. On average, subjects showed a decrease in power of 13.6% by the fourth week, with over half that decrease occurring in the first week.

These results suggest that athletes trained to a high level of aerobic fitness can reduce training by 70% for four weeks without significantly losing aerobic capacity or strength. However, **power**, the ability to deliver strength over time, decreases quite quickly with reduced training. ❏

Effect of Reduced Training on Muscular Strength and Endurance in Competitive Swimmers
P. D. Neufer et al.
Medicine and Science in Sports and Exercise
V 19 #5: 486-490, 1987

Endurance athletes can improve performance and time to exhaustion by drinking carbohydrate solutions during an event. The carbohydrate consumed gets readily metabolized: some 98% of glucose taken in during prolonged exercise gets burned during the exercise as fuel. It is thought that this outside source of carbohydrate prolongs internal stores of glycogen, thus delaying exhaustion. Taking carbohydrate during exercise seems to do more than just prolong glycogen stores, however. It also decreases perceived exertion.

Seven subjects cycled for three hours on stationary bicycles at 70% of their maximum work output. Every 30 minutes, they were given either an 8% carbohydrate/electrolyte solution or a water placebo to drink. Every 15 minutes throughout the experiment they were asked to give a subjective rating of how hard they thought they were working (a rating of perceived exertion, or RPE). RPE's were tabulated both for leg fatigue and for overall fatigue.

Those who drank the carbohydrate/electrolyte solution reported ratings of perceived exertion significantly lower than those who drank just water. The lower RPE's were reported for both leg fatigue and overall fatigue.

The lower perceived exertion probably resulted from changes in factors contributing to fatigue. For example, two factors most likely to contribute to leg fatigue are low blood glucose and high blood lactate levels. Athletes who drank the solution had significantly *higher* blood glucose levels and *lower* blood lactate levels than the athletes who drank only water.

Similarly, factors most likely to contribute to overall fatigue are maximum oxygen uptake, respiratory rate, and total ventilation. These factors were significantly improved in the carbohydrate group.

These findings suggest that intermittently drinking a carbohydrate/electrolyte solution during endurance exercise does more than just prolong glycogen stores. It also affects the perception of peripheral and central fatigue. When you're pounding the pavement with another ten miles to go, that might make the going just a little easier. ❏

Effect of Intermittent Carbohydrate/Electrolyte Supplementation on Ratings of Perceived Exertion During Prolonged Cycling
M. Lonnett et al.
International Journal of Sports Medicine
V 9: 148, 1988

EFFECT OF CARBOHYDRATE AND ELECTROLYTE REPLACEMENT DURING EXERCISE

USING PERIODIZATION TRAINING TO IMPROVE STRENGTH

Weight training is generally considered the most effective method of increasing strength. However, there is disagreement among coaches and other sports professionals about which method of weight training is best.

Many studies have indicated that performing three sets of five to six repetitions with maximum weight (3 x 5-6 RM) produces maximum strength gains in minimum time. More recent studies suggest that training with **periodization** produces the greatest results.

Periodization refers to a training method in which the athlete begins by lifting relatively light weights a high number of times (high rep/low weight). Over the course of the next two to three months, the athlete changes to heavier weights and fewer repetitions (low rep/high weight). This training cycle is then repeated several times during the year.

The theory is that the initial high rep/low weight phase increases anaerobic capacity, better preparing the athlete to tolerate the heavier weights of the subsequent low rep/high weight phase.

Does periodization work? Ninety college-age men were divided into two groups and trained using either periodization or the standard 3 x 6 RM method over the course of eleven weeks. Subjects were evaluated for changes in squat strength and short-term cycle ergometer (stationary bicycle) power output.

Both groups improved squat strength. However, the periodization group showed significantly greater improvement at eight and eleven weeks than the standard-training group. Similarly, although both groups improved power output, the periodization group showed significantly greater improvement than those who trained with the standard 3 x 6 RM method.

This study demonstrates that weight training can improve maximum leg and hip strength, power, and short-term high intensity power output simultaneously. Periodization appears to be superior to standard methods for achieving these gains.

[Ed. note: As this study shows, strength training improves short-term high-intensity cycling endurance. As each motor unit becomes stronger with training, fewer motor units are needed for a given power output. This creates a "training reserve," and prolongs endurance.] ❏

Cycle Ergometer Performance and Maximum Leg and Hip Strength Adaptation to Two Different Methods of Weight-Training
H. O'Bryant, R. Byrd, and M. Stone
Journal of Applied Sport Science Research
V 2 # 2: 27-30, April/May 1988

SPEED OF REPETITIONS IN STRENGTH TRAINING

What is the optimal rep speed, fast or slow? There has long been disagreement among coaches and athletes on this question. It turns out that both are appropriate, depending on training goals.

If the goal is maximum strength and size, then training with slow reps and heavy weights is most effective. Lifting slowly eliminates use of momentum. This results in higher, more even levels of tension in the muscles, and increases the length of time the muscles are under tension—all favoring development of strength and size.

On the other hand, training with fast reps and lighter weights favors development of **power**, the ability to deliver strength quickly. Training with fast reps produces somewhat lower levels of strength than training with slow reps, but it also produces adaptations to the nervous system that allow for more rapid production of force. Power is particularly useful in sports requiring explosive movements, such as football. Indeed, most sports involve repeated short bursts of activity, for which power is more useful than raw strength.

It is recommended that, when training with slow reps, a total of no more than 60 seconds of work should be done in any given set. For example, if an athlete is doing bench presses at the rate of five seconds up and five seconds back down, he or she should do no more than six reps per set. (5 seconds up + 5 seconds back down = 10 seconds/rep x 6 reps = 60 seconds.) This limits total tension on the muscle to 60 seconds per set.

Training with fast reps is safest and most effective among athletes who already have some weightlifting experience. Many European weightlifting coaches, for instance, recommend using slow-to-moderate reps (4 to 6 seconds per rep) during the first year of weight training, and using progressively faster reps after that. That way, the athlete has some solid muscle strength training on which to base subsequent gains in power. Varying rep speed from slow to moderate is a good idea, as muscle strength increases faster when rep speed is varied.

Coaches and athletes might want to consider using slow-to-moderate reps for strength training during the pre-season, gradually changing to faster reps as the competitive season approaches, and switching over to fast reps for power once the competitive season begins. ❏

Five Steps to Increasing the Effectiveness of Your Strength Training Program
C. Poliquin
National Strength and Conditioning Association Journal
V 10 # 3: 34-39, June/July 1988

IMPROVED RESULTS THROUGH TASK-SPECIFIC TRAINING

The body can call on several different energy sources, depending on the duration and intensity of exercise. For brief, high-intensity anaerobic bouts (those lasting less than six seconds), the primary energy source is the ATP-PC system. For marathons, the primary sources are fat and glycogen stores.

An athlete can train to develop the energy sources appropriate for the specific exercise. For example, training with repeated bursts of explosive activity (anaerobic training) helps develop the ATP-PC system. Training with prolonged periods of moderate exercise (aerobic training) helps develop efficient delivery of energy from fat and glycogen stores. Interestingly, cross-training does not seem to occur: some studies have indicated that aerobic training does not improve the ATP-PC system, and that aerobic training may actually worsen anaerobic performance.

There are several ways to train to develop the ATP-PC system for anaerobic performance. In this study, researchers compared three of these—**static training, dynamic training,** and a new method called **motivational jumping**—to see which was most effective at improving performance of an anaerobic task, vertical jumping.

Thirty-four men and women trained five times a week in this six-week experiment. All were evaluated before and after for vertical jumping ability, flexibility, and stair climbing ability.

Static Training

Static training is a variation on isometric training. Subjects performed a single leg and hip extension at greater than 75% of maximum exertion, and held it for 30 seconds. They worked against a digital strength apparatus, receiving constant digital feedback about the intensity of their effort. Some researchers feel that static training provides the ultimate high intensity anaerobic stimulus needed to tax the ATP-PC system.

Dynamic Training

Dynamic training is the most common method of strength training in this country. It involves lifting sets of heavy weights in predetermined numbers of sets and repetitions. In this study, the subjects in the dynamic group performed three sets of eight to twelve leg presses on a Universal weight machine. Subjects were allowed a two minute rest between sets, and weight was set so that the athletes approached failure with the last reps of the second and third sets.

Motivational Jumping

Motivational jumping is a training method in which subjects are given task-specific feedback, with the task very similar to the performance to be improved. Here, the performance to be improved was the vertical jump, and the task to perform was also the vertical jump.

A lever, attached to a bell, was positioned one inch below the subjects' maximal jumping height. The task was to do vertical jumps and ring the bell ten times in a row. A five second rest was allowed between jumps. If a subject failed on the ninth try, he or she had to start over. This continued until the bell had been rung ten times in a row, or until forty jumps had been performed. If the subject could ring the bell ten consecutive times in under twenty tries, the lever was raised half an inch for the following day. If the subject couldn't ring the bell ten consecutive times in forty tries, the lever was lowered half an inch for the following day.

The static group failed to show significant improvement in any of the measured variables. The dynamic group significantly increased power output and stair climbing speed, but not vertical jump ability. The motivational jumping group significantly improved power output, and was the only group to improve vertical jumping ability. No group showed any improvement in flexibility.

The static method has the advantage of limited time commitment (30 seconds per workout), but also appears to be the least effective. The dynamic method has the advantage of being standardized and performable on equipment available in most gyms, and it produces some gains. The motivational method appears to produce the greatest task-specific gains. This suggests that task-specific training produces greater gains faster than static or dynamic training.

Other studies with basketball players and swimmers concur with these findings, showing four to five inch improvements in vertical jump with only five weeks of task-specific training.

There are several drawbacks to task-specific training. It may require specialized equipment (as it did here for vertical jump training). It is time-consuming. Also, because the feedback is so immediate and so strong, the method can be mentally stressful. Subjects reported considerable anxiety, especially upon missing the tenth effort after nine successful ones. In addition, there was often a discouraging decrease in jumping ability after the first few days. In any intense training session, athletes typically show a small performance loss right at the beginning. Given the strong feedback of the motivational jumping method, it is easy to understand why subjects could get discouraged under these circumstances.

These drawbacks aside, by the end of six weeks the motivational jumping group showed significant improvement in vertical jump. The emotional intensity of this method, while producing anxiety and some initial discouragement, probably also helped improve concentration and mental focus.

[Ed. note: Similar motivational methods can be used for task-specific training of other sports skills, such as sprinting. It appears the athlete must be given a well-defined task, receive immediate and unequivocal feedback, be positively reinforced for successful performance, and negatively reinforced for unsuccessful performance. The goal should be one that can be made easier or harder in small increments, so that the athlete can work on small but manageable gains. It may be that emotional intensity, raising anxiety but also improving concentration, is necessary for improvement.

Task-specific training is probably more applicable to anaerobic skills, requiring the ATP-PC system, than to aerobic skills. Anaerobic tasks are briefer, so they can be done many more times with much more frequent feedback. Aerobic skills, coming into play during longer tasks, lend themselves to less-frequent feedback.] ❏

Anaerobic Power Changes Following Short Term, Task-Specific, and Static Overload Training
B. Brown, D. Gorman, R. DiBrezzo, and I. Fort
Journal of Applied Sport Science Research
V 2 # 2: 35-38, April/May 1988

Recommendations for amount of weight to be lifted in weight training programs are often given in terms of the **one repetition maximum**. The one repetition maximum, commonly known as the **one rep max** or **RM**, is the maximum amount of weight an athlete can lift once. For every athlete, each maneuver—bench press, biceps curl, squat, and so on—has its own one rep max.

Percentage of one rep max used in a weightlifting program can have a pronounced effect on metabolic rate, total work done, and lactic acid production, which in turn can affect overall weightlifting results.

Seventeen subjects participated in a study that was designed to evaluate more precisely the relationship between percentage of one rep max, metabolic rate, total work done, and lactic acid production. Subjects performed the given number of bench presses at each of the following intensities:

- 4 sets of 30 reps at 20% of RM
- 4 sets of 20 reps at 30% of RM
- 4 sets of 20 reps at 40% of RM
- 4 sets of 10 reps at 60% of RM
- 4 sets of 5 reps at 80% of RM

At least two days' rest separated performance at each intensity. Researchers measured metabolic rate, work performed, weight training economy (a measure of how efficiently the athlete is lifting), and blood lactic acid levels in subjects at each intensity.

Metabolic rate, calculated from oxygen uptake, steadily increased with increasing percentage of rep max. Work performed also steadily increased, *but not as fast as metabolic rate*. As a result, weight training economy, calculated as calories expended per amount of work done, steadily *decreased* as percentage of one rep max increased. For example, at 80% of one rep max, subjects used almost twelve times as much energy performing one rep as they did performing one rep at 20% of one rep max, even though they performed only 4 times as much work.

Why does it take disproportionately more calories to lift higher amounts of weight? It may be that the muscles work less efficiently at higher weights, or that stabilizing muscles participate more, or that changes in form (for example, tremors in the arms, or not lifting as smoothly as with lighter

EXERCISE INTENSITY AND METABOLIC RATE VARIATION

weights) increase the energy required to lift. Or perhaps all three contribute to decreased total efficiency at heavier weights.

Lactic acid levels increased when weight went from 30% to 60% of RM, but actually decreased when weight increased above 60%. This indicates that, for bench press, 60% of RM may be the best weight training intensity for athletes working to improve tolerance to higher lactic acid levels.

The authors conclude that those who are interested in body composition changes should train at 60% to 80% of RM. Other studies have shown that lifting in this intensity range produces muscular size and strength changes that do not occur at lower intensities, and that the higher metabolic rates at this level result in burning more calories (although not nearly as many calories as are burned by aerobic work).

This study shows that high rep/low weight programs and low rep/high weight programs are not interchangeable. Even though the same amount of work may be done in both, higher lactic acid production and caloric expenditures in the 60% to 80% intensity range may make a higher-intensity workout better for many athletes. ❑

Bench Press Metabolic Rate as a Function of Exercise Intensity
G. Hunter et al.
Journal of Applied Sports Science Research
V 2 # 1: 1-6, Feb 1988

PAIN MANAGEMENT DURING EXERCISE

Pain and discomfort are common companions of athletes, especially those pushing to the limits of their physical capabilities. Indeed, pain and discomfort are often the limiting, and thus deciding, performance factors in a competition.

Since there are recognized psychological techniques for management of pain in medical patients, the question exists whether these techniques can help in lessening exercise-induced pain, perhaps thereby improving physical performance.

Most theories about pain hold that the perception of pain is a result of the interaction of **peripheral** (sensory) and **central** (cognitive and emotional) factors. This suggests that reduction in perceived pain can be accomplished by addressing peripheral and central input. For athletes, influencing both peripheral and central input has been demonstrated to improve physical performance.

Peripheral input (input from sensory nerves) is what is called a **capacity-bound process**, that is, only a certain amount of peripheral input can be processed and reach the consciousness at one time. This means that distracting stimuli may reduce the perception of pain. In fact, with athletes, this has been shown to be true. Subjects exercising while listening to unrelated sounds (traffic noise, for example) experienced less fatigue with similar tasks than subjects forced to monitor their own breathing.

Central input, such as any pre-existing mental or emotional state, can also influence the perception of pain and exercise performance. Women who were led to believe an exercise task was "very tolerable" reported much lower ratings of perceived exertion than did women who were led to believe the same task was "intolerable."

Most medical pain and distress management programs involve multiple simultaneous approaches, rather than just one approach. Because of this, in the current study researchers investigated the effects of a multi-approach distress management training program on mood, ratings of perceived exertion, and running efficiency in novice runners.

The multi-approach pain and distress management program consisted of teaching and practicing a number of coping behaviors. These coping behaviors included relaxation techniques, concentrating on positive sensations of running, not concentrating on negative sensations of running, and others. In a submaximal run, those subjects who participated in the program reported a decrease in perceived exertion and improved mood at the end compared to controls. In a run to exhaustion, those who participated in the program again reported improved mood over controls but *no* improvement in performance. No changes in running efficiency were noted.

Finding no improvement in performance in runs to exhaustion contrasts with several previous studies, which have demonstrated improvements in performance with pain and stress management techniques.

The authors offer several possible explanations for the disagreements. Previous studies showing improved responses have used exercise with much lower intensity. It may be that higher-intensity exercise is less responsive to stress-management techniques than lower-intensity exercise. Other studies showing improved responses have employed six months of stress management training, as opposed to the five weeks used here. Perhaps this study was too short to bring about a change in performance. A third possibility centers around the fact that other studies showing improved responses have involved experienced collegiate runners, rather than novices. Perhaps experienced athletes are more responsive to stress-reduction training than novices. Another study showing a difference relied more heavily on relaxation techniques, which may have had an effect.

In any event, this study has demonstrated that is it possible to reduce ratings of perceived exertion and improve mood in runners placed on a relatively short pain and distress management program. Such a program may be successful in deterring beginning athletes from quitting exercise programs.

[Ed. note: Though it is possible to improve performance by decreasing the perception of pain, it must be remembered that the primary function of pain is protective—if your knee is hurting while you are running, it is hurting for a reason. Decreasing the perception of pain to try to improve performance may work under some circumstances, but it may not always be the best thing to do. The authors of this study fail to draw a distinction between reduction of exercise distress and reduction of pain perception; this may be a distinction that, from the standpoint of athletic performance, is difficult, if not impossible, to draw.] ❑

Managing Exercise Distress: The Effect of Broad Spectrum Intervention on Affect, RPE, and Running Efficiency
Elizabeth A. Kenney et al.
Canadian Journal of Sports Sciences
V 12 # 2: 97-105, June 1987

FLEXIBILITY AND STRENGTH TRAINING

For years many athletes and coaches have believed that strength training causes a loss of flexibility. As a result, some athletes whose performance depends on flexibility—martial artists, divers, gymnasts, dancers—have avoided strength training. Some athletes in sports that require less flexibility have also avoided strength training, out of fear of becoming "muscle bound," even though increased strength may enhance performance of their sport.

Over the past twenty years little research has been done on this issue, leaving the concept of "muscle boundness" largely unchallenged. However, a recent study shows strength training *doesn't* cause a loss of flexibility.

Researchers tested thirteen male college students for flexibility in trunk, shoulders, and ankles, and for strength in all major muscle groups. The subjects then participated in an eleven-week weight training program for all major muscle groups.

In preparation, subjects were taught proper lifting technique, with emphasis on performing each exercise through its full range of motion. Subjects were encouraged to increase the amount of weight used as rapidly as possible.

After twenty-nine training sessions over eleven weeks, the subjects' strength and flexibility were measured once again.

Subjects demonstrated significant strength increases for each of the exercises. In addition, subjects showed *increases* in flexibility for all joint actions measured, and significant increases in flexibility for two of those joint actions. The authors conclude that use of a properly performed weight training program does not decrease flexibility, and may in fact increase it.

[Ed. note: This experiment failed to ensure the subjects did not consciously or subconsciously stretch on their own. Any stretching they may have done would make it difficult to determine how much of the increase in flexibility is attributable to strength training. Still, the concept of "muscle boundness" has gone unchallenged for years. If these results are borne out by further research, it may pave the way for improved performance for martial artists, gymnasts, and others currently avoiding strength training for fear of losing flexibility.] ❑

Flexibility and Strength Training
Journal of Applied Sport Science Research
V 1 #4: 74-75, October/November 1987

FLEXIBILITY IN POWERLIFTERS

Powerlifters are athletes who train to maximize the amount of weight they can lift in a single rep. In so doing, they experience substantial muscle hypertrophy and increase lean body mass. Muscle hypertrophy has the potential to reduce joint flexibility. As such, one might expect powerlifters to have impaired flexibility.

How flexible are powerlifters?

Ten powerlifters and ten matched non-lifters were evaluated for joint flexibility. Seven single-joint systems—shoulders, elbows, forearms, wrists, hips, knees, and ankles—were measured using a **goniometer**, a device designed to measure joint flexibility. In addition, two multi-joint systems—the upper back/shoulder girdle/upper extremities system, and the lower back/hamstrings system—were tested for flexibility.

With the exception of the forearms, the non-lifters showed significantly more flexibility in all goniometer measurements than did the powerlifters. In addition, non-lifters were significantly more flexible in the behind-the-back stretch than were the powerlifters. This suggests that powerlifting does indeed result in loss of flexibility.

However, the researchers note that this need not be the case. There is evidence that a good stretching program can counteract the flexibility-limiting effects of powerlifting, and may also decrease incidence of common powerlifting injuries, such as low back pain, shoulder pain, and knee injuries. ❑

Limited Joint Mobility in Power Lifters
D. Chang MD et al.
American Journal of Sports Medicine
V 16 # 3: 280- 284, 1988

PNF STRETCHING

A recent study now indicates that using the advanced PNF flexibility technique, less is just as effective. Done properly, quick (fifteen second) stretches seem to be just as effective as longer (two minute) ones.

PNF, or Proprioceptive Neuromuscular Facilitation, is a stretching technique usually involving three steps: passive stretch of a muscle, contraction of the same muscle *without* moving its limb (isometric contraction), then another passive stretch.

For example, one way to do PNF stretching of your right hamstrings would be:

- lie on your back
- have a partner passively raise your right leg to a point of tension, keeping your right knee straight (passive leg raise)
- gradually try to bring your right leg back down against the resistance of your partner, who is holding your right leg up, immobile. This forces an isometric contraction of your right hamstrings
- hold the isometric contraction for a number of seconds
- lower the right leg and repeat passive leg raise

PNF can be used for any muscle group, and has been shown to be more effective at increasing flexibility than traditional techniques such as ballistic ("bouncing") stretches and straight passive stretches.

However, earlier PNF studies have involved different numbers of isometric contractions (from one to six), leaving unresolved the question of how many isometric contractions is best. This current study looked at whether doing three PNF repetitions of a particular stretch increases flexibility more than doing one rep.

Thirty female subjects, ages 25 to 31, were randomly assigned to one of two PNF treatment groups. Both groups used the same PNF technique for hamstrings, as described above, holding isometric contractions for six seconds.

The first group did only one PNF repetition, the second group did three. Maximum hip flexibility was measured before and after exercise.

Both groups showed significant increases in range of motion at the hip. However, there was no significant difference in the flexibility increases for the two groups.

This suggests that three isometric contractions per PNF exercise is no more effective than one. Since the entire one-contraction PNF hamstring routine takes only about twenty seconds, this should save considerable time for athletes using this technique! ❏

A Comparison of Single vs. Repeated MVIC Maneuvers Used in PNF Flexibility Techniques for Improvement in ROM
William L. Cornelius and Karen K. Hayes
Journal of Applied Sport Science Research
V 1 #4: 71-73, October/November 1987

BENEFITS OF STRENGTH TRAINING FOR THE FINGERS AND TOES

You may not know it, but you're probably leaving twenty important body parts out of your workout: your fingers and toes!

In most sports activities, you bring into play both the major muscles, such as those of the legs, and the small muscles, such as those of the fingers and toes. It has long been recognized that strength training for the major muscle groups can significantly improve sports performance. However, strength training for the muscles of the fingers and toes has been largely ignored. Two recent studies have looked at strength training for these areas, with promising results.

In one study, researchers investigated the effects of finger and toe strength training on 40-yard dash acceleration and baseball pitching velocity; in the other study, on vertical jump and shot-put distances. In both studies, subjects trained either toe flexors (muscles responsible for curling the toes), or finger flexors (muscles responsible for making a fist) on special "digit exercising machines." Training programs lasted twelve weeks.

Toe flexor strength training resulted in significant increases in 40-yard dash acceleration (2.2%), baseball pitching velocity (3.5%), and vertical jump (5%—almost 1 inch). Control subjects, who did not train, showed no significant improvement.

Finger flexor strength training resulted in significant increases in baseball pitching velocity (4.3%), and shot-put distance (4.4%—almost 2 feet). Again, control subjects showed no significant improvement.

These results are in agreement with several earlier studies that showed that strengthening toe flexors can increase acceleration, and strengthening finger flexors can increase throwing power.

Sports such as baseball, basketball, football, soccer, tennis, track and field, and volleyball require quick acceleration, vertical jumping ability, and/or throwing power. Athletes and coaches involved in these sports may want to consider adding toe and finger strengthening exercises to the workout routine.

[Ed. note: These athletes trained on specially designed machines. The lack of suitable weight-training equipment for these bodyparts is probably the primary reason little research has been done on finger and toe training. These areas can be trained with conventional equipment, albeit with difficulty. Widespread use of finger and toe flexor

routines will probably have to await introduction of suitable machines into the marketplace.] ❏

Effect of Toe and Wrist/Finger Flexor Strength Training on Athletic Performance
T. Adams et al.
Journal of Applied Sports Science Research
V 2 # 2: 31-34, April/May 1988

Improved Performance Through Digit Strength Gains
J. Kokkonen et al.
Research Quarterly for Exercise and Sport
V 59 # 1: 57-63, 1988

Certain sports skills, such as the basketball tip-off and the volleyball spike, require a sudden burst of power in the form of a vertical jump. Training for these skills often includes use of **plyometric** techniques.

Plyometrics refers to a training approach that works specific movements by starting with the opposite movement. The most common example is **drop jumping**, which is a method of training for the vertical jump. In drop jumping, the targeted movement (jumping *up*) is preceded by the opposite movement (jumping *down*). The athlete jumps down from a platform, then jumps up again.

A number of experiments have shown that drop jumping increases vertical jumping ability. The likely mechanism behind the increase is that the combination of jumping down followed by jumping up overloads the muscles involved, resulting in improvements in muscular strength. Indeed, muscular forces and power output reach greater levels with drop jumping than with standard vertical jumping.

Investigators have tried several modifications of the drop jumping technique, in attempts to improve the results further. One of these modifications involved use of the "bounce drop jump" rather than the "counter-movement drop jump."

The "bounce drop jump" is a drop jump in which the jump down is followed as quickly as possible with a jump up. The "counter-movement drop jump" involves a slower, more-controlled absorption of the force of the downward jump, with a deeper bend at the knees.

Result: muscular forces and power output reached greater levels with bounce drop jumping than with counter-movement drop jumping. This suggests that bounce drop jumping puts a greater overload on the participating muscles, making bounce drop jumping more likely to result in improvements in muscular strength and vertical jump performance.

What about height? What is the best height from which to jump for the "jump down" part of the technique?

The recommendation is to limit the height to twenty to forty centimeters, roughly eight to sixteen inches. Heights greater than that do not increase the plyometric results, but do increase potentially injurious stress on joints and ligaments.

Skills such as basketball tip-offs and volleyball spikes require more than just vertical jumping ability, however. These athletic tasks require the coordination of a number of different

PLYOMETRIC DROP JUMPING

motor abilities. As a result, training for these sports skills requires more than just application of one plyometric technique. While drop jumping can help improve vertical jumping ability, it should be just one component of an overall training program

[Ed. note: Plyometric drop jumping exercises are often referred to as "depth jumps."] ❑

Drop Jumping I. The Influence of Jumping Technique on the Biomechanics of Jumping

Drop Jumping II. The Influence of Dropping Height on the Biomechanics of Drop Jumping
M. F. Bobbert et al.
Medicine and Science in Sports and Exercise
V 19 # 4: 332-46, 1987

BEST POSITIONS FOR TRAINING THE ROTATOR CUFF MUSCLES

The shoulder is a complex joint, capable of a variety of movements over a broad range of motion. Two shoulder movements common to a number of different sports skills are **internal rotation** and **external rotation.**

The muscles responsible for internal and external rotation are called the **rotator cuff muscles.** These muscles are a common site for injury, particularly for muscle tears (*rotator cuff tears*). Strengthening the muscles of the rotator cuff decreases their risk of injury. However, because the shoulder is capable of such a variety of movements, rotator cuff strengthening exercises can be done in many possible positions. Which is best?

To find out, researchers evaluated internal and external rotation strength in twelve subjects using Cybex isokinetic resistance machines. Isokinetic machines are ideal for evaluating strength because the muscle is forced to work against maximal resistance at every point throughout the movement. This is in contrast to most weightlifting equipment, such as dumbbells and barbells, which are **isotonic**. With isotonic devices, the amount of resistance remains constant throughout the movement; consequently, the weight is often too heavy where the muscle is weakest and too light where the muscle is strongest.

The researchers tested internal and external rotation in three positions.

- ■ **Position One.** Subject standing up, upper arm hanging straight down, with the axis of internal and external rotation parallel to the axis of the body.

- ■ **Position Two.** Subject sitting, upper arm parallel to the floor and pointing straight ahead, with axis of rotation along a line going straight out from the body.

- ■ **Position Three.** Subject lying on the back, upper arm parallel to the floor and pointing straight out to the side, with the axis of rotation along an imaginary line passing through both shoulders.

The greatest torque values for internal rotation were achieved in Position One, with the upper arm hanging straight down. The greatest torque values for external rotation were achieved in Position Two, with the upper arm pointing straight ahead.

These findings suggest that the best orientations for exercising the internal and external rotators are different. The

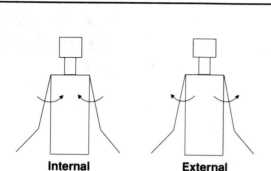
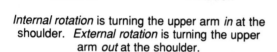

Internal rotation is turning the upper arm *in* at the shoulder. *External rotation* is turning the upper arm *out* at the shoulder.

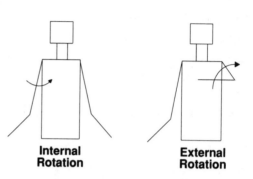

Best exercise positions for internal and external rotation: Internal rotation, Position 1; External rotation, Position 2.

most efficient way to exercise the internal rotators is with the upper arm hanging straight down. This is the anatomically most "natural" position, in which the internal rotator muscles are acting most directly against resistance.

Similarly, the most efficient way to exercise the external rotators is with the upper arm pointing straight ahead.

Given that strengthening the internal and external rotation muscles decreases the risk of damaging the often-injured rotator cuff, athletes would be well-advised to take the time to train these muscles. This study provides some needed guidelines for the best way to approach this kind of training.

*[Ed. note: Although isokinetic machines are the most efficient way of **testing** the internal and external rotation muscles, this does not mean that isokinetic machines are necessary to **train** these muscles. Ordinary isotonic equipment, such as dumbbells or cables, can also be used to train these muscles, taking advantage of the above-mentioned ideal orientations for internal and external rotation.]* ❑

A Comparative Study of the Torque Generated by the Shoulder Internal and External Rotator Muscles in Different Positions and at Varying Speeds
R. Walmsley and C. Szybbo
Journal of Orthopaedic and Sports Physical Therapy
V 9 # 6: 217-222, Dec 1987

ISOMETRIC VERSUS ISOTONIC TRAINING

Isometric and isotonic contractions are both used in resistance (weight) training. **Isometric contraction** refers to the development of tension in a muscle that does *not* result in motion—for example, pushing against a wall, or suspending a weight in mid-air. **Isotonic contraction**, on the other hand, refers to the development of tension in a muscle that *does* result in motion—for example, the standard biceps curl or bench press.

While the advantages and disadvantages of isometric versus isotonic training have been debated for years, few studies have directly compared the strength gains from an isometric program with gains from an isotonic one. Those which have made the comparison have often produced conflicting results—some finding greater strength increases with isometric, some with isotonic, some finding no differences. This is the first study to compare the two methods directly in the same subjects.

Nineteen healthy males participated in this ten-week study in which they trained their right knee extensor (quadriceps) isotonically and their left knee extensor isometrically. The subjects trained three times a week, three sets per workout, basing the workout load on the six-rep max (the maximum amount of weight which can be lifted six times in succession). One-rep and six-rep maximums were re-evaluated weekly, and workout loads adjusted upward accordingly.

By the end of the ten weeks, both the isometrically and the isotonically trained quadriceps showed significant increases in strength. However, the strength gains from the isometric training were significantly greater than the strength gains from the isotonic training.

Researchers noted a decline in strength after the first week of training for both isometrically and isotonically trained quadriceps. Strength returned to baseline after three weeks, and steadily increased from there. The reason for the initial decline is not known, but the authors speculate that it was somehow related to muscle soreness. For the second through fourth weeks, the isotonic training showed greater strength gains; after the fifth week, however, the isometric training showed greater gains.

Why isotonic training showed greater gains early on, while isometric showed greater gains later is unclear. However, this study demonstrates that both isometric and isotonic methods are successful at increasing strength. For training schedules longer than four weeks, the authors recommend the isometric program.

[Ed. note: For those athletes whose goal is to increase strength and whose workouts are built entirely around isotonics, perhaps isometrics are worth a second look.] ❑

Static Versus Dynamic Training Programs for Muscular Strength Using the Knee
Extensors in Healthy Young Men
O. Amusa DPE. et al.
Journal of Orthopaedic and Sports Physical Therapy
V 8 # 5: 243-247, November 1986

Isometrics can be an effective mode of training. Indeed, under certain circumstances, isometric training can be more effective than isotonic training (see previous article).

Many athletes shy away from isometrics, however, believing that isometrics are limited by **angular specificity**. *Angular specificity* is the theory that, with isometrics, the muscle only gets stronger at the specific angle trained. For example, if someone trained their biceps isometrically by holding a weight with the elbow bent at 90°, under the angular specificity theory the biceps should get stronger at 90°, but not at any other angle. It follows that training a muscle throughout its range of motion requires a whole series of separate isometric maneuvers, each at a different angle, an arrangement that is both inefficient and time-consuming.

It turns out that little research has been done to evaluate the theory of angular specificity. What little research has been done is contradictory—some studies show the existence of angular specificity, others do not. In an attempt to resolve the conflict, these investigators re-evaluated the question of angular specificity, with some surprising results.

Twenty-four men, divided into three groups of eight, participated in this five-week study. All three groups trained their biceps isometrically, each subject using 80% of the maximum amount he could hold. They performed sets of five five-second contractions, five sets per workout, three workouts per week. The first group trained with the biceps at almost full length (a 25° angle; 0° is full extension), the second group near halfway (80°), and the third group with the biceps almost fully shortened (120°). A fourth group of subjects, who didn't train, served as controls.

Result: All subjects showed increases in strength. Those who trained with the muscle most shortened (that is, the 120° group) showed strength improvements only around 120°. On the other hand, those who trained with the muscle most lengthened (that is, the 25° group) showed strength improvements not only at the trained angle but throughout the biceps' range of motion as well. The middle group (80°) showed some angular specificity, but less than the 120° group.

In other words, the shorter the muscle length at which the isometric contraction is performed, the greater the angular specificity.

The investigators then went back to the earlier studies to see if this pattern might reconcile the earlier conflicting results. In

ANGULAR SPECIFICITY AND STRENGTH GAIN IN ISOMETRICS

fact, it did. Earlier studies supported the relationship—the shorter the muscle length, the greater the angular specificity.

This isometric program resulted in some impressive strength increases. The 25° group increased strength by 54% at the trained angle, and by an average of about 25% throughout the rest of the range of motion. The 80° group increased strength by 30% at the trained angle, and by about 25% throughout the rest of the range of motion. The 120° group increased strength by 25% at the trained angle, and by about 7% throughout the rest of the range of motion.

This study demonstrates that, if performed with the muscle in a relatively lengthened position, isometrics can produce substantial strength gains, not only at the angle trained, but throughout the muscle's range of motion. ❏

Myoelectrical and Mechanical Changes Linked to Length Specificity During Isometric Training
C. Thepaut-Mathieu, et al.
Journal of Applied Physiology
V 64 # 4: 1500-1505, 1988

B*ody shaping* salons are one of the more recent entrants into the world of health and fitness. These organizations promise improvements in muscle tone, strength, and endurance without exercise, using external application of electricity to muscles. There are some Soviet reports of increased muscle size and localized fat loss with electrical stimulation, but until now no well-controlled Western studies had examined the question.

Two new studies have now looked at **electrical muscle stimulation (EMS)**, also called **neuromuscular electrical stimulation (NMES)**. One study used the same regimen as the Soviet report, the other study used a regimen similar to those used in body shaping salons in the United States.

Subjects received electrical stimulation three times a week for six weeks (for the Soviet regimen) or seven weeks (for the body salon regimen). In neither study did subjects show any improvement in body weight, total body fat, fat weight, muscle hypertrophy, or lean body mass. Consequently, both studies reach the same conclusion: there is no scientific basis for claims of muscle hypertrophy or fat reduction using externally-applied electrical muscle stimulation. ❏

Electrical Stimulation Effects on Muscle and Fat
B. Keller et al
Medicine and Science in Sports and Exercise
V. 20 # 2: S22, April 1988

Neuromuscular Electrical Stimulation Does Not Decrease Body Fat
D. Lake & W. Gillespie
Medicine and Science in Sports and Exercise
V. 20 # 2: S22, April 1988

CONSEQUENCES OF ELECTRICAL STIMULATION ON MUSCLE AND FAT

THE SAFETY OF WEIGHT TRAINING FOR CHILDREN

Weight training, with its potential to improve performance and reduce injury, is becoming an increasingly common mode of training for participants in a variety of sports across a variety of ages. However, for children and adolescents, lifting heavy weights places considerable stress on still-growing bones, muscles, and hearts. This raises the obvious question: is weight training safe for growing bodies?

In search of the answer to this question, researchers from the Center for Sports Medicine and Health Fitness in Peoria, Illinois, placed eighteen boys, aged seven to nine, on a fourteen-week supervised strength training program. An additional ten age-and-activity-matched boys did not go through the training program, and served as comparison controls.

The weightlifting subjects underwent three forty-five minute training sessions a week, working eight upper body and seven lower body motions per workout on hydraulic machines.

Those who trained showed significant strength increases in all fifteen motions exercised compared to those who did not train. In addition, those who trained showed significant increases in flexibility and in height of vertical jump.

A type of bone scan was done to evaluate any damage that may have occurred to bone, muscle, and growing bone end plates (epiphyses). The test revealed no damage from weight training. A blood test for muscle damage (creatine phosphokinase) also showed no damage.

There were no significant changes in resting heart rate, blood pressure, height, sexual maturity rating, hemoglobin, or blood testosterone levels between the trained and untrained groups. The trained group gained significantly more weight, but showed no change in body composition.

Only one of the subjects suffered from a weight-training related injury, a mild shoulder strain that resolved with one week of rest.

Thus, supervised strength training appears safe for prepubescent males. It does not seem to cause bone, muscle, or growing bone end plate damage, nor does it decrease growth, development, or flexibility, nor does it have a high rate of injury.

However, the authors add two cautionary notes: the type of training done here involved almost exclusively concentric work, and those participating in the study were under very close supervision by trained professionals.

Concentric work refers to a way resistance is applied in a weight training program. With free weights (barbells and dumbbells), the weights act on you both as you lift them up and as you let them back down. For example, when doing a biceps curl with a dumbbell, the target muscle (biceps) shortens in a controlled manner on the way up (*concentric contraction*), and lengthens in a controlled manner on the way back down (*eccentric contraction*).

Hydraulic machines, the type used in this study, differ from free weights, Nautilus machines, and almost all other kinds of weightlifting devices in that hydraulic machines provide resistance *only to concentric contractions*. (Think of the hydraulic cylinders in a rowing machine. They provide resistance on the "stroke" part of the movement, the concentric contraction, but not on the "forward" part of the movement, the controlled-lengthening eccentric contraction.)

In adults, concentric and eccentric training have different effects, including changes at the microscopic level. Thus, the results of this study (demonstrating the overall safety of concentric weight training on prepubescent males) cannot be generalized to predict the safety of training with nonhydraulic machines and free weights, which require both concentric *and* eccentric contractions.

The other cautionary note involved the close supervision under which these seven-to-nine-year-olds trained. This close supervision was probably a major factor resulting in the low rate of injury noted in this study. At many points during the fourteen weeks, subjects reported technique-related pain or discomfort while performing lifts; because of the close supervision, it was possible to provide early correction of technique for these subjects. With early correction, symptoms subsided readily, probably preventing some injuries that might otherwise have occurred.

These caveats noted, weight training in prepubescent males using concentric contractions under close supervision appears to be reasonably safe. ❑

Strength Training for Prepubescent Males: Is it Safe?
C. B. Rians MD et al.
American Journal of Sports Medicine
V 15 # 5: 483-9, Sep/Oct 1987

LEARNING AND ATHLETIC PERFORMANCE

Sports skills can be looked at as complex learned movements. Because the movements are learned, the learning process plays an important role. Optimizing the learning process can help optimize sports performance.

Every time a sports movement is executed, a bit of learning goes on. Learning for sports skills typically takes the following form:

- A movement is executed
- The result is evaluated
- This result is compared to the desired result, and differences noted
- Mental error correction takes place to lessen differences in subsequent movements
- The movement is repeated, incorporating the error correction

All these steps are necessary for learning and improvement of sports skills.

Step 1: Movement Execution

With no movement, there is no physical learning. Conversely, the more times a movement is executed, the more learning takes place. Put another way, *practice makes perfect*. Practice is nothing more than repeated execution of a movement, with the athlete coming closer and closer to the desired result. The more times a movement is executed, the more subtle and refined the error corrections become.

Step 2: Movement Evaluation

Sometimes movement results are easy to evaluate ("Did my free throw make it in the basket?"); sometimes not ("Was my dismount from the parallel bars as smooth as last time?"). Whether easy to evaluate or not, knowledge of results from movement evaluation (**feedback**) is essential for learning to take place. If feedback is not made available to the athlete, no learning takes place, and an opportunity for improvement is lost.

The magnitude and direction of differences between the actual results and the desired results are noted, and from this a mental *degree of error* is calculated.

Step 3: Comparing Actual Results to the Desired Results, and Noting Differences

The recollection of the physical "feeling" of the movement just executed is combined with the calculated degree of error to come up with a mental error correction. This correction is then applied to subsequent movements to lessen the differences between the desired results and the actual results.

Step 4: Mental Error Correction

The movement must be repeated soon after the initial execution for the mental error correction to be incorporated. If the movement is not repeated, no learning takes place. Likewise, if too much time elapses between initial movement and repetition of the movement, no learning takes place. (It is difficult to say exactly what *too much time* means, and it probably depends on the nature of the movement involved. However, the more time elapses, the more the mental details of error correction fade, and the less learning takes place.)

Step 5: Repeating the Movement, With Incorporation of the Error Correction

This study addressed steps 3 and 4, the "comparing results" and "mental error correction" steps. These steps require a few moments of thinking. Deliberately distracting someone right after a movement might interfere with the thinking necessary for these steps; thus distraction might interfere with the learning process.

In fact, it does. This study demonstrated that distracting someone right after a movement does indeed interfere with the learning process.

Subjects were given a hand movement to do, with the task of completing it in exactly 150 milliseconds. All subjects were informed of how long they took to complete the movement either 10 or 15 seconds into the post-movement period. Half the subjects, though, were distracted during the post-movement period with arithmetic questions.

The subjects who were distracted during the post-movement period made significantly larger errors than those who were not distracted. This suggests that post-movement distraction interferes with the mental tasks of comparing results and making error corrections.

Furthermore, when asked to estimate how long they thought they had taken to do the movement, the distracted subjects were significantly farther off on their estimations. This suggests post-movement distraction interferes with self-evaluation of performance.

Several approaches for optimizing learning for sports skills follow from this research.

- **Practice.** The more times a movement can be repeated, the more learning can take place.

- **Get feedback** as soon as possible after a movement. Athletes should always get some kind of feedback, whether directly from seeing the result themselves, or indirectly from seeing the result on videotape or hearing specifics on how they did.

- **Minimize distractions** for ten to fifteen seconds after execution of a movement. The athlete should take a few moments to go through the mental steps of comparing results and making error corrections.

- **Concentrate** on every movement. The learning process doesn't stop when athletes get sloppy. If the athlete gets sloppy during practice, poor habits get ingrained.

- **Repeat** the skill movement as soon as possible after getting the feedback. The longer the lapse between initial execution and repetition, the less effective the feedback and error correction. ❑

Post-Knowledge of Results Delay: Effects of Interpolated Activity on Learning and Performance
C. Bendetti and P. McCullagh
Research Quarterly for Exercise and Sport
V 58 # 4: 375-381, Dec 1987

Running speed is important in many sports, including football, baseball, basketball, and track. While there are a number of external factors that can affect running speed (such as wind speed, ambient temperature, type and condition of the running surface, type and condition of running shoes), there are only two physical factors that can directly affect running speed: stride frequency and stride length. To increase running speed, the athlete must increase stride frequency, stride length, or both.

Stride length is more responsive to improvement with training than is stride frequency. The keys to improving stride length are improving leg strength and flexibility. However, simply improving strength and flexibility is not enough; these changes need to be incorporated into the stride in a fluid and efficient manner.

The stride can be divided into four phases:

- planting
- shock absorption
- takeoff
- airborne

The **planting phase**, also called **touching down**, is that part of the stride when the foot strikes the ground. Because of the nature of planting, there can be a tendency to brake, causing a loss of speed. Certain techniques used by experienced sprinters can minimize braking. The most important of these involves optimal foot positioning just before planting.

In the middle of the previous stride, the non-weight-bearing leg (the one preparing for planting) needs to be brought forward with the knee bent until the toes pass the knee of the weight-bearing leg. The planting foot should touch down about twelve inches in front of the anticipated center of gravity, with the weight-bearing knee slightly flexed.

Bringing the leg forward and planting the foot in this way increases stride length and keeps the runner's inertia moving forward horizontally, minimizing braking and increasing running speed. These motions can be facilitated by strength improvements in the gluteus, hamstring, and quadriceps muscle groups.

TRAINING TO INCREASE RUNNING STRIDE LENGTH AND EFFICIENCY

Phases of the Stride

Planting

Shock Absorption

Immediately after planting, there is a period in which the body's center of gravity continues moving downward. This is the **shock absorption** phase, also called **amortization**. During this phase, the runner has to absorb the energy of landing and quickly convert that energy into forward momentum while providing drive. The optimal angles for doing this are 80 to 85 degrees of flexion at the ankle, and 140 to 150 degrees of flexion at the knee.

Takeoff

Also called **get-away**, this is the period from when the center of gravity begins to rise until the moment contact with the ground is lost.

Airborne

This is the "flying" part of the stride, when neither foot is in contact with the ground.

Stride Rhythm

The way these four phases flow from one into another is the **rhythm** of the stride. Stride rhythm is affected by the constantly changing angles and velocities of the runner's limbs and torso. These can be looked at as changes in **posture, swing, support, flying action,** and **arm action.** Each can be optimized to improve running speed.

Posture

Posture is the position of the athlete's trunk during running. At the gun, when the runner is accelerating from a dead stop, the trunk goes from leaned-over to a progressively more upright position. Once a steady speed is established, the trunk angle changes slightly through the course of the stride—from 2 to 4 degrees at takeoff, to a more leaned-over 4 to 6 degrees at planting, and back to 2 to 4 degrees at takeoff.

This slight two- to four-degree change in angle of posture is optimal. Any further leaning forward (beyond 6 degrees) causes the foot to be planted prematurely, shortening stride. Any further leaning backward (to less than 2 degrees) decreases the power of the drive, also shortening stride.

Swing is the action of bringing the back leg forward during the takeoff and airborne phases. During the swing, the swinging leg acts essentially as a pendulum. As with any pendulum, the shorter the length of the pendulum the less momentum it has, and the less energy required to move it. In the case of the leg, this means that if the runner can bend at the knee and bring the foot up under the hip, the hip-foot distance (length of the pendulum) is lessened, reducing the energy required to swing the leg forward. The amount which the hip-foot distance can be shortened is limited by the length of the leg bones and the flexibility of the knee.

Once the foot is brought up under the hip, with the knee flexed at 20° to 30°, the leg should be carried forward in this position until the toes of the swinging leg pass the knee of the supporting leg. Forward rotation of the swinging leg is limited in part by hamstring elasticity; speed of the swing is limited by quadricep strength and hip flexibility. These limitations can be lessened by training.

Swing

At the moment of touchdown, the swinging leg becomes the supporting leg. The foot, which was moving forward, now comes to a dead stop.

The supporting leg should be rigid enough to prevent the center of gravity from dropping too low, but flexible enough to allow shock absorption and transfer of momentum. Optimum angles at the amortization phase appear to be 160° to 170° flexion at the hip, 135° to 145° flexion at the knee, and 70° to 85° flexion at the ankle. At the end of the support phase, at the moment of takeoff, a slightly bent knee (170° to 175°) provides the best conditions for acceleration of the center of gravity. A fully extended (180°) leg increases stride length, but also decreases stride frequency, slowing down overall speed. As a result, a slightly bent knee is better at takeoff.

The supporting phase takes only about 0.1 second, during which the supporting leg overcomes braking forces and propels the center of gravity forward. About 45% of the athlete's effort during this 0.1 second is directed at landing and amortization, and the other 55% is spent on the forward drive. Exercises designed to optimize the supporting phase should address both components. Several such exercises are given on the next page.

Support

Flying Action

During this phase, the leg that had been the supporting leg moves upward and backward, while the swinging leg rotates upward and forward. As a result, the legs move in opposite directions. The farther the legs can be separated, the quicker and stronger they can move toward each other on landing. Moving in opposite directions like this requires the quadriceps of the supporting leg and the hamstrings of the swinging leg to stretch. Good flexibility of the gluteals, quadriceps, and hamstrings improves knee-lift and helps lengthen stride.

Arm action

The arms move opposite the legs, providing a counterbalance to leg thrust. When running in a straight line, the direction of movement for all body segments should be linear. However, the anatomy of the arms and shoulders makes the arms tend to move to the side on the backswing. Any side-to-side motions of the arms causes tension in the upper body, potentially decreasing velocity.

Exercises

The stride is clearly a complex movement, with a variety of events occurring simultaneously. Having looked at the primary components of the stride, we can address the training of each component with specific exercises.

No athlete should be expected to do all of the following exercises. A variety is presented to allow maximum flexibility in terms of available equipment, and to allow the athlete to create the best individualized program. However, every program should include at least one exercise from every category.

Posture

These exercises help to maintain the optimum postural angles during running, maximizing stride length and minimizing trunk weaving.

Toes rising. Stand upright, with your hands on your hips. Go from standing flat-footed to standing on tip-toe. Hold for a moment. Let yourself back down and repeat.

Rocking walk. Stand upright. Raise the right knee and bring it up to your chest by grabbing it below the kneecap and pulling. Simultaneously stand on tip-toe with the left foot. Hold for a moment, lower and repeat with other leg.

Skipping. This is regular step-hop-step-hop skipping. Concentrate on taking big steps and long hops.

These exercises facilitate knee, quadriceps, and hamstring strength and flexibility.

Forced knee flexion. Stand on your left foot, supporting yourself against a table with your left hand. Using your right hand, grab your right foot behind your back. Pull up on your right foot, tilting your pelvis forward. Hold, relax, and repeat with left leg. This improves knee and quadricep flexibility.

Forced swing. Stand next to a table in the same position as for forced knee flexion. Once you have pulled your right foot up behind your back, slowly flex at your right hip, providing isometric resistance with your hand. Then pull your leg back again, providing isometric resistance with your quadriceps.

Back swing. Steady yourself against a wall. Lift your right leg straight out in front of you, and have a partner hold it at 90°. Slowly try to press your leg back down again, with your partner isometrically preventing movement. Hold, and repeat with other leg.

Front swing. Steady yourself against a wall. Lift your right leg out behind you, and have a partner hold it. Slowly try to bring your right leg forward, with your partner isometrically preventing movement. Hold, and repeat with other leg.

Hip kick in place. Lean over and support yourself against a table. Lift one leg and kick back as high as you can, keeping your knee bent as tightly as possible. Repeat with other leg.

Knee lift in place. Lean over and support yourself against a table. Lift one knee forward as high as you can, keeping it bent as tightly as possible. Repeat with other leg.

Hip kick run. Run at a moderate pace, kicking back the rear leg with every step.

Knee lift run. Run at a moderate pace, lifting the swinging leg as high as you can with every step.

Front circle run. Run at a relatively slow pace, concentrating on moving your feet in a circular motion. This requires kicking your foot backward as your foot leaves the ground, and deliberately bringing it up and forward in a circular path.

Bike in air. Straddling an elevated beam (such as a gymnastics balance beam), move your legs in circles as if you are bicycling in the air, paying attention to lifting your knees

Swing

high on the forward swing and your feet far back on the backward swing.

Sitting bike. Sitting on the edge of a table or chair, hold both feet off the ground and move your legs in circles as if you are bicycling in the air. Pay attention to lifting your knees high on the forward swing.

Rubber resistance swing. Fasten one end of a rubber strap to a wall and the other end to your right ankle. Face away from the wall, leaning over a table. Support yourself on the table with both hands. Position yourself so the rubber strap is at resting length with your right leg straight out behind you. Bring your leg from out behind you to a position with your knee tucked up under your chest. Return to original position. Repeat, then repeat with other leg.

Hops in place. Hop on your right foot, bringing your left knee up as high as you can. Then hop on your left foot, bringing your right knee up as high as you can. Alternate left and right. Repeat.

Swing-lunge jumps. Start by kneeling with your right knee down and your left knee up (the "about to be knighted" position). Lunge up and forward, propelling yourself with your left leg and bringing your right knee up as far as it will go. Land on your left foot. Repeat with legs reversed.

Support

As mentioned above, in this phase the supporting leg overcomes braking forces and propels the center of gravity forward. These exercises improve landing, amortization, and the forward drive.

One-leg depth jumps. Stand with your feet together on a box eight to twelve inches high. Jump off the box, landing on your right foot, then immediately push off with your right leg and land with your feet together. Try to jump as far as you can with each jump. Repeat with other leg.

Two-leg depth jumps. Stand with your feet together on a box eight to twelve inches high. Jump off the box, landing on both feet, then immediately push off with both feet and land with your feet together. Try to jump as far as you can with each jump. Repeat.

Alternating-leg depth jumps. Stand with your feet together on a box eight to twelve inches high. Jump off the box, landing on your right foot, then immediately push off with your right leg and land on your left foot. Immediately push off with your left leg and land with your feet together. Try to jump as far as you can with each jump. Repeat, leading with your left foot.

Elevated skipping. Set out several eight-to-twelve-inch boxes at two-pace intervals. Start with your feet together on one box. Jump down and land on the ground on your right foot. Hop up onto the next box, landing again on your right foot, then jump down from that box and land on the ground on your left foot. Hop up onto the next box, landing again on your left foot, and so on.

Low hurdle jumps. Place low hurdles or boxes at appropriate intervals. Practice successive broad jumps (feet together) over them.

Incline jumps. Practice standing long jump, triple jump, and multi-jumps up a hill (15˚ to 30˚).

Increasing strides. Run short distances (e.g. 100 yards), increasing the length of every stride as you go. Do this both without weights and with a six-to-ten-pound weight vest.

Low hurdles. Practice sprinting over low hurdles placed seven to nine strides apart.

The next two exercises require a medicine ball (a soft ball with a heavy central weight).

Legs rebound. Lie on your back with your feet together and your knees brought up to your chest. Have a partner toss a medicine ball to you. Catch it with the bottoms of your feet and toss it back to your partner.

Squat catch. Sit in a semi-squatting position, holding a medicine ball with both hands. Throw the ball upward as you straighten out from the squat. Catch the ball as you go into the squat again.

These exercises improve leg split.

Stationary swing lunge. Start by kneeling with your right knee down and your left knee up (the same "about to be knighted" position as for *swing lunge jumps*)

Lunge straight up, swinging your right knee up and bringing your left knee down. Land kneeling, with your left knee down and your right knee up. Repeat with legs reversed.

Stationary split jump. Stand upright. Jump straight up, kicking right leg forward and left leg backward in mid-air as

Flying Action

far as you can. Land with both legs together. Repeat with legs reversed.

Arm action. These exercises are intended to minimize side-to-side arm motion in running.

Mirror test. Run in place in front of a mirror. Watch your elbows to make sure they don't drift too much to the sides. Get the feel of running without lateral arm motion, and incorporate this feeling into your stride.

Hurdle test. Place two high hurdles (or any two barriers that are about 42" high) about three feet apart. Run in place between them, keeping your elbows from touching the hurdles.

Arm pumping. Basketball dribbling and boxing speed bag punching are excellent exercises for training arm pumping.

Effort

Finally, good stride length is dependent on giving a good, consistent effort to keeping strides long. Many resistance exercises, such as chin-ups, bench press, and arm curls, are good for training concentration and effort.

Each of these exercises is good for improving stride length, which, in turn, improves running speed. Given the primary role that running plays in many sports activities, training to improve stride has the potential to have a major impact on sports performance. ❑

Training With the Objective to Improve Stride Length
R. Korchemny
National Strength and Conditioning Association Journal
V 10 # 2: 21-25, April/May 1988
V 10 #3: 61-64, June/July 1988

MOTIVATIONAL STATES AND ATHLETIC COMPETITION

Butterflies in the stomach before competition sometimes enhance performance, but, if too severe, may hinder it. On the other hand, insufficient excitement can also interfere with optimum performance.

Sports psychology aims to understand the athlete's feelings and behavior and identify effective methods of modifying those feelings and behavior to improve performance.

The general concern of sports psychologists has been to enable athletes to adjust their **level of arousal** to the level that encourages the best performance. Usually, emphasis is placed on *reducing* arousal levels, in the belief that excessive nervousness is most likely to interfere with winning the gold.

Recommended techniques for reducing arousal have included biofeedback, visualization, and transcendental meditation. Some sports psychologists are now suggesting a new way of looking at the athlete's emotional states, called **Reversal Theory**.

Reversal Theory suggests that an athlete may interpret feelings in one of two ways, depending on which of two underlying emotional states (called *metamotivational states*) he or she is in at a given instant.

The authors list a number of pairs of metamotivational states, including one called the **telic vs. paratelic**.

You are in a *telic state* when you feel goal-oriented, interested in ends rather than means, are future-oriented, planned, generally realistic, and exhibit a preference for controlled, stable, "low arousal" activity.

You are in a *paratelic state* when you feel process-oriented, interested in means rather than ends, are present-oriented, spontaneous, off in a land of make-believe, and exhibit a preference for exciting, "high arousal" activity.

Although most people demonstrate a preference for one of these two states, the authors suggest that it should be possible to learn to switch back and forth between them at will. This would give the athlete much greater control of his or her emotional responses at critical times, such as before competition.

Consider:

A highly aroused athlete in the *telic state* interprets that pre-competition arousal as *anxiety*.

A highly aroused athlete in the *paratelic state*, on the other hand, interprets pre-competition arousal as *excitement*. Same arousal, different emotional response. A switch from *telic* to *paratelic* would allow the athlete to use the energy of the moment as excitement, possibly improving performance—rather than as anxiety, possibly worsening performance.

Likewise, an athlete experiencing *low* arousal in a *paratelic state* interprets that low arousal as *boredom*.

An athlete experiencing low arousal in the *telic state* interprets that low arousal as *relaxation*. Again, same arousal, different emotional response. Again, same potential for turning an emotion that might interfere with performance into one that might enhance it.

The key to taking advantage of the metamotivational states is the ability to change from one to another. The authors suggest that visualizations and other techniques might be used to accomplish this change between states.

Both Reversal Theory and its application to sports are in their infancy. However, if a reliable strategy for changing states could be developed, it could be a powerful pre-competition tool for the athlete. ❑

Cognitive Intervention with Elite Performers: Reversal Theory
J.H. Kerr, BEd, MA
British Journal of Sports Medicine
V 21: 29-33, June 1987

REACTION TIME AND MENTAL FOCUS

In sprinting events, some of which may last less than ten seconds, a fast start out of the blocks can make the difference between winning and losing. Speed out of the blocks is largely determined by reaction time.

Much research has looked into ways to minimize reaction time. Earlier studies have identified two types of mental focus that can be adopted at the starting gun: a **sensory set**, in which the athlete concentrates on the sensory input (sound of the starting gun), and a **motor set**, in which the athlete concentrates on what the muscular response to the sound of the gun will be.

More recent research has further divided the motor set into two subtypes: **execution emphasis** and **initiation emphasis**. *Execution emphasis* involves concentration on the details of the impending movement. *Initiation emphasis* involves concentration on details of just the first few moments of the impending movement, focusing on producing a rapid movement initiation.

Fourteen members of a university track team (eleven male, three female) were studied to determine which of these methods is the most effective at reducing reaction time.

Upon interviewing the subjects before the study, the authors noted that each athlete came to the study with a "set preference"; through the course of individual experience, each had spontaneously adopted for his or her own use either a sensory or motor set at the starting gun.

Each subject was tested on a track in standard starting blocks, five starts per day over twelve days for a total of sixty starts. Reaction time was measured electronically, from the firing of the starting gun to the moment pressure-sensitive pads in the blocks sensed pressure from the runner's foot. Subjects were told to concentrate either on the sound of the gun (sensory set), on the details of the impending movement (motor set, execution emphasis), or on producing a rapid movement initiation (motor set, initiation emphasis).

None of the mental sets consistently produced the shortest reaction times. However, the athletes who reported a spontaneous preference for the sensory set exhibited fastest reaction times when directed to perform under sensory set instructions. Those who reported a spontaneous preference for the motor set exhibited fastest reaction times when performing under motor set instructions. Among those with motor set preference, execution emphasis produced slightly shorter reaction times than initiation emphasis.

These results indicate that coaches may be able to minimize reaction times by identifying the spontaneous set preferences in their athletes and reinforcing each individual's preference. Among those with motor set preferences, slight further reductions in reaction times may be gained by promoting execution emphasis over initiation emphasis. ❏

Sprint Start Reaction Time: On the Advisability of Sensory vs Motor Sets
E. Buckolz and B. Vigars
Canadian Journal of Sports Sciences
V 12 # 1: 51-53, March 1987

Exercise produces heat, and the ability to dissipate that heat can influence performance. If heat is not dissipated well enough during exercise, body temperature rises and heat exhaustion sets in. In marathon runners, body temperatures in excess of 105.8 °F have been reported.

Athletes who have trained in the heat have lower body temperatures both at rest and during exercise; this is the result of a change in their thermoregulation, with a lowering of their thermal "set-point." By having lower body temperatures during exercise, heat-trained athletes can exercise longer before raising their body temperatures to levels that limit performance.

Since, by virtue of lower body temperatures, heat-trained athletes can exercise longer, can artificially lowering body temperature before exercise allow non-heat-trained athletes to exercise longer?

To find out, subjects were tested in a "climate chamber" in which ambient temperature was controllable. Temperature was dropped from room temperature to 41 °F to 50 °F, and held there for thirty minutes of relaxation. The temperature was then raised to 64.4 °F for exhaustive stationary bicycle exercise. For control values, the experiment was repeated without the temperature drop.

The precooling caused slightly below-normal body temperatures, but increased endurance time by an average of 12%. Precooling also caused some changes in oxygen consumption during exercise, changes usually characteristic of endurance-trained athletes. In addition, during the precooled trial the athletes had heart rates that were significantly lower than during the non-precooled trial, even though they were performing at the same level of exertion.

Subjects also showed a decreased tendency to shiver at the lower temperatures. This is interpreted as a short-term adaptation to cold, an adaptation that appears necessary for precooling procedures to have an effect on exercise.

Why does precooling work? It may be that precooling decreases blood supply to the skin, increasing the amount of blood and oxygen available to the exercising muscles. Or it may be that precooling provides a "thermal debt" that must be repaid, delaying onset of temperature-induced stress.

In any event, an increase in endurance of 12% is considerable. Perhaps a pre-race "cool down" (using a water-cooled jacket or other device) rather than a pre-race

IMPROVING PERFORMANCE BY LOWERING BODY TEMPERATURE

"warm up" will become the standard for endurance events in the near future.

[Ed. note: It has long been felt that "warming up" before an event improves performance. How that fits in with precooling, and whether precooling increases risk of injury, has yet to be evaluated.] ❏

Thermoregulatory, Cardiovascular, and Muscular Factors Related to Exercise After Precooling
H. Olschewski and K. Bruck
Journal of Applied Physiology
V 64 # 2: 803-811, Feb 1988

CONDITIONING FOR TENNIS

Tennis, a popular sport year-round, is especially popular during the summer. Because so many people play tennis, it accounts for a considerable percentage of sports injuries seen by doctors during the summer months. Some of these injuries are due to poor technique, some to inadequate conditioning. Injuries of either type are potentially preventable.

The elbow is the most common site of injury, accounting for about 31% of all tennis injuries. Next are the ankle (8%), shoulder (5%), knee (4%), wrist (2%), and forearm (1%). Generally, men have more shoulder and knee injuries, and women more wrist and forearm injuries. This may be because men tend to have greater upper body strength, tend to serve harder, and often play more aggressively than women.

The best-known tennis injury is "tennis elbow." Tennis elbow is an inflammation of the tendons that originate from the bump on the outside of the elbow. (Technically speaking, that bump is the *lateral epicondyle*, and tennis elbow is *lateral epicondylitis*). Tennis elbow is most common in players who play often, play hard, play long, or have poor technique, especially poor backhand technique. It is also common in adult beginners, who are usually predisposed to tennis elbow by having poor forearm strength.

The tendons that originate from the lateral epicondyle connect to muscles that bend back the wrist and fingers. Consequently, anything that increases the stress on those muscles increases stress on those tendons. Examples include "leading elbow" backhand, off-center ball contact, poor timing, poor bodyweight transfer, wet or dead balls, tightly strung racquets, too small or too large a grip, and fast court surfaces. If a player starts with poor strength, endurance, or flexibility in the muscles that bend back the wrist and fingers, overloading those muscles with any of these factors can lead to injury.

Shoulder injuries are often caused by incorrect stroke technique, inappropriate equipment, or poor muscle strength, flexibility, or endurance. These tend to be impingement or stretch injuries.

Lower extremity injuries can be from either trauma or overuse. Traumatic injuries are those occurring acutely on the tennis court, such as sprains. Overuse injuries are those occurring from repeated muscular and tendinous stress, and include patello-femoral pain, tibial stress syndrome, tendonitis, and bursitis. The quick starts, stops, and changes of direction common in tennis bring on these repeated stresses and make overuse injuries common. As with tennis elbow, the players predisposed to lower extremity injuries are those who play often, play hard, and play long, and those who have poor lower extremity strength, endurance, or flexibility.

Many tennis players play once a week or less, and do no training in between. As a result, they have inadequate aerobic capacity, strength, flexibility, and, often, poor technique and neglected equipment—all predisposing them to injury. A pre-season (and ongoing) conditioning program should address the following:

- aerobic training
- anaerobic training
- muscle strength
- muscle flexibility
- technique
- equipment

Aerobic Training

According to the recommendation of the American College of Sports Medicine, exercise intended to promote aerobic fitness should meet the following criteria:

- **Activity.** "Any activity that uses large-muscle groups and that can be maintained continuously and is rhythmical and aerobic, such as running, walking, swimming, skating, cycling, rowing, cross-country skiing, rope skipping, and various endurance-game activities."
- **Frequency.** 3 to 5 times per week
- **Intensity.** Of sufficient intensity to raise the heart rate to 60% to 90% of maximum heart rate (where maximum heart rate is approx. 220 minus age)
- **Duration.** 15 to 60 minutes of continuous exertion, depending on intensity

If you are just starting to get into shape, the most important precaution is to begin *slowly* and increase intensity and duration *gradually*. Don't try to reach 90% of maximum heart rate for an hour the first time out. Allow time for your body to adapt, both to increase aerobic capacity and to decrease risk of injury.

Does tennis itself meet the American College of Sports Medicine recommendations? According to a recent study (see *Sports Research Monthly*, December 1987), singles tennis raises heart rates to about 61% of maximum, barely meeting the ACSM recommendation. Doubles raises heart rate to only about 33% of maximum, well below the ACSM recommendation. Since singles tennis barely qualifies as promoting aerobic fitness, adding a second aerobic activity is probably advisable.

Anaerobic Training

Tennis is characterized by a continual succession of brief, rapid explosive movements. Players may perform hundreds of these anaerobic movements in a game. Anaerobic training can improve performance of these movements, in turn decreasing fatigue and increasing stroke control.

Anaerobic training involves a series of short (30 to 45 second) all-out movements with a two- or three-minute rest between movements. Common anaerobic training movements include track sprints, stairs, hills, and on-court drills.

As with aerobic exercise, start slowly and work up gradually, to decrease risk of injury. Eventually work your way up to sets of ten.

Muscle Strength

Tennis requires both upper and lower body strength, in particular the muscles of the shoulder girdle, elbow, forearm, hand, quadriceps, hamstrings, calves, back, and abdomen. Unless otherwise noted, for each of the following exercises do 3 sets of 15, with a 30 second rest between sets.

Abdomen

The abdominal muscles ("abs") run from the bottom of the rib cage to the top of the pelvis. Most exercises designed to work the abdominals in fact target the *psoas*, one of the muscles responsible for bending at the hip, rather than the abdominals, the muscles responsible for bringing the bottom of the rib cage closer to the top of the pelvis. "Ab machines" are generally not satisfactory because they typically target the psoas, not the abdominals. One way of targeting the abs and not the psoas is as follows:

Lie on your back, knees bent, arms across chest. Raise your head and shoulder blades off the ground and hold for 5 to 10 seconds. Avoid bending your neck too far forward. Lower and repeat.

Quadriceps

The quadriceps is the set of four muscles (*quad* means *four*) in the front of the thigh. The quadriceps are primarily responsible for straightening out the knee.

Stand upright, then drop to a squatting position, being careful not to drop below horizontal (to minimize risk of knee injury). Rise and repeat.

Alternatively, stand with your back to a wall, with heels 1 to 2 feet from the wall. Lean back flat against the wall, then slowly slide down until your thighs are horizontal. Hold 20 seconds; slowly rise. Repeat 10 times.

Most quad machines are acceptable for this exercise.

Hamstrings

The hamstrings are the muscles in the back of the thigh, primarily responsible for bending the knee.

Place an ankle weight around your right ankle. Stand upright, facing and steadying yourself against a wall. Lift your right foot back by bending at the knee to 90°. Hold for 8 to 10 seconds; lower and repeat. Repeat with left leg. Increase weight as you improve.

Most hamstring machines are acceptable for this exercise.

Calves

The calf muscles, the *gastrocnemius* and *soleus*, are primarily responsible for bending the foot down at the ankle.

Stand on a stair or stable block, with the ball of your foot on the edge of the stair and your heels extending out over the edge. Lower your heels so they are as far below the level of the stair as you can get them. Then raise your body by standing on your toes. Hold for 5 seconds, then lower again. Repeat. As you improve your calf strength, do each leg separately. As you improve further, repeat with toes pointed in and toes pointed out.

Skipping is also a good calf exercise.

The hip abductors are responsible for moving the leg out to the side. Lying leg lifts are a good way to work the hip abductors.

Lie on your side. Keeping your knee straight and your hips perpendicular to the ground, lift your upper leg up as high as you can (stop short of 90°), keeping your heel higher than your toes. Hold for 5 to 10 seconds. Lower and repeat.

Hip abductors

The hip adductors are responsible for moving the leg in from the side.

Lie on your side. Bend your upper leg at the knee and bring it forward. Keeping your lower leg straight and your hips perpendicular to the ground, lift your *lower* leg up as high as you can, keeping your heel higher than your toes. Hold for 5 to 10 seconds. Lower and repeat.

Hip adductors

The paraspinal muscles are located on either side of your backbone, and are responsible for straightening out the back from a bent-over position.

Lie face-down on a table, with your hips on the edge of the table and your upper body hanging off the edge. Place a pillow under your hips for comfort. (You may need to get someone or something to hold your legs in place.) Lower your upper body down, bending at the hips. Keep your back straight. Then, arching your back, bring your upper body up to horizontal. Lower and repeat. Do not raise your upper body above horizontal. Not rising above horizontal minimizes the risk of low back injuries.

Paraspinals

The shoulder girdle and elbow are responsible for the motions of the shoulder and arms. The best way to work these muscles is with a progressive-weight system using free weights or machines. Some competitive tennis players have complained that high-resistance, low-rep training affects their timing. This problem can be minimized by use of low-resistance, high-rep training.

Since tennis can involve arm motions in any direction, the athlete should train all the motions of the shoulder and arm. These include:

Shoulder girdle

- **shoulder flexion** (bringing the arm straight out in front)
- **shoulder extension** (bringing the arm from straight-out-in-front down to parallel with the trunk)
- **shoulder abduction** (bringing the arm straight out to the side)
- **shoulder adduction** (bringing the arm from straight-out-to-the-side down to parallel with the trunk)
- **shoulder internal rotation** (rotating the upper arm inward)
- **shoulder external rotation** (rotating the upper arm outward)

Biceps and triceps

The biceps bend the arm at the elbow; the triceps straighten the arm at the elbow.

The standard biceps exercise, the biceps curl, is still the best. Start with a dumbbell or barbell down at waist level, holding it with palms up. Bring it up to shoulder level, then lower it back down to starting position.

Be careful not to let your elbows drift back while you lift.

To work your triceps, find a stable chair. Sit as close as possible to the edge of the chair, with your arms securely placed on either side of you on the edge of the chair. Put your feet about four feet in front of you. Placing all your weight on your arms, slide off the edge of the chair and lower yourself as far down as you can go. Then raise your body up to the starting position, keeping your back as close as possible to the edge of the chair. Repeat. As this exercise becomes easier, start with your feet elevated on another chair.

Biceps and triceps machines also work well for these muscles.

Forearm

The most important forearm muscles for tennis are the wrist and grip muscles.

Work the wrist extensors (muscles that bend the wrist back) as follows. Lay your arm on a table, your palm facing down, with your hand off the edge of a table. Hold a 1 to 2 pound weight in your hand, and rock your wrist back as far as it will go. Lower and repeat.

The wrist flexors (muscles that bend the wrist forward) are exercised in a similar manner. Lay your arm on a table, your hand off the edge of the table, with your palm facing *up*. Hold a 1 to 2 pound weight in your hand, and rock your wrist *forward* as far as it will go. Lower and repeat.

Work the grip muscles by squeezing a tennis ball for 10 seconds at a time.

Muscle Flexibility

The same muscles that need to be strong also need to be flexible. Stretch both before and after working out or playing tennis. You should briefly warm up before stretching to minimize injury to muscles, tendons, and ligaments. *Do not bounce.* You should feel tension, but no pain. Work slowly and gradually. Hold each stretch for 15 to 30 seconds, repeat 3 to 4 times.

Quadriceps

Stand on your left foot. Grab your right foot with your right hand behind your back. Tilting your pelvis forward, pull up on your right foot with your hand. Hold and repeat.

Hamstrings

Sit on a low stool. Place your right leg out in front of you, with your toes pointing straight up. Lean forward, with your back straight, and feel the stretch in the back of your thigh. Hold and repeat. Repeat with left leg. Now repeat the entire process with your toes pointed inward, and again with your toes pointed outward.

Calves

Stand facing a wall, with one foot about four feet from the wall and the other foot about two feet from the wall. Lean against the wall with your forearms, and gradually move your hips forward, shifting all of your weight onto your rear foot. Hold with rear knee straight, then repeat with rear knee bent. Switch feet and repeat.

Paraspinals

Lie on your back, knees bent. Keeping the small of your back against the floor, rotate your hips so your knees move as far to one side as possible. Hold. Now rotate your hips so

your knees move as far to the other side as possible. Hold.
Repeat.

Shoulder girdle

For each of these, hold 20-30 seconds; repeat 3-4 times.

Shoulder extension: Move your arms straight out in front of
you and over your head as high as you can hold them. Hold
and repeat.

Shoulder abduction: Move your arms straight out to the
side and over your head as high as you can hold them. Hold
and repeat.

Shoulder internal rotation: With your arms dangling at
your sides, rotate your arms inward (right arm
counterclockwise, left arm clockwise) as far as you can.
Holding the rotated position, move arms straight out to the
side as far as you can. Hold. Repeat.

Shoulder external rotation: With your arms dangling at
your sides, rotate your arms outward (right arm clockwise, left
arm counterclockwise) as far as you can. Holding the rotated
position, move arms straight out to the side as far as you can.
Hold. Repeat.

Forearm

Grasp the right hand with the left. With the right elbow
straight and the right arm rotated as far counterclockwise as
possible, gently bend (flex) the right wrist forward. Hold and
repeat. Now with the right elbow straight and the right arm
rotated as far *clockwise* as possible, gently bend (flex) the right
wrist *backward*. Hold and repeat. Repeat for left wrist.

Technique

Technique refers to the set of skills gained through experience
and training. Good technique can help prevent injuries; bad
technique can predispose to injuries. Part of technique is
recognizing and adapting to the specific characteristics of a
variety of playing conditions.

For example, grass and cement courts maintain ball velocity,
so the ball travels faster and at a lower angle. Consequently,
the ball encounters the racquet with more force and impact.
This calls for a particular technique. On the other hand, clay
and other rough-surface courts decrease ball velocity, so the
ball travels slower and at a higher angle. Here, the ball

encounters the racquet with less force and impact, calling for a different technique.

Poorly maintained courts, or wet, dirty, or leaf-strewn courts present their own hazards that affect both mode of playing and risk of injury.

Equipment

Racquets

The type of racquet and the type of stringing will vary depending on the skill and experience of the player. For beginners, a wooden racquet is satisfactory. More experienced players often benefit from metal, graphite, or composite racquets. Larger racquets provide a larger hitting surface, which decreases the number of misses and decreases risk of injury.

Grip is an important consideration, and can make a big difference in arm forces. The correct grip size is determined by measuring from the tip of the ring finger to the palmer crease between the middle and ring fingers. This should equal the grip circumference. As mentioned above, a racquet that has too large or too small a grip, or is too heavy, can increase stress on muscles and tendons and predispose a player to overuse injuries.

Type of stringing also depends on the skill and experience of the player. Gut strings are more sensitive than nylon, but they lose their responsiveness in 3 to 4 weeks and they are expensive. Nylon is less expensive and lasts longer. For players with tennis elbow, lower string tensions result in lower tendon stress.

Balls

It is worthwhile using balls that are in good condition. Wet, dead, bald, or otherwise suboptimal balls bounce and fly differently from well-conditioned balls. Trying to improve your game using balls with poor bounce and flight characteristics may slow your improvement.

Shoes

Good tennis shoes should provide support for all aspects of the game—running, stopping, turning, jumping, pushing off.

The sole should absorb the force of repeated foot strikes. The upper (preferably of reinforced leather) should provide firm side-to-side support for sudden starts and stops. The heel should be rigid and strong to provide rear foot control and help protect the Achilles tendon. A slight heel lift shifts some of the weight to the ball of the foot, putting the player in a responsive playing position and helping to reduce the stress on the Achilles tendon. The choice of tread pattern can vary, depending on the court surface. Nubbed tread patterns, with rows of alternating high and low nubs, are good for hard surfaces. Level herringbone tread patterns, on the other hand, are best for clay courts. ❑

Pre-Season Tennis Conditioning
C. Peterson
Canadian Family Physician
V 34: 141-145, Jan 1988

CONDITIONING FOR SKIING

When winter approaches, many people prepare to take to the slopes in search of the perfect powder. Unfortunately, as noted in this article from the *Journal of Orthopaedic and Sports Physical Therapy*, "skiing is probably the sport in which the largest proportion of people who participate, especially adults, do not condition themselves."

Little research has been done on the effect of ski conditioning on risk of injury. However, it has been demonstrated that conditioning delays the onset of fatigue, and fatigue plays a major role in causing ski injury.

Author Matthew Morrissey and associates examined the biomechanical and physiological demands that skiing places on the body, as well as common types of skiing injuries. Based on this information, they suggest a conditioning program to increase skiing safety and pleasure.

The program employs three modalities: **resistance (weight) training** to increase strength and endurance in appropriate muscles; **flexibility training** to prevent various parts of the body from being overstretched during a fall; and **aerobic training** to improve cardiovascular capacity.

Resistance Training

Increased strength in the muscles surrounding a joint improves stability at that joint and decreases risk of injury. It also increases the finesse with which movements that rely on muscular strength—such as many skiing movements—may be performed.

To increase muscular strength and endurance, the authors recommend that resistance exercise be performed for the following muscle groups:

Upper Body
- **shoulder flexors** (the muscles that raise the arms forward; mostly anterior deltoids).
- **shoulder extensors** (the muscles that pull the arms down from a "raised-forward" position; mostly latissimus dorsi)
- **shoulder internal rotators** (the muscles that turn the upper arm in toward the body)
- **shoulder horizontal adductors** (the muscles that pull the arm in across the chest; mostly pectorals)

- **elbow extensors** (the muscles that straighten the elbow; triceps)
- **finger flexors** (the muscles that curl the fingers)

Trunk

- **neck extensors** (the muscles that pull the head back)
- **trunk flexors** (the muscles that pull the trunk forward, or, looking at it from another perspective, pull the legs up toward the trunk; abdominals and psoas)
- **lateral trunk flexors** (the muscles that bend the trunk to the side; obliques and spinal erectors)

Lower Body

- **hip flexors** (the muscles that raise the leg straight forward; rectus femoris, psoas)
- **hip extensors** (the muscles that pull the leg down from a "raised-forward" position; gluteals, hamstrings)
- **hip abductors** (the muscles that pull the leg out to the side; gluteus medius, tensor fascia latae)
- **hip adductors** (the muscles that pull the leg in from an "out-to-the-side" position; adductor magnus, longus, and brevus)
- **knee extensors** (the muscles that straighten the knee; quadriceps)
- **knee flexors** (the muscles that bend the knee; hamstrings)
- **tibial internal and external rotators** (the muscles that turn the feet inward and outward without motion at the ankle)
- **ankle invertors** (the muscles that rock the ankle out so your weight is on the outer edge of your foot; tibialis anterior and posterior)
- **ankle evertors** (the muscles that rock the ankle in so your weight is on the inner edge of your foot; peroneals)
- **ankle plantarflexors** (the muscles that bend your ankle down so your toes move away from your shin; gastrocnemius and soleus, more commonly referred to as your calf muscles)

Exercises for these muscle groups can be performed using a variety of equipment, including free weights, cable-and-pulley devices, and weight machines.

Flexibility

Movement at most joints is limited at least in part by soft tissue, including muscle. Stretching increases the range of motion at joints by increasing the flexibility of soft tissue. This decreases risk of injury from a fall while skiing by allowing joints to flex more before soft tissue damage occurs.

The authors recommend static stretching (stretches in which you relax into the stretch and hold the stretched position) for the actions listed below. Hold stretches for 10 to 20 seconds (except trunk stretches: 2 to 4 seconds) and repeat 10 to 15 times.

Shoulder external rotation with horizontal abduction. This exercise stretches the front of the shoulders. Hold your arms straight out to your sides, palms up. Have a partner gently pull your arms back. (Alternative if no partner: in the same position, stand in a doorway with your arms against the walls on either side of the doorway. Gently lean forward.) Hold and repeat.

Trunk flexion. This exercise stretches the back. Stand up straight. With your knees bent, bend at the waist until your chest touches your legs. Feel for the stretch in your back. Hold and repeat.

Trunk rotation. This exercise increases trunk mobility, which is helpful in turning. Stand in a doorway. With your feet planted, rotate your upper body as far to the right as you can, using your arms in the doorway to help balance. Hold, then do the same motion turning to the left. Repeat.

Hip flexion. This exercise stretches the back of the leg (hamstrings), and helps prevent hamstring strains and tears. Stand up straight. With your knees straight, cross one leg over the other, bend at the waist and try to touch your toes. Do not bounce. Hold, reverse legs, and repeat.

Ankle dorsiflexion (calf). This exercise stretches both major calf muscles (gastrocnemius and soleus). Stand facing a wall, with one foot about four feet from the wall and the other foot about two feet from the wall. Lean against the wall, and gradually move your hips forward, shifting all of your weight onto your rear foot. Hold with rear knee straight, then repeat with rear knee bent. Switch feet and repeat.

Ankle inversion (peroneals). This exercise increases ankle flexibility. Stand facing a wall, with one foot about four feet from the wall and the other foot about two feet from the wall. Roll the ankle of your rear foot outward, so weight is on the outside edge of the foot. Lean against the wall, and *gradually* move your hips forward, shifting *some* (not all) of your weight onto your rear foot. You will not be able to support nearly as much weight on your rear foot in this exercise as you did in ankle dorsiflexion. Feel for the stretch along the outside of your ankle. Hold. Switch feet and repeat.

Aerobic work

Alpine (downhill) skiing makes demands both on aerobic and anaerobic systems. The typical ski run consists of many one-to-two-and-a-half-minute bouts of high-intensity exertion followed by brief rests (on the slope on the way down), with occasional longer rests (on the chair on the way back up). These bouts of high-intensity exertion rely on the aerobic system for approximately 65 to 70% of their energy.

Because of this, the authors recommend a conditioning program including "exercises of brief duration that will tax both the anaerobic and aerobic systems." Several (seven to ten) one- to two-and-a-half-minute runs at slightly faster than a jogging pace would appropriately address these criteria.

Other exercise

Finally, the authors recommend an exercise they call the "pillow jump," which mimics skiing movements and will improve the skier's balance, agility, and endurance.

Perform the exercise by standing parallel to a pile of pillows and jumping sideways from one side of the pillows to the other. Increase number of jumps and height of the pile of pillows as the exercise becomes easier.

This entire routine can be performed in about one hour. It should be performed at least twice a week during the off-season and at least three times a week during the ski season. If the routine eliminates three or four days of soreness on the slopes, or prevents a broken leg or torn hamstring, it is well worth the time spent. ❏

Conditioning for Skiing and Ski Injury Prevention
M. Morrissey et al., J. of Orthopaedic and Sports Physical Therapy
V 8 # 9: 428-437, March 1987

SWIMMING QUICKLY TO FITNESS

Swimming has often been called "the ideal exercise" because it involves all of the major muscle groups, has a low risk of injury, and provides aerobic and anaerobic benefits. But how great are these benefits, how soon do you see them, and do they translate into improved performance in other athletic endeavors?

Twelve previously sedentary (physically inactive) men and women aged 30 to 48 participated in a 12-week intensive swim-training program. They swam 30 to 45 minutes a day, 6 times a week, supplementing their swimming with 3-times-a-week weight training.

At the end of the twelve weeks, the subjects were tested for changes in heart, peripheral circulation, and oxygen uptake values.

Testing revealed improved cardiac pump capacity, increased muscle blood flow, increased lean muscle mass (in leg), and decreased subcutaneous fat (in leg) by the end of the program.

Since these favorable changes were measured on a stationary bicycle, it is reasonable to assume that changes obtained from swimming do indeed translate into improvements in other areas of athletic endeavor.

Remember, these appreciable improvements were noted in previously sedentary people after only 12 weeks of exercise. This degree of improvement in such a short time should be good news to those just beginning an exercise program. ❏

Cardiovascular Adaptations to Intense Swim Training in Sedentary Middle-Aged Men and Women
Circulation, V 75 #3: 323-330, 1987

BALLROOM DANCING FOR FITNESS

Bored with running? Tired of the same old aerobics routine? Is one more lap in the pool one more than you can stand? Take off your sweats, don your tuxedo or evening gown, and hit the dance floor!

Ballroom dancing is enjoying a resurgence of popularity in this country. And—surprise!—it's better exercise than you might have thought.

A recent study looked at the energy expenditure of ballroom dancing. Ten competitive ballroom dancing couples were evaluated for maximum heart rate on the dance floor using remote radio-controlled heart rate devices. Maximum oxygen consumption was calculated from heart rate. Couples danced either Modern (Modern Waltz, Tango, Foxtrot, Quickstep, and Viennese Waltz) or Latin American (Samba, Rumba, Paso Double, Cha Cha, and Jive) dance routines, 15 seconds for each dance, with a 15 to 20 second rest between dances. This arrangement simulates competitive ballroom dancing.

Men achieved heart rates averaging 170 beats per minute (bpm) for Modern, and 168 bpm for Latin American. Women averaged 179 bpm for Modern, and 177 bpm for Latin American. This is not because the dancers were out of shape; by treadmill test they all showed above-average fitness.

Exercise which elicits heart rates in this range qualifies as either "heavy" or "extremely heavy," depending on the classification scheme. Oxygen uptake averaged over 80% of maximum for both men and women, indicating they were exerting themselves at over 80% of their maximum. This degree of exertion is enough to provide a training effect, and to increase anaerobic threshold.

According to this study, competitive ballroom dancing is as physically demanding as basketball, squash, and cross-country running. Of course, not all ballroom dancers perform at competitive levels. Still, for those looking for some variety in their workout schedule, an evening on the dance floor may be just the ticket. ❑

Heart Rate and Estimated Energy Expenditure During Ballroom Dancing
B. Blanksby and P. Reidy
British Journal of Sports Medicine
V 22 # 2: 57-60, June 1988

PHYSIOLOGY

A number of recent findings about the body's physiologic processes bear strongly on athletic performance. New discoveries about the conditions affecting muscle growth and repair, aerobic conditioning, circadian rhythms, and blood cholesterol—among many other factors—carry subtle but significant implications in structuring an athlete's routine.

MUSCLE ANATOMY

The muscular system is one of the most adaptable in the body. The kind of adaptation depends on the type, duration, and intensity of muscle stress; the most common stress is *exercise*. To understand muscle response to exercise, however, we first need to look at the structure and function of normal muscle tissue.

Basic Structure

Skeletal muscles vary greatly in size and shape, from the large muscles controlling locomotion (gluteus, hamstrings, quadriceps, and others) to the tiny muscles of the inner ear. At a more microscopic level, however, skeletal muscles are very similar in structure and function.

Muscles are organized in several levels (see illustration, next page). At the highest level is the whole muscle. The whole muscle is made of many **fascicles**—the strands of muscle tissue you can see when you look at a piece of roast beef.

LEVELS OF MUSCLE ORGANIZATION

Whole muscle

Fascicle

Bundle of
muscle fibers

Muscle
fiber

Myofibril

Sarcomere

Thin filaments
made of actin

Thick filaments
made of myosin

- The whole muscle is made of *fascicles*
- Each fascicle is made of *muscle fibers*
- Each muscle fiber is made of *myofibrils*
- Each myofibril is made of *sarcomeres* laid end-to-end
- Each sarcomere is made of overlapping *thick* and *thin filaments*
- The thick and thin filaments are made of the proteins *myosin*

Each fascicle is made of many **muscle fibers**. Each fiber, in turn, is made of 500 to 10,000 **myofibrils**. Each myofibril is made of 1,000 to 2,000,000 **sarcomeres** laid end-to-end. Each sarcomere is made of overlapping **thick** and **thin filaments**. Finally, the thick and thin filaments are made of contractile and regulatory proteins—actin, myosin, tropomyosin, troponin, and others. The contractile and regulatory proteins are the foundation of muscle contraction.

Voluntary muscle contraction requires a number of steps. It starts with an electrical signal in the brain, a signal to contract. The signal travels along a nerve, first to the spinal column, then to the muscle. When the nerve approaches the muscle, the nerve branches into many tiny fibers. These fibers go throughout the muscle; the electrical signal travels along the nerve fibers and reaches all parts of the muscle essentially simultaneously.

At the end of each nerve fiber is a place where the nerve actually meets the muscle fibers, called the **neuromuscular junction**. The electrical signal crosses the neuromuscular junction and is transmitted deep inside the muscle fibers.

Here, the signal stimulates release of calcium inside the muscle, which causes the thick and thin filaments to slide across one another. When the filaments slide in this way, the sarcomere shortens, generating force. Billions of sarcomeres shortening in a muscle all at once result in contraction of the whole muscle.

The energy that causes the thick and thin filaments to slide across one another comes from **mitochondria**, the "factories" inside muscle cells that generate energy from glucose. Inside the mitochondria are enzymes that control the chemical reactions involved with breaking down glucose. Both resistance and strength training cause changes in mitochondria and mitochondrial enzymes.

Muscle Fiber Types

Not all muscle fibers are created equal. In humans, there are three main types of fibers: 1, 2A, and 2B. Type 1 fibers are slow to contract but slow to fatigue. Type 2A are fast to contract and intermediate to fatigue. Type 2B are fast to contract and fast to fatigue.

One of the reasons Type 1 fibers are slow to fatigue is that they have more mitochondria, making them capable of producing more energy. This decreases fatigability. Type 1 fibers also are smaller in diameter than Type 2A and 2B fibers, and have increased capillary blood flow around them. Having a smaller diameter and increased blood flow improves oxygen delivery and waste product removal from muscle fibers, also decreasing fatigability.

All muscles contain all three fiber types, but in differing amounts. The postural muscles of the back, for instance, have to be contracted much of the time to keep your upper body upright. These muscles have a high percentage of Type 1 (slow) fibers, so they fatigue slowly and recover quickly.

The biceps, on the other hand, are at rest most of the time. When called into action, they usually have to do brief bouts of intense activity—for example, a set of bicep curls. Your biceps tend to fatigue quickly and recover slowly, because they have a high percentage of Type 2 (fast) fibers.

When a muscle begins to contract, primarily Type 1 fibers are activated first, then Type 2A, then 2B. This sequence of fiber recruitment allows very delicate and finely tuned muscle responses to brain commands. It also makes Type 2B fibers difficult to train; most of the Type 1 and 2A fibers have to be activated already before a large percentage of the 2B fibers participate.

One way to remember the differences between muscle with predominantly type 1 (slow) fibers and muscle with predominantly type 2 (fast) fibers is to think chicken.

Everyone is familiar with dark meat and white meat. Chicken legs—dark meat—have to hold up the chicken most of the day. Not surprisingly, the chicken leg consists of muscle tissue that is slow to fatigue and fast to recover. This corresponds to muscle with predominantly type 1 (slow) fibers in humans. Dark meat is dark because it has a greater number of mitochondria (mitochondria are dark). Having more mitochondria gives chicken legs a greater capacity to make energy, making them slow to fatigue and fast to recover.

On the other hand, chicken breasts—white meat—are at rest most of the time but are called on for brief bouts of intense activity, for example a few seconds of flying around the barnyard. Chicken breast consists of muscle tissue that can contract quickly, but is fast to fatigue and slow to recover. Breast meat is whiter in color because it has fewer mitochondria.

The darkest meat of all is heart muscle, which can never afford to tire. Heart muscle cells are over 50% mitochondria by volume.

In addition to more mitochondria, dark meat has greater fat stores in its muscle fibers. These fat stores serve as a source of energy for the mitochondria. Result? The extra fat in dark meat makes it moister, but higher in calories, than white meat.

Response to Endurance Exercise

As mentioned above, the kind of muscle adaptation depends on the type, duration, and intensity of muscle stress. With endurance exercise, the primary response is *increased capacity for energy production*.

In rats, a 3-to-4-month program of treadmill running can double rat muscle capacity to oxidize carbohydrate and fat, with a parallel increase in energy production. The increase is due to increases in energy-producing enzymes in the mitochondria, and in size and number of mitochondria. Other studies in animals have shown similar results.

Human studies have agreed with the animal studies, showing increases in energy-producing enzymes and mitochondrial size. However, in humans, if intensity of exercise is only 75% of maximum, only the Type 1 (slow) fibers show increased enzyme activity. The Type 2A and 2B do not. For an athlete to target Type 2 (fast) fibers, the exercise must be close to maximum intensity. This observation is in line with the theory of sequential recruitment of muscle fibers: as exercise intensity increases, muscles sequentially activate Type 1, then 2A, then 2B. To train Type 2A or 2B (fast) fibers, exercise must be very intense—at least 75% of maximum exertion.

These changes seem to occur fairly rapidly. Significant increases in enzyme levels and capillary density have been seen after just a few weeks of moderate training. However, these changes rapidly return to baseline after training is stopped.

Can training change a muscle's fiber composition? In general, no—a muscle's fiber composition is mostly genetically predetermined. Thus, sprinters (who have a high percentage of fast-twitch fibers in their muscles) and marathoners (who have a high percentage of slow-twitch fibers) are thought to have the fiber compositions that they do primarily because they are genetically programmed to. In other words, successful sprinters are successful because they are born with a high percentage of fast-twitch fibers in their muscles, not because they developed them with training. However, some recent evidence suggests that many years of systematic training may in fact cause a limited amount of fiber conversion.

In addition to changes in mitochondria, enzymes, capillary density, and possibly fiber type, endurance exercise results in changes in muscle fuels.

Endurance training causes a slight increase in muscle concentration of ATP and CP, intracellular fuels that are the end product of glucose metabolism. However, their increases are too small to be of importance except for very brief contractions.

Endurance training also causes a slight increase in fat deposits in the muscle cells. Again, though, these increases are too small to be of major significance in performance.

Response to Resistance Exercise

While the primary response of muscle to endurance exercise is increased capacity for energy production, the primary response of muscle to resistance exercise is *increased size*.

Muscle hypertrophy (increased size) is mostly the result of increased myofibril volume. Resistance training increases volume of myofibrils in both fast-twitch and slow-twitch fibers, but appears to affect fast-twitch fibers more.

Long-term resistance training may increase overall muscle size not only by increasing fiber size (fiber **hypertrophy**) but also by increasing fiber number (fiber **hyperplasia**). However, hyperplasia, if it occurs at all, is a relatively minor contributor; most of the increase in size seems to come from fiber hypertrophy.

Contrary to endurance exercise, resistance exercise causes a *decrease* in mitochondrial volume and enzymes of energy production. These changes may reduce endurance in athletes training with resistance exercise.

Most people think that muscles are fairly static, that the protein in muscle is locked in. In fact, protein turnover in muscle is quite rapid. Myosin, for example, has a half-life of only a few days. This means that in the matter of two days or so half of all the myosin in your body has been broken down and replaced by new myosin.

This rapid turnover helps to explain why the muscular system is so adaptable. With muscle proteins being broken down and rebuilt this quickly, the tissue can readily respond to changes in muscle stress. For example, when you increase the intensity of your training, your muscles can readily add more muscle protein to compensate for the increased stress.

Conversely, it also helps explain why training gains are lost so quickly with inactivity. Without consistent muscle stress, the muscle can lose some of the protein that it added with training. If the inactivity goes on long enough, performance is impaired. Consistent training remains the cornerstone for peak performance. ❑

Skeletal Muscle Adaptability I: Review of Basic Properties
R. Lieber
Developmental Medicine and Child Neurology
V 28: 390-7, 1986

Skeletal Muscle Adaptability III: Muscle Properties Following
Chronic Electrical Stimulation
R. Lieber
Developmental Medicine and Child Neurology
V 28: 662-70, 1986

The Adaptive Response of Skeletal Muscle to
Increased Use
S. Sammons MSc PhD, J Henriksson MD PhD
Muscle and Nerve
V 4 # 2: 94-105, March/April 1981

Skeletal Muscle Adaptations Consequent to
Long-Term Heavy Resistance Exercise
P. Tesch
Medicine and Science in Sports and Exercise
V 20 # 5 (Supplement): S132-4, October 1988

Developmental and Functional Adaptation of
Contractile Proteins in Cardiac and Skeletal Muscles
B. Swynghedauw
Physiological Reviews
V 66 # 3: 710-770, July 1986

Response of Skeletal Muscle to Training
H. Matoba and P. Gollnick
Sports Medicine
V 1: 240-51, 1984

The last section looked at how muscles respond to exercise. But there's more to strength than just muscles alone. Strength comes from the entire motor system—muscles and nerves working together. A lot of strength improvements in athletes are attributed to muscular responses to training, when in fact they are due to nervous system responses.

The nervous system is divided into two parts: the **central nervous system**, and the **peripheral nervous system**. The central nervous system is the brain and spinal cord; the peripheral nervous system consists of the nerves traveling to and from the spinal cord, serving the muscles, skin, and all organs.

Muscle contraction calls on both the peripheral and central nervous systems. The signal to contract begins in the central nervous system, in the brain, and travels to the spinal cord. From there it moves to the peripheral nervous system, where it travels along nerves to the muscles.

When a nerve nears a muscle, the nerve splits into many tiny branches. Each branch supplies a number of **muscle fibers**. The nerve branch, together with the muscle fibers it supplies, is called a **motor unit**.

Not all motor units are activated with every contraction. If a gentle, slow contraction is needed, the brain sends a weak signal down the nerve, and only a small percentage of the total motor units are activated. If a strong, fast contraction is needed, the brain sends a strong signal and a larger percentage of the total motor units are activated. The brain has a great deal of control over the number of motor units it can activate, which is why muscles can move with such precision over such a wide range of strength demands.

Certainly, total strength is related to total muscle mass. The more muscle tissue you have available for contraction, the greater strength you can potentially deliver. However, this is only part of the story. Even with substantial muscle mass, if you can activate only a small percentage of the total motor units, strength will be limited. This is where nervous system adaptations come in: strength training increases *how much* of that muscle mass you can activate for a contraction, *how frequently* you can get individual motor units to fire, and *how long* each motor unit can sustain a contraction.

THE NERVOUS SYSTEM AND MUSCULAR RESPONSE

The Nervous System

These changes increase peak strength, allow strength to be delivered more rapidly, and allow strength to be sustained longer.

Increased Muscle Activation

Most of the evidence for nervous system adaptations to exercise has come from electromyographic (EMG) studies. EMG's measure the electrical activity of a muscle. Since muscle contraction is an electrical process, the stronger the signal from the brain to contract, the greater the electrical activity in the muscle.

As mentioned, not all motor units are activated with every contraction. Training increases the maximum number of motor units that can be activated during a contraction, increasing strength.

EMG's have demonstrated increased motor unit activity after training with weight lifting, isometric contractions, isokinetic (constant velocity) eccentric contractions, and "explosive" jumping. This suggests that a variety of methods of strength training increase the degree to which the brain can activate a prime mover muscle.

How does training increase motor unit activation? It seems that untrained people may have either some kind of motor unit inhibition or insufficient motivation that prevents full activation under normal conditions.

Motor unit inhibition

Contraction of a prime mover is often associated with simultaneous contraction of its antagonists. This may seem paradoxical—like having your foot on the accelerator and the brake at the same time. However, simultaneous contraction of a prime mover and its antagonist does have a purpose: it increases precision. Thus, it occurs most prominently in movements requiring precision.

Contraction of the antagonist also occurs when the action of the prime mover is strong and rapid, especially in untrained subjects. Here, the "braking" action of the antagonist may have a protective function. It may limit full prime mover activation, preventing the beginner from lifting much more than he or she is accustomed to—thus decreasing risk of injury. With training and experience, antagonist braking is reduced and apparent strength increases.

The second nervous system adaptation to strength training involves changes in *how frequently* individual motor units fire.

Motor units don't just fire once per contraction; rather, they fire repeatedly. The more frequently motor units fire, the greater the strength, with maximum strength occurring at a firing rate of about 50 times a second. Trained athletes are able to come closer to the 50/second maximum than untrained athletes.

In some small muscles, such as those of the hand, most if not all motor units are called upon when you contract with half of your maximum strength. To increase force to greater than half of maximum, the athlete must increase the firing rate of the motor units already recruited.

In other muscles, such as the biceps and delts, motor units are recruited throughout the range of force. In these muscles, force is increased by increasing both motor unit firing rate and number of motor units activated. Training probably improves strength in biceps, delts, and other large muscle groups by facilitating both these changes.

It is possible for motor units to fire at rates higher than 50 times per second. For example, during the first one-tenth of a second at the beginning of a maximal contraction, motor units may fire 100 times per second. This very high firing rate increases the rate of force development, increasing speed of contraction.

Athletes participating in sports requiring quick reaction times can train to increase firing rate and speed of contraction. Training with "explosive" movements, such as vertical jump, sprint starts from blocks, or line-of-scrimmage exercises can increase speed of contraction even if there is no change in maximum strength.

The third neurological adaptation to exercise is an increase in *how long* each motor unit can sustain a contraction.

While a motor unit may start out contracting 50 or even 100 times per second, it can't sustain these rates for long. Within a matter of a few seconds, some motor units drop to a rate of 30 to 40 cycles per second. Along with the drop in firing rate comes a loss in overall muscle strength.

However, training appears to delay the drop in firing rate for at least some individual muscle fibers. In one experiment,

Increased Motor Unit Firing Rate

Prolonged Motor Unit Contraction

untrained subjects could keep certain motor units active for only about three seconds. After training, the same subjects could keep these motor units active for about 20 seconds. In addition, they were able to fire these motor units more rapidly.

This kind of adaptation probably prolongs time to overall muscle contraction failure.

Other Neurological Adaptations

There are other neurological adaptations to training that are not as well understood. These are changes in strength that seem to be adaptations of the central nervous system.

Learning

The best-known of these adaptations is **learning**. Everyone knows that "practice makes perfect." But *how* practice makes perfect is not well understood at all. Feedback from repeated performance of specified movements somehow gets incorporated into the nervous system so that the movement comes a little closer to ideal every time. This involves carefully balancing speed and strength of contraction in both prime movers and antagonists.

Motivation

Trained athletes seem to be better at focusing their attention and energies on the immediate sports activity than do non-athletes. This increased mental focus results in activating a greater number of motor units. Motivation can also be increased with hypnosis, or with feedback during an event (for example, when the coach, teammates, or crowd shouts encouragement at a player).

Cross-training

Another such adaptation is **cross-training**. Cross-training is an odd phenomenon: believe it or not, training one limb increases strength in the other. If, for example, an athlete trains just the right arm, strength will increase in both right *and* left arms. The left arm shows increases in strength, even though it was never trained.

In one study, eight weeks of training one biceps resulted in a 36.4% increase in strength in that arm, and a 24.7% increase in the other, untrained arm.

The cross-training effect is not attributable to local changes within the muscle or to changes in the peripheral nervous system. It is probably due to changes in the central nervous system, in the cross-communication networks between limbs.

Another central nervous system adaptation is the **bilateral deficit**, in which exerting one limb decreases strength in the other.

For example, let's say you squeeze a hand grip strength-testing device with one hand. If you retest that same hand while testing the other hand simultaneously, strength in the first hand will drop. The drop is usually about 5% to 25% of maximum strength, and is not attributable to changes in posture or positioning.

What causes the bilateral deficit? It seems to come from the way we use our limbs. We generally use our limbs separately, instead of together. For example, we use both legs separately (as with walking) more often than we use them together (as with leg press or vertical jump).

With training, however, it is possible to turn a bilateral deficit into an increase. For example, the deficit in the legs is usually fairly large, except in athletes such as weightlifters who train with both legs together with leg presses. These athletes can actually have "bilateral facilitation" rather than a bilateral deficit. This suggests that the bilateral deficit is a central nervous system phenomenon that will adapt with training.

How can the athlete use all this information? In general, you don't have to train the nervous system separately beyond applying the **Law of Specificity.**

The Law of Specificity states that the most efficient way to train *for* a movement is to train *with* that movement.

The most efficient way to improve vertical jump is not with leg presses, although leg presses can help. The most efficient way to improve vertical jump is to train with vertical jump. The most efficient way to train for running endurance is with endurance running. The most efficient way to train for powerlifting is by lifting heavy weights.

Bilateral deficit

Law of Specificity

97

This is because the neurological adaptations to exercise are very movement-specific. For example, training with squats results in neural adaptations in the quadriceps that increase strength in the squat. You would think that this would translate into comparably increased strength in knee extensions, since knee extensions also require the quads. But it doesn't. The adaptations in the quads that come from training with the squat are specific to the squat. And the adaptations from training with light weights are probably different from those gained by training with heavy weights.

The same is true for muscle groups all over the body. The closer an athlete can come to training with the actual movements required for sports performance, the more likely he or she will gain neurological adaptations that will be of benefit on the playing field. ❑

Neural Adaptation to Resistance Exercise
D. Sale
Medicine and Science in Sports and Exercise
V 20 # 5: S135-145, October 1988

Muscle Strength and Its Development
R. Enoka
Sports Medicine
V 6 # 2: 146-68, February 1988

Many athletes have heard that "exercise tears down muscle tissue," meaning that exercise causes a breakdown in muscle tissue protein. Attempting to protect against this, some athletes take protein or amino acid supplements, particularly branched-chain amino acid supplements. They believe that eating more protein and amino acids will decrease muscle tissue breakdown, increase muscle tissue rebuilding, or both.

In fact, exercise does cause breakdown of muscle tissue protein. But muscle tissue protein undergoes breakdown (degradation) and rebuilding (synthesis) all the time, not just during exercise. For example, about 17% of the energy your body uses *at rest* comes from protein breakdown, and most of that is from muscle tissue protein.

At rest, the rate of muscle protein breakdown is quite close to the rate of protein synthesis, and the total muscle neither shrinks nor grows.

Exercise, however, changes muscle protein breakdown and synthesis. During exercise, the rate of breakdown *increases* and the rate of synthesis *decreases*. How much this happens depends on the duration and intensity of exercise, with greater changes generally occurring in longer and more-intense exercise.

The culprit behind the decrease in muscle protein synthesis during exercise appears to be an energy shortage. An exercising muscle diverts most of its energy supply to the business of contraction, so the muscle protein synthesis machinery gets comparatively little of the available energy. Without enough energy, the rate of protein synthesis decreases.

Increased breakdown of muscle protein results in an increase in the release of amino acids from muscle into the bloodstream. The predominant amino acid released from exercising muscle is **alanine**. Alanine is the predominant amino acid released not because alanine is the predominant amino acid in muscle; rather, it's because most of the assorted amino acids freed in the breakdown of muscle protein are converted into alanine before being released into the blood.

DEGRADATION AND SYNTHESIS OF MUSCLE TISSUE PROTEIN IN RESPONSE TO EXERCISE

Degradation and Synthesis

At the same time exercise increases release of alanine from muscles, exercise also increases release of the branched-chain amino acids from the liver.

What happens to all of these amino acids released during exercise? One of two things: they get converted into a form of fuel and burned in the muscles; or they get incorporated into other proteins. Which occurs depends in part on individual amino acid structure.

Amino Acid Structure

All amino acids share some structural similarities. They all have a nitrogen part, called the **amino group**. The amino group is identical for all amino acids. They also all have a carbon part, called the carbon skeleton. The carbon skeleton is different for every amino acid, and is what distinguishes one amino acid from another.

For example, the amino acids valine and alanine have identical amino groups, but differ in their carbon skeletons (see illustration). Because their carbon skeletons are different, they are different amino acids. (The carbon skeletons of valine, leucine and isoleucine have a branched configuration, so they are called branched-chain amino acids.)

Valine

CH_3

NH_3^+ —CH—CH—CH_3

COOH

amino groups

carbon skeletons

NH_3^+ —CH—CH_3

COOH

Alanine

All amino acids have an amino group and a carbon skeleton.

Converted Into Fuel

Amino acids that are released from the muscles in the form of alanine travel to the liver, where the amino group is removed. The remaining carbon skeleton is converted into *glucose* (blood sugar), which is then released from the liver and travels back to the muscles to be used as fuel. This is the primary avenue of amino acid utilization during exercise.

The branched-chain amino acids released from the liver are transported to the muscles. This fact has led some athletes into thinking that the branched-chain amino acids are being used for muscle growth. In fact, after the branched-chain amino acids are taken up by the muscles, the amino group is removed, leaving only a carbon skeleton. The carbon skeleton is rearranged in the muscles to form a fuel that can be burned for muscle contraction. So rather than being used for muscle growth, the branched-chain amino acids are being used for fuel. Branched-chain amino acid supplements are an expensive source of calories.

Although there is decreased muscle protein synthesis during exercise, some synthesis still occurs. However, it tends to be synthesis of enzyme and regulatory proteins, rather than muscle contractile proteins. Some of the essential amino acids released in muscle protein breakdown are used in synthesis of other proteins.

Re-incorporated Into Other Proteins

As noted, during exercise muscle protein synthesis decreases and breakdown increases. After exercise, though, muscle protein synthesis *increases*. The amount of synthesis during recovery is related to the amount of breakdown during exercise. The greater the breakdown, the greater the synthesis.

Post-exercise Recovery

In addition, the pathways responsible for amino acid breakdown during exercise work in reverse during recovery. During exercise, various muscle amino acids are converted to alanine in the muscles; the alanine travels to the liver where the amino group is removed and the carbon skeleton is converted to glucose. During recovery, the reverse happens: glucose is converted into alanine in the liver, then the alanine travels to the muscles where it is converted into various amino acids. These various amino acids are then incorporated into muscle proteins.

It appears that recovery is characterized not just by increased protein synthesis, but by increased protein *breakdown* as well. Increased protein breakdown is important for removal and repair of damaged muscle components and for improvements in muscle function and growth. In fact, high levels of muscle protein synthesis *and* high levels of muscle protein breakdown are probably both necessary for rapid muscle growth.

It is important to note that, in general, the muscle proteins broken down during exercise are structural elements and enzymes, *not* muscle contractile proteins. Muscle protein breakdown that occurs during exercise *spares* muscle contractile protein. In contrast, muscle protein synthesis that occurs during recovery *includes* muscle contractile protein. This suggests that exercise and recovery together cause a net increase in amount of muscle contractile protein.

So during exercise, amino acids mobilized from muscle tissue are primarily used as *fuel*; during recovery, amino acids are still mobilized from muscle tissue, but are now used for

AMINO ACID PATHWAYS DURING EXERCISE AND RECOVERY

DURING EXERCISE

2. *Alanine* from muscle protein breakdown travels to the liver, where the alanine amino group is removed. The remaining carbon skeleton is converted into glucose.

3. *Glucose* from alanine breakdown is released into the bloodstream

5. *Branched-chain amino acids* from breakdown of liver proteins are released into the bloodstream.

1. *Non-contractile muscle protein* is broken down into different component amino acids. Many of these amino acids are converted into the amino acid *alanine* and released into the bloodstream.

4. *Glucose* from the liver is taken up by the muscles and burned as fuel for contraction.

6. *Branched-chain amino acids* from the liver are taken up by the muscle. The amino group is removed, and the remaining carbon skeleton is burned as fuel for contraction.

DURING RECOVERY

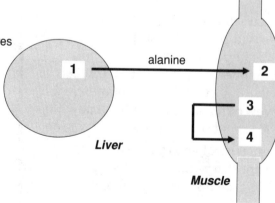

1. *Glucose* from glycogen stores and from lactic acid metabolism is converted into carbon skeletons. An amino group is added to make the amino acid *alanine*. This alanine is released into the bloodstream.

2. *Alanine* from the liver is taken up by the muscle, and is converted into different component amino acids. These amino acids are used to manufacture new muscle protein, including contractile

3. and **4.** *Muscle protein* is broken down into different component amino acids. These amino acids are used to make new muscle protein.

protein synthesis. In addition, during recovery glucose is used in the manufacture of new amino acids for protein synthesis.

And what of the protein and amino acids supplements? Will they protect against muscle protein breakdown, or increase muscle protein synthesis? There is no evidence that they decrease breakdown any more than any other source of calories. Nor is there any evidence that they increase post-exercise synthesis for an athlete with an otherwise balanced diet. ❏

Mobilization of Structural Proteins
During Exercise
Atko Viru
Sports Medicine
V 4: 95-128, 1987

TRAINING AND THE RATE OF MUSCLE REPAIR

Some types of exercise seem to produce a "protective effect" against later muscle fiber damage. As well, the muscle fiber damage that occurs with subsequent exercise bouts is *repaired at a faster rate*. Moreover, it doesn't require much exercise to produce this "faster-repair" adaptation.

Eight college-age women participated in an experiment in which both the right and left forearm flexors were subjected to 70 maximal eccentric contractions. In one arm (the "pre-stressed" arm, randomized for dominance), muscle damage had been induced two weeks before by doing 24 maximal eccentric contractions. Serum creatine kinase (CK), muscle soreness and pain, and isometric strength were evaluated before, immediately after, and for five days after each exercise session.

Subjects showed significant losses in strength immediately after all exercise sessions. (Decreased strength is common after an intense workout.) The pre-stressed arm recovered full strength after only one day. The arm that was not pre-stressed, however, had not recovered full strength even after *five* days.

Similarly, the arm that was not pre-stressed showed greater release of CK (indicating greater muscle fiber damage), greater pain sensations, greater muscle soreness, and slower pain and soreness recovery than did the pre-stressed arms.

This suggests that there is a training effect, at least with eccentric exercise, that results in faster recovery and decreased damage. This effect may be attributable to increases in strength of muscle fiber membranes or surrounding connective tissue caused by the initial muscle stress.

One important training implication from this study is that consistent training may have the potential to maximize recovery and minimize damage.

[Ed. note: Downhill skiing involves almost exclusively eccentric contractions. Talk to any skier 48 hours after the first day on the slopes and you are likely to here about some considerable muscle soreness. However, later in the season the soreness is usually not nearly as bad. This is probably a reflection of the "protective effect" of eccentric exercise, with the first day's exercise protecting against muscle fiber damage and muscle soreness later in the season.] ❏

Exercise-Induced Muscle Damage, Repair, and Adaptation in Humans
P. Clarkson and I Tremblay
Journal of Applied Physiology
V 65 # 1: 1-6, July 1988

MUSCLE FATIGUE

Muscle fatigue is defined as the failure to maintain the desired or expected muscular force. It is one of the two factors most commonly limiting exercise performance. (The other is cardiovascular/respiratory capacity. Less common limiting factors include limitations imposed by skill at a specific task or by pain.) What exactly is it that causes muscle fatigue? For years it had been assumed that build-up of lactic acid was solely responsible. New research indicates there are in fact three different components of fatigue, only one of which involves build-up of lactic acid. These are:

- An impairment in the **electrical stimulus** the muscle receives
- A decrease in muscle cell **phosphocreatine** and an increase in muscle cell **acidity**
- A decrease in **neuromuscular efficiency**.

Understanding these new findings about muscle fatigue requires a brief review of some of the biochemical and physiological events of muscle contraction.

Muscle Contraction

The following events happen when a muscle contracts:

- The brain sends an electrical signal to contract along a nerve to a muscle.
- The muscle gets the electrical signal from the nerve.
- This electrical signal spreads across the membranes of the muscle cells.
- The spreading electrical signal causes **calcium** to be released within the muscle cells.
- The release of calcium causes a series of changes within the muscle cell, eventually resulting in the breakdown of a substance called **adenosine triphosphate**.
- Adenosine triphosphate, also called **ATP**, is a molecule that stores energy; ATP releases its energy when it is broken down.
- The energy released from the breakdown of ATP is used to power muscle contraction.

If a muscle contracts repeatedly, it uses up the ATP present in the muscle. More ATP fuel must be synthesized if the muscle is going to continue to contract. For short-term exertion, ATP is synthesized primarily from one of two sources: **phosphocreatine** or **glucose** (blood sugar).

Like ATP, phosphocreatine is an energy-storage molecule that releases its energy when it is broken down. Phosphocreatine is naturally present in muscle tissue, but cannot be replenished during exercise. Because of this, the amount of phosphocreatine present in a muscle steadily decreases as the muscle gets more fatigued.

Glucose is also naturally present in muscle tissue, but, unlike phosphocreatine, glucose supplies *can* be replenished during exercise. Additional glucose is brought into exercising muscle tissue via the bloodstream. The amount of ATP that can be regenerated from glucose depends not on how much glucose is available to the exercising muscle (there's usually plenty), but on how much **oxygen** is available.

The amount of oxygen available dictates in which of two ways glucose will be metabolized. Glucose can be metabolized *aerobically* if there is enough oxygen around, or *anaerobically* if there is not enough oxygen around. Aerobic metabolism of glucose is much more efficient, producing nineteen times more ATP per glucose molecule than anaerobic metabolism. While anaerobic metabolism of glucose produces some ATP, it also produces the byproduct *lactic acid*, which accumulates in muscle tissue.

Fatigue

Returning to the topic of muscular fatigue, researchers in this experiment examined progressive fatigue of a grip muscle in the hand. Various muscle characteristics were measured as subjects squeezed a specially designed cylinder for four minutes.

The force of contraction dropped by 90%, decreasing to 10% of original force after the four minutes. This indicates substantial fatigue of the grip muscles of the hand.

Impairment in the electrical stimulus

Accompanying the fatigue was an impairment in the electrical stimulus the muscle fiber receives. The stimulus at the muscle cell membrane was found to be weaker but more prolonged for the fatigued muscle when compared to rested muscle. With rest, there was rapid recovery from this fatigue effect, with electrical stimulus back to normal values after *four to six minutes*. This change is unrelated to lactic acid level.

The second fatigue effect was a decrease in muscle cell phosphocreatine and an increase in muscle cell acidity. As mentioned above, exercise results in the progressive depletion of the energy-storage molecule phosphocreatine, and, if there is not enough oxygen around, a build-up of lactic acid with a progressive increase in muscle cell acidity. With rest, muscle cell phosphocreatine and muscle cell acidity return to normal in *fifteen to twenty minutes*.

Decrease in phosphocreatine and increase in acidity

The third fatigue effect is a decrease in neuromuscular efficiency. Neuromuscular efficiency is a measure of how many muscle fibers must be stimulated to generate a given muscular force. When a muscle is tired, it takes stimulation of a greater number of fatigued muscle fibers to achieve the same amount of force. Of the three components of fatigue, neuromuscular efficiency is the slowest to recover with rest, returning to normal in about *sixty minutes*. This change is also unrelated to lactic acid level.

Decrease in neuromuscular efficiency

These findings suggest a new way of thinking about muscle fatigue and recovery. All three components of fatigue begin recovering during the first few minutes of rest, but progress at different rates. Impairment in electrical stimulus recovers in four to six minutes, muscle cell phosphocreatine and acidity recover in fifteen to twenty minutes, and neuromuscular efficiency recovers in about sixty minutes.

Thus, if you fatigue a muscle, rest for six minutes, then work that muscle again, you will tire quickly because you have recovered from only the first of the three components of fatigue. The muscle's electrical activity will be back to resting levels and ready to go again, but the phosphocreatine, acidity, and neuromuscular efficiency levels will still be in a partly fatigued state.

Likewise, if you fatigue a muscle, rest for *twenty* minutes, then work that muscle again, you will tire quickly (although less quickly than after only six minutes of rest) because you have recovered from only two of the three components of fatigue. The muscle's electrical activity, phosphocreatine, and acidity will be back to resting levels and ready to go again, but the neuromuscular efficiency will still be in a partly fatigued state.

If these studies on the grip muscle are representative of muscle physiology throughout the body, it takes an hour or more for a muscle to recover fully from substantial fatigue. Athletes and coaches may want to bear this in mind for sports events involving successive bouts of all-out exertion. ❑

Effects of Fatiguing Exercise on High-Energy Phosphates, Force, and EMG:
Evidence for Three Phases of Recovery
R. Miller MD et al.
Muscle and Nerve
V 10 # 9: 810-21, Nov/Dec 1987

MUSCLE MASS AND PERFORMANCE LIMITING FACTORS

Generally, there are two types of factors that limit muscle performance: **peripheral factors** and **central factors.**

Peripheral factors, such as metabolic capacity of a muscle, local muscle blood supply, local obstruction of blood supply, or a ceiling on muscle power, are specific for every muscle group. *Central factors,* such as cardiac output, are not specific to any muscle group. (Cardiac output refers to the volume of blood the heart can pump per minute. There are occasions when the exercising muscles need oxygenated blood delivered faster than the heart can pump; under these circumstances, cardiac output becomes the limiting factor for muscle performance.)

This study looked at the effects of exercise on large-mass muscle groups (legs) and small-mass muscle groups (arms). Each subject was exercised to exhaustion on ergometers using each of four different exercise programs: one-arm, one-arm-plus-shoulder, one-leg, and two-leg.

The researchers found that arm work was limited by peripheral factors, one-leg work was limited by a combination of central and peripheral factors, and two-leg work was almost entirely limited by central factors. The larger the mass of muscle involved, the more likely the limitation will be central.

This has important implications for training. If an athlete wants to increase endurance of small muscles, that athlete should use resistance rather than aerobic exercise. This is because with resistance exercise the athlete is directly targeting the limiting factors of small-muscle performance, and training to improve the peripherally based limitations. For example, an athlete who wants to increase biceps endurance can lift weights, increasing local muscular capillarization and helping to increase local blood supply.

On the other hand, if an athlete wants to increase endurance of large muscles, that athlete should use aerobic rather than resistance exercise. With aerobic exercise, the athlete is directly targeting the limiting factors of large-muscle performance, and training to improve the centrally based limitations. For example, an athlete who wants to increase gluteus endurance can train with running, thereby improving central circulatory transport. ❑

Muscle Mass as a Factor Limiting Physical Work
R. Shephard et al.
Journal of Applied Physiology
V 64 # 4: 1472-1479, 1988

STRENGTH TRAINING AND ANDROGEN LEVELS IN WOMEN

Androgen is the term given a family of male sex hormones, which includes testosterone, androstenedione, and dihydrotestosterone, among others.

Although called "male sex hormones," they are also normally found in women in small amounts. Increases in androgens have frequently been associated with increases in muscle strength, muscle hypertrophy, and lean body weight in men; this study investigated the relationship between androgen levels, strength, and body composition in women.

Eighteen college women, none competitive athletes, participated in a ten-week, maximal-effort, hydraulic resistance exercise program. Serum androgens were measured before and after the training program, controlling for menstrual changes (elevated androgen concentrations routinely occur mid-cycle). Strength (bench press and squat) and lean body weight changes were also determined.

Although there were significant increases in strength, there were no significant increases in androgen hormone concentrations or in lean body weight.

In fact, androgen hormone concentrations went *down*. This was attributed to either decreases in psychological stress from the beginning to the end of the experiment (stress increases release of corticotropin, which in turn increases release of androgens), or to possible seasonal or yearly variations in androgen concentrations.

This study suggests that high androgen levels are not associated with greater strength or muscle mass in women, at least over the course of a ten-week training period. ❏

Exercise and Serum Androgens in Women
The Physician and Sportsmedicine
V 15 # 5: 87-94, May 1987

Runner's high, a euphoric feeling experienced by some distance runners during prolonged exercise, is caused by a set of chemicals called **endorphins**. These occur naturally in the brain. Certain drugs, such as heroin and morphine, mimic the action of endorphins and produce a similar euphoric state.

Endorphins have generally been looked upon as benign substances.

However, according to an article in *Internal Medicine News*, "high beta-endorphin levels may be the key factor enabling individuals to run until they are confused, dehydrated, and hyperthermic [overheated], without first experiencing considerable pain."

The article chronicles the collapse of eleven runners near the end of two consecutive half-marathon (13 mile) runs. All showed beta-endorphin levels averaging almost 4 times higher than levels in eleven healthy runners.

The unusually high endorphin levels may have allowed these runners to keep going, masking symptoms that would have made other runners slow down or stop. ❑

Internal Medicine News
Endogenous Opioids Play a Role in
Runner's Collapse
V 20 #16: 42, August 15-31, 1987

NEGATIVE CONSEQUENCES OF ENDORPHIN RELEASE

MUSCLE ACTIVITY AND WEIGHT-LOAD INTENSITY

Small differences make a big difference. In this study, a small increase in workout intensity in elite weightlifters resulted in a big increase in muscle electrical activity and an increase in strength.

"Muscle electrical activity" refers to the electrical processes occurring in a muscle during a contraction. Muscle fibers are given the signal to contract by electrical impulses from nerves.

With training, the nerves stimulate a greater number of muscle fibers, resulting in greater muscular power. (This effect is more pronounced in beginning weightlifters, and is why beginning weightlifters show bigger strength gains early on.)

The amount of stimulation can be measured with an **EMG** (electromyograph), a machine that measures electrical activity in muscles. Amount of electrical activity is related to muscular power.

Thirteen elite male weightlifters, all with five to nine years' experience, were followed through one year of training. All subjects were Finnish champions and/or national record holders in various weight categories.

The one-year experiment was divided into three four-month periods. The subjects followed individualized programs designed by their own coaches, and trained an average of five times per week. Training included standard Olympic and power lifts, as well as supplementary pulling and pushing exercises and squats.

Subjects trained at an average intensity of 79% of one-rep max (the maximum weight they could lift for one repetition) for the first four-month period, at a slightly lower intensity (averaging 77% of one-rep max) for the second four-month period, then returned to the initial intensity (79% of one-rep max) for the final four-month period.

At zero, 4, 8, and 12 months, researchers measured maximum strength and EMG response for a number of muscle groups.

From the first to the second four-month period, when intensity dropped an average of 2%, electrical activity in leg muscles dropped an average of 16%. From the second to the third four-month period, when intensity increased by the same 2%, electrical activity in leg muscles increased by the same 16%.

   Individual changes in workout intensity were paralleled by
statistically significant changes in muscular strength. This
suggests that training intensity plays an important role in
determining the nervous system's ability to stimulate muscle,
and that small differences in training intensity can translate
into big differences in muscle fiber stimulation and strength.❏

EMG, Muscle Fibre and Force Production
Characteristics During a 1 Year Training Period in Elite Weight-Lifters
K. Häkkinen et al
European Journal of Applied Physiology
V 56: 419-427, July 1987

THE CARDIO-VASCULAR EFFECTS OF WEIGHT TRAINING

All forms of exercise, when pursued vigorously, result in physiologic changes to the body. The type and extent of these changes depends on the type of exercises performed and the vigor with which they are pursued.

Weight training is no exception. Whether as a primary endeavor or as an adjunct to other forms of exercise, weight training results in characteristic changes in the body. The type and extent of these changes depends on the type of weightlifting and the vigor with which the weights are lifted.

Among these changes to the body are a variety of effects on the heart. What are these cardiac changes, and how do they differ from changes seen in aerobic training? What happens to heart rate, blood pressure, and oxygen consumption? Are these changes good or bad?

The Aerobic Heart

The cardiac changes seen with weight training are considerably different from those seen with aerobic conditioning. In aerobic conditioning (running, bicycling, and swimming, for example), the demand for oxygen delivery is increased. This translates into a demand for the heart to pump more blood per minute, in order to deliver more oxygen. If the demand for increased oxygen delivery is high enough over a long enough period of time, the cardiac tissue changes by increasing ventricle cavity size, that is, increasing the diameter of the heart's main pumping chambers.

A bigger ventricle can pump more blood with every stroke (increased stroke volume); therefore, at a given heart rate, more blood gets pumped per minute (increased cardiac output), and more oxygen gets delivered to the tissues. (To keep a big-chambered heart from pumping too much blood at rest, the resting heart rate goes down. That's why highly aerobically trained athletes often have resting heart rates in the 40's.)

The Anaerobic Heart

For the highly weight-trained athlete, the demands on the heart are quite different. Instead of needing to increase oxygen delivery for prolonged periods of time, the heart needs to increase its ability to pump against high resistance for very short periods of time.

During a lift, a weightlifter's blood pressure may go as high as 280/350. While the weightlifter's heart needs to sustain such incredibly high pressures for only short periods of time, these high pressures still place considerable demand on the heart. If this demand occurs repeatedly over a long-enough period of time, the cardiac tissue changes by increasing ventricle wall thickness, without changing chamber size.

A thicker ventricle pumps the same amount of blood with every stroke, but can generate a much greater pressure when needed.

These heart changes, both in aerobically trained and in weight-trained athletes, come on fairly quickly—measurable differences have been noted in as little as one week. However, it appears these changes persist only as long as the training continues. If training is stopped, the heart thickness and chamber sizes eventually return to pre-training dimensions.

Blood Pressure

As mentioned above, during a lift blood pressure can reach very high levels. Blood pressure increases with every rep, reaching the highest levels when submaximal lifts are repeated to failure, and is related to the amount of weight lifted and the muscle mass involved. The rise appears to be significantly less in experienced bodybuilders than in inexperienced bodybuilders. Other than the momentary increases during a lift, however, weightlifting does not seem to increase baseline blood pressure. In fact, there is some evidence that weightlifting may actually decrease baseline blood pressure.

Heart Rate

Resting heart rate is unchanged in weight-trained athletes. This contrasts with aerobically trained athletes, who have a decrease in their resting heart rate. During a 10 to 12 rep max set, a trained weightlifter's heart rate increases to 80 to 85% of the maximum heart rate attainable during aerobic activity. This increase is a result of a combination of neural and hormonal influences, but heart rate quickly returns to normal once the exertion is stopped.

When trained weightlifters lift to exhaustion, they have higher heart rates and lactate levels than untrained subjects, but recover more quickly. This is attributable not only to the fact that by the time they reach exhaustion trained weightlifters have performed more work, but also that they have "well-developed fast glycolytic systems." This means that, by training, they have geared up the muscle glucose-metabolism machinery so that their muscles can metabolize a greater amount of glucose in a shorter period of time. This is similar to glucose metabolism changes seen in aerobically trained athletes.

Oxygen Consumption

Trained weightlifters and bodybuilders also show an increase in VO_2 max, the maximum rate they can consume oxygen under aerobic conditions. However, this increase is only proportional to the increase in muscle mass. If corrected for the increase in muscle mass, weightlifters show no increase in VO_2 max. Weight training is not an efficient way of increasing VO_2 max; traditional aerobic-type exercises are much better for this.

The Bottom Line

Are the heart changes seen in weightlifters good or bad? Although the jury is still out, there is no solid evidence that these changes are detrimental, and some evidence that they may in fact be beneficial. The increased ventricular wall thickness and momentary increases in blood pressure do not appear to be harmful or injurious to otherwise healthy athletes. Resting heart rate remains at normal levels and resting blood pressure may decrease slightly. There is evidence to suggest that weight training may improve serum cholesterol and lipid (fat) profiles in steroid-free bodybuilders comparably to aerobic training, thus decreasing the risk of heart disease. ❑

Cardiovascular Effects of Weight Training: a Roundtable Discussion
National Strength and Conditioning Association Journal
V 9 # 2: 10-20, 1987

Characteristics of Anabolic-Androgen Steroid-Free Competitive
Male and Female Bodybuilders
The Physician and Sportsmedicine
V 15 # 6: 169-179, June 1987

Body Composition and Maximal Aerobic Capacity of Bodybuilders
Journal of Sports Medicine
V 20: 181-188, 1980

Effects of Physical Deconditioning After Intense Endurance Training on
Left Ventricular Dimensions and Stroke Volume
Journal of the American College of Cardiology
V 7 # 5: 982-9, May 1986

Structural Features of the Athlete Heart as Defined by Echocardiography
Journal of the American College of Cardiology
V 7 # 1: 190-203, 1986

Heart Rate and Lactate Levels During Weight-Training Exercise
in Trained and Untrained Men
The Physician and Sportsmedicine
V 15 #5: 97-105, May 1987

Weight Training and Strength, Cardiorespiratory Functioning and
Body Composition of Men
British Journal of Sports Medicine
V 21 # 1: 40-44, March 1987

AEROBIC CONDITIONING AND WEIGHTLIFTING PERFORMANCE

Two muscular energy production processes—aerobic and anaerobic—contribute in varying degrees to all athletic endeavors. Both processes take place within muscle cells.

Aerobic energy production requires oxygen. Prolonged low intensity exercise—such as jogging—relies heavily on the aerobic energy process.

Anaerobic energy production does not require oxygen. Brief bouts of high intensity exercise—such as single repetitions of heavy weightlifting—rely primarily on the anaerobic energy process.

Energy for the performance of most exercises is not derived solely from one process, aerobic or anaerobic. Instead, both processes contribute, with degree of contribution depending on the type of exercise performed.

When you run, for example, the anaerobic process supplies the energy at first, until your heart and lungs get up to speed. Then the aerobic system takes over and supplies most of the energy (as long as you are running slowly enough that it can handle the demand). If you suddenly sprint, the anaerobic mechanism steps back in to handle a greater part of the load.

It has been assumed for years that, since weightlifting primarily involves the anaerobic process, an athlete's aerobic condition doesn't impose much of a limitation on his or her weightlifting performance. A new study calls this belief into question.

Fourteen male elite weightlifters, average age 22.5 years, were tested to determine their maximal oxygen uptake, a measure of aerobic capacity. The subjects' anaerobic power was also determined, by having them pedal a bicycle ergometer (stationary bicycle) against extreme resistance for sixty seconds. Power was measured at fifteen second intervals.

Results showed a significant correlation between maximal oxygen uptake and *an*aerobic power after the first thirty seconds. In other words, the athletes' *aerobic* capacity was strongly correlated with their ability to perform what is considered to be primarily an *anaerobic* task.

What does this mean? It has been generally thought that energy production due to aerobic processes doesn't really contribute until at least two minutes into maximal exertion, and that energy production in the first two minutes is almost entirely due to anaerobic processes. But this correlation at thirty seconds indicates that aerobic processes may play a greater role in energy production earlier on than was previously thought. This suggests that those athletes whose events are almost entirely anaerobic ought not ignore the possible benefits of aerobic training to their performance. ❏

Aerobic, Anaerobic, Assistant Exercise and Weightlifting Performance Capacities in Elite Weightlifters
Journal of Sports Medicine
V 27: 240-6, June 1987

EFFECTS OF INCREASED LOAD ON AEROBIC AND ANAEROBIC PERFORMANCE

Performing endurance exercises with the addition of weights has long been a method of increasing intensity of a workout. The increase in intensity is dependent on the amount of weight and their positions: heavy loads cause a greater increase than light loads, loads on the feet cause a much greater increase than loads on the hands (for workouts involving primarily leg work, such as running).

These greater loads increase heart rate, carbohydrate metabolism, and stress on the muscles.

Most studies have been done using weights only during the exercise periods; this study examined whether continuous wearing of a weight vest during all waking hours, both during exercise and non-exercise periods, affected energy metabolism and exercise performance.

Twenty-four trained endurance athletes (twelve runners, twelve cross-country skiers) were studied. Half wore vests weighing 9 to 10% of their body weight morning to night, including every workout (for the skiers) or every other workout (for the runners). The other half (six runners, six skiers) served as controls.

The vests were worn for four weeks, at which time the subjects were given several aerobic and anaerobic tasks.

Those who wore the weight vests demonstrated improved anaerobic performance but *worsened aerobic performance.*

The most likely explanations for this are changes in running efficiency and muscle fiber recruitment (the pattern with which different muscle fibers participate at different intensities). Those who trained with weight vests showed a *decrease* in running efficiency. The vests had altered their pace, so that even when tested without the vests they were taking shorter steps and exerting more energy per step.

It is probable that muscle fiber recruitment changed as well. During low-intensity running, most of the power is supplied by slow-twitch fibers (the moderate-strength, slow-to-tire fibers). As intensity increases, or as the slow-twitch fibers begin to tire, progressively more fast-twitch fibers (the high-strength, fast-to-tire fibers) are recruited. The extra weight may have altered the pattern of muscle fiber recruitment in athletes who trained with vests such that fast-twitch fibers were recruited earlier and at lower intensities. This would mean that they would exhibit more power (improved anaerobic performance) but would tire more quickly (worsened aerobic performance), as was seen in this study.

[Ed. note: Weights appear to alter gait and muscle fiber recruitment in a way that persists (at least temporarily) even when the weights are not worn. While wearing weights did improve anaerobic performance, it is not the most efficient way to do so (weight training is better); wearing weights also decreased running efficiency, which ought not be the goal of any running program. These athletes wore moderately heavy vests, but even lighter weights may have similar effects if carried in the hands.] ❏

Metabolic Response of Endurance Athletes to Training with Added Load
Heikki Rusko and Carmelo Bosco
European Journal of Applied Physiology
V 56 # 4: 412-418, July 1987

IMPROVEMENT IN BLOOD CHOLESTEROL THROUGH EXERCISE

Exercise is good for you. Among many beneficial changes are changes in amounts of various kinds of cholesterols in the blood. But how much exercise do you need to see an effect?

According to researchers at Brown University, a single exercise session is enough to bring about a temporary improvement in blood cholesterols.

There are several different kinds of cholesterols in the blood. HDL cholesterol (the "good" kind) has been associated with lower risk of heart disease and is increased with exercise, diet rich in omega-3 fatty acids (the fish oils you've been hearing so much about) and diet low in saturated fats. LDL cholersterol (the "bad" kind) has been associated with higher risk of heart disease and is increased with smoking, inactivity, and diet high in saturated fats.

In this experiment, untrained subjects pedalled stationary bicycles for one hour at 80% of maximal heart rate; trained subjects for two hours. Increases in HDL cholesterol appeared beginning 48 hours after exercise, and remained elevated to 72 hours, the duration of the experiment. HDL cholesterol levels in the trained athletes both started at a higher level and increased by a greater percentage than did levels in the untrained subjects.

While noting the improvements in blood cholesterols seen with a single exercise session, the authors also note that these beneficial changes are probably rapidly reversed by physical inactivity. ❑

Exercise Acutely Increases High Density Lipoprotein-Cholesterol and Lipoprotein Lipase Activity in Trained and Untrained Men
Metabolism
V 36 # 2: 188-192, Feb 1987

TRAINING AND CAPILLARY DEVELOPMENT

Capillaries are the smallest blood vessels. Muscle tissue gets its nutrients, such as oxygen, glucose, vitamins, and minerals, and gets rid of its waste products, such as lactic acid and carbon dioxide, by diffusion of these substances across the walls of the capillaries.

Training changes not only muscle fiber characteristics, but also the number and geometry of muscle capillaries. This alters the characteristics of blood supply to muscle.

In a comparison of muscle tissue samples from untrained, trained, and elite athletes, the trained and elite athletes showed significantly more capillaries per cross-sectional area, more capillaries per muscle fiber, and an altered capillary/muscle fiber geometry. The altered geometry has each capillary in contact with greater muscle fiber area. This greater area is thought to contribute to enhanced oxygen diffusion across the capillary wall, which increases oxygen supply to muscle tissue; this, in turn, leads to greater aerobic capacity. ❏

The Capillary Supply of Human Skeletal Muscle:
Effect of Training
M. J. Plyley
Canadian Journal of Sports Sciences
V 12 # 3: 19P, Sept 1987

REPLACING FLUIDS AND CARBOHYDRATE DURING EXERCISE

When winter bears down upon us, it may seem a strange time to take a look at sports drinks. But dehydration doesn't hibernate. Endurance activities—cross-country skiing, ultra-long distance cycling races, and distance runs undertaken to take advantage of cooler weather—put the athlete at risk for the same dangers associated with water and electrolyte loss as in the summer.

The manufacturers of sports drinks say their products are the best line of defense against those dangers. Just how do those products stack up against each other, and against other beverages?

Sweating

To function properly, your body must maintain an appropriate environment for the chemical reactions taking place within it. When you exercise, that environment is threatened by the heat generated by muscular contraction. The body uses a number of mechanisms for ridding itself of that heat. Most important is sweating, which cools the body by evaporation.

Sweating itself can threaten the body's internal environment, however. Endurance exercise can lead to dehydration, and prolonged endurance exercise (greater than four hours) in which sweat losses are replenished only with water can cause hyponatremia (abnormally low blood sodium concentrations).

The goal of sports drinks is to offset water and mineral losses from sweating. Another goal is to provide the athlete with additional energy "fuel," usually in the form of glucose or sucrose.

Research has centered on determining the formulation which gets the fluid, minerals, and carbohydrate (glucose) into the athlete's blood stream the fastest, and at finding the optimum concentrations of those ingredients.

Gastric Emptying Rate

There are two major factors affecting the time required for the ingredients in a sports drink to find their way into the athlete's bloodstream. The first is **gastric emptying rate**. This term refers to the speed with which the contents of the stomach empty into the small intestine, where they can be absorbed. A number of factors that affect gastric emptying rate are discussed below.

In general, the greater the amount of stomach contents, the faster those contents enter the small intestine. This factor has little impact on design of sports drinks. Any drink consumed in large enough quantities to bring volume-accelerated emptying into play would leave the athlete feeling bloated, and most likely would interfere with sports performance.

Volume

The higher the caloric content, the slower the gastric emptying rate. Caloric content seems to be the most important factor influencing gastric emptying rate. This has led some researchers to suggest that glucose and other forms of carbohydrate be left out of sports drinks because they retard emptying time. Inclusion of these substances, they hypothesize, might slow absorption of fluid enough to interfere with optimum sports performance.

However, current research indicates that under exercise conditions, plain water and a 10% (or less) carbohydrate solution exhibit similar emptying rates.

Caloric content

This term refers to the *concentration* of particles in a given amount of fluid. For example, a cup of water with three teaspoons of sugar has a higher osmolarity than a cup of water with one teaspoon of sugar.

For many years, higher osmolarities were thought to slow gastric emptying. However, higher-osmolarity drinks are usually higher in calories as well, and researchers now believe the higher caloric values, not the difference in osmolarity, have been responsible for the slower emptying rate demonstrated in many studies.

Osmolarity

The second major factor affecting the time required for the in-gredients of a sports drink to get into the athlete's blood is the **rate of intestinal absorption**.

Studies show:

- ■ Water is absorbed much more quickly in the presence of both glucose and sodium.
- ■ Glucose is absorbed much more readily in the presence of sodium.

Intestinal Absorption

As mentioned, both the rate of gastric emptying and the rate of intestinal absorption affect how long it takes for the ingredients in a sports drink to find their way into the athlete's bloodstream. In turn, carbohydrate content affects both the rate of gastric emptying and the rate of intestinal absorption, slowing gastric emptying and hastening intestinal absorption. The benefits that glucose provides by hastening intestinal absorption and providing extra fuel outweigh the drawbacks of slowed gastric emptying time. Stimulation of intestinal water absorption by glucose is the basis for the efficacy of carbohydrate-electrolyte beverages.

Concentrations

It has been determined that maximal water absorption in the small intestine occurs when glucose concentration in the small intestine is about 1% to 3%, and sodium content is 90 to 120 mmol/liter. Most sports drinks contain higher glucose concentrations (usually 6% to 7%) and lower sodium contents (10 to 20 mmol/liter) than this (see chart on next page).

However, there is evidence that even though a sports drink may supply glucose and sodium in less-than-optimal concentrations, a better balance of glucose and sodium may result once the sports drink mixes with intestinal fluids.

Carbohydrate Type

Although many studies demonstrate that carbohydrate feeding during exercise effectively increases endurance, there is some controversy as to the best type of carbohydates to include in sports drinks.

Glucose polymers

Some manufacturers see **glucose polymers** as the carbohydrate-of-choice. Glucose polymers are long chains of glucose molecules. Since the glucose molecules are all tied up in long glucose polymer chains, the osmolarity (particle concentration) of a glucose-polymer drink is *low*, even though the calorie content is *high*.

The thinking here is that the lower osmolarity will increase the gastric emptying rate, improving the efficacy of the drink.

Research indicates this is not the case. Ingestion of a glucose polymer solution during exercise results in similar gastric emptying and intestinal absorption times as ingestion of an equal-calorie, equal-volume glucose solution.

CARBOHYDRATE AND ELECTROLYTE CONTENT OF SELECTED SPORTS DRINKS (APPROX.)

| BEVERAGE | CARBOHYDRATE | | ELECTROLYTE (mmol/L) | |
	Content (% carbohydrate)	Type	Sodium	Potassium
Body fuel 450	4.5	Glucose Polymer	16	2
Exceed	7.0	Glucose Polymer, Fructose	10	5
Gatorade	6.0	Sucrose, Glucose	20	3
Gookinaid E.R.G.	5.0	Glucose	16	10
Isostar	7.0	Sucrose, Glucose, Fructose	23	5
Max	7.5	Glucose Polymer, Fructose	0	0
Recharge	7.5	Fructose, Glucose	5	10

This indicates that glucose polymer solutions are no more effective than glucose in achieving the goals of sports drinks.

Fructose

Fructose stimulates slightly less intestinal water absorption than the same concentration glucose solution, and thus is slightly less effective in accomplishing this most important goal of sports drinks. Also, high-concentration fructose solutions have been shown to cause gastrointestinal distress and diarrhea, both during rest and exercise, diminishing the attractiveness of fructose as a carbohydrate source in sports drinks.

Sucrose

Sucrose is rapidly broken down in the small intestine to glucose and fructose. The fructose portion is associated with slightly less water absorption, as indicated above. So sucrose is slightly less effective than glucose in sports drinks.

Electrolyte Content

Sweat contains small quantities of sodium, postassium, and other minerals important for fluid balance. Losses of these minerals, called **electrolytes**, through sweating normally pose no threat either to health or performance. A post-exercise meal replenishes all electrolyte losses.

However, performance of extreme endurance events—triathlons, marathons—in the heat may necessitate some electrolyte supplementation during exercise.

Most sports drinks contain low concentrations of electrolytes, including sodium, potassium, and chloride.

Electrolytes in sports drinks serve three functions. They:

- can replace electrolytes lost through sweating and thus help maintain the body's electrolyte and fluid balance
- increase the absorption of water in the small intestine
- increase the palatability of the solution, raising the likelihood that the athlete will drink enough to meet fluid requirements of heavy exercise

Conclusions

Athletes lose both water and electrolytes during prolonged exercise. If they lose enough of either, performance suffers. Sports drinks can replenish both, and contribute carbohydrate fuel as well. However, what constitutes an "ideal" sports drink is far from settled, and intense research continues.

Nevertheless, sports drinks containing all three nutrients—water, electrolytes, and carbohydrate—represent a convenient vehicle for maintaining the athlete's fluid and electrolyte balance and energy during exercise, and can help maintain peak performance—winter or summer. ❑

The Effects of Consuming Carbohydrate-Electrolyte Beverages on
Gastric Emptying and Fluid Absorption During and Following Exercise
Robert Murray
Sports Medicine
V 4: 322-351, September/October 1987

GENETICS AND ATHLETIC ABILITY

Certain physical characteristics tend to run in families. One of these is athletic ability. However, as with any trait that runs in families, a question arises: does the trait run in families because it is genetically transmissible from parent to offspring or because of the environment in which the offspring was raised?

In an attempt to find out, Canadian researchers tabulated the results of the 1981 Canada Fitness Survey. Fitness information, including weight, height, skinfold measurements, extremity and trunkal girths, endurance, strength, submaximal power output, flexibility, and resting heart rate was gathered on some 13,800 Canadians. Statistical comparisons were made between siblings and between parents and siblings to evaluate the effect of heredity versus environment.

For weight, height, waist-to-hip ratio, and submaximal power output the transmissibility from parent to offspring was less than 30%, indicating that environment contributed over 70%; for strength and flexibility the transmissibility was less than 40%, indicating an environmental contribution of over 60%. For none of the measured indices was the transmissibility ever over 50%, indicating that, for all the fitness characteristics measured, environment accounts for over 50% of the variation.

This calls into question the concept of the "natural athlete," suggesting that environmental factors, such as training, may play a bigger role than previously thought. Although there will always be people who seem to excel effortlessly at a variety of sports, it may be that these athletes are made, not born. ❏

Inter-Generational Transmission of Physical
Fitness in the Canadian Population
L. Perusse, et al.
Canadian Journal of Sports Science
V 13 # 1: 8-14, 1988

CIRCADIAN RHYTHMS

Everyone knows a "morning person," someone who is always bright-eyed and chipper first thing in the morning. Everyone also knows an "evening person," someone who can barely drag out of bed in the morning and is sluggish for the first several hours of the day. For morning people and evening people, the tables turn late in the evening: morning people can barely keep their eyelids open, while evening people are full of energy.

Whether you are a morning person or a evening person is determined by your internal biological clock, called your **circadian rhythm** (from Latin *circa dies*, meaning *about a day*). For some people, their circadian rhythm dictates they are best in the morning; for others, best in the evening. Not surprisingly, circadian rhythms can affect sports performance. Knowing your circadian rhythm may help you get the competitive edge.

Functions Affected by Circadian Rhythms

A number of physiologic functions follow a roughly 24 hour cycle and are presumed to be under circadian control. These include sleep, body temperature, strength, arousal, heart rate. blood pressure, urinary excretion, and hormonal output.

For example, resting heart rate and blood pressure show daily maximums in late morning or early afternoon, and daily minimums from about 2 to 4 am. This may be related to daily maximums and minimums in certain hormones, such as cortisol and epinephrine (adrenaline).

The increase seen in resting heart rate in late morning or early afternoon also translates into an increase in exercise-induced heart rate. So your heart rate will get up to higher levels while doing submaximal exercise in late morning or early afternoon compared to the same amount of exercise done at other times of the day. Those who gauge their exercise by following their heart rate need to be aware that circadian changes in heart rate may throw off their exercise measurements.

Body temperature varies by about 1° F over the course of 24 hours, with a maximum from about 4 to 6 pm, and a minimum from about 4 to 6 am. Two factors relating to getting rid of excess body heat, sweating and blood flow to the surface of the skin, show maximums and minimums at about the same times as body temperature. These circadian variations probably have less influence on performance in the heat than do other factors, such as ambient temperature and clothing type.

One circadian-controlled factor that *does* significantly influence performance, though, is **arousal**. Arousal includes feelings of mood, alertness, vigor, and overall well-being, and probably shows more variation from person to person than most factors under circadian control. Arousal generally shows one peak in the morning, a drop-off after lunch, and then a second, greater peak in the afternoon. Arousal may affect performance in that exercise is generally perceived to be more strenuous and fatiguing when arousal is low, and less strenuous and fatiguing when arousal is high.

There is some evidence to suggest that flexibility and strength are greatest in the late afternoon or early evening. If this is true, then, all else being equal, an athlete might get in a better workout by hitting the gym after work rather than before work.

Other factors affecting performance, such as maximum oxygen uptake (a measure of aerobic capacity) and pain threshold, have shown no clear circadian pattern.

Performance

Since such factors as heart rate, body temperature, arousal, flexibility, and strength are under circadian influence, it is reasonable to wonder if sports performance as a whole might be influenced by circadian rhythms. Several studies have looked into this.

In one study, sixteen swimmers, six runners, three shot putters, and four rowers were tested for maximum performance in the morning and in the evening. All athletes competed at the intercollegiate or Olympic level. Nine of the sixteen swimmers, all six runners, all three shot putters, and all four rowers performed better in the evening (5 to 7 pm) than in the morning (7 to 9 am). In another study, results of all-out swimming performed at five different times of the day showed steady improvement from 6:30 am to 8:00 pm, with an overall improvement of 2.5 to 3.5%. In a third study, subjects tested on stationary bicycles at either 6:30 am or 10:00 pm showed significantly greater tolerance to intense exercise, performed more work, and produced more lactic acid (a measure of how hard the muscles are working) in the evening than in the morning. Several other studies have reported similar results.

Thus, it appears that sports performance progressively improves throughout the day.

But what of morning people and evening people? How do their circadian rhythms specifically affect their performance?

Experiments that have shown improved sports performance later in the day have generally shown that performance parallels circadian variations in body temperature. On average, body temperature peaks from about 4 to 6 pm. However, people identified by questionnaire as morning people hit peak body temperature about 70 minutes earlier than do evening people. Morning people may therefore be at their sports performance "prime" somewhat earlier than evening people.

Morning people produce more of the hormone *epinephrine* (adrenaline) in the morning; evening people produce more epinephrine in the evening. Since epinephrine is one of the hormones contributing to arousal, and arousal affects performance, having higher circulating levels of epinephrine may allow morning people to perform better earlier in the day.

It has been estimated that peak time of day for performance by an evening person is two to five hours later than peak time of day for performance by an "intermediate," one who is neither a morning nor evening person. To bring out peak performances, then, athletic competitions are best scheduled in late afternoon or early evening. For evening people, they are best scheduled even later than that.

Athletes crossing several time zones to attend a competition should try to minimize jet-lag changes, going to bed earlier or later in preparation. This same technique can be used by an athlete to prepare for an event scheduled at the biologic "wrong time of day" (e.g. a morning 10K for an evening person). Be aware that setting the biological clock back (by getting up earlier) is not nearly as easy as setting it forward (by going to bed later).

If you have a choice, it is probably advantageous to work out during a time that is in concert with your natural circadian rhythm. ❑

Circadian Timekeepers in Sports
Edward R. Eichner, MD
The Physician and Sportsmedicine
V 16 # 2: 79-86, Feb 1988

EYE-HAND DOMINANCE

Why do some people seem to be naturally good baseball pitchers, and others naturally good batters? Often, such abilities are chalked up to an athlete's innate "talent," some sort of mystical gift that defies analysis. According to a recent letter in the *New England Journal of Medicine*, however, at least some factors contributing to baseball ability may not be all that mystical after all.

Everyone knows that most people exhibit strong hand dominance—the preference for using the right hand or the left hand for manual tasks. For example, most people write with their right hand; a smaller number write with their left hand. A still smaller number can write with either hand, and are ambidextrous.

Just as humans exhibit hand dominance, they also exhibit eye dominance, called **ocular sighting dominance.** Ocular sighting dominance is the preference for using one eye over the other for sighting tasks. For example, a pitcher with right ocular sighting dominance will use primarily his right eye in aiming a pitch. Some people have neither right nor left ocular dominance, and sight as if they are looking through one central eye at the bridge of the nose. These people are said to have **central ocular dominance.**

It turns out that hand dominance and ocular sighting dominance are not independent of one another. Most people (65%) have **uncrossed dominance,** meaning they show preference for both their right hand and their right eye, or both their left hand and left eye. Eighteen percent show **crossed dominance**, that is, right hand/left eye or left hand/right eye preference. Seventeen percent show central ocular dominance.

In an evaluation of hand-eye dominance patterns among 23 college varsity baseball players, those with central ocular dominance were the best batters and pitchers, as reflected in batting and earned-run averages. Those with crossed dominance were good batters but poor pitchers, and those with uncrossed dominance were good pitchers but poor batters. This suggests that hand-eye dominance is a partial determinant of baseball success.

Not surprisingly, when the college varsity baseball players were compared to normal controls, the baseball team had a disproportionately high number of players with central ocular dominance (good batters/good pitchers). Since a team needs more good batters than good pitchers, there was a relative preponderance of players with crossed dominance (good batters/poor pitchers), and relatively few with uncrossed dominance (good pitchers/poor batters).

Can a player's hand-eye dominance be changed? Possibly, but it is probably not a good idea to try. Ocular sighting dominance seems to be genetically predetermined, and trying to change it may cause permanent double vision and other visual problems. Most developmental specialists also recommend against trying to change handedness.

However, knowledge of hand-eye dominance can be used to help guide young athletes into activities in which they are most likely to succeed. ❏

Patterns of Eye-Hand Dominance in Baseball Players
J. Portal MD and
P. Romano MD
New England Journal of Medicine
V 319 # 10: 655-6, Sept 8 1988

ACCURACY AND HYDROSTATIC WEIGHING

Body fat is in the news. A growing number of athletes are paying attention to percentage body fat as an indication of fitness. Bodybuilders, in particular, are interested in achieving the minimum percentage body fat, to maximize their muscular definition. Other athletes, such as wrestlers, want to minimize body fat to maximizing lean body mass for their weight class.

One of the most accurate ways of measuring percentage body fat is hydrostatic weighing. With this method, the athlete is weighed in air, then submerged and weighed underwater. The two weights are compared, and from these values percentage body fat is calculated.

Food has the potential to throw off measurements. Since water is more dense than fat, a high-water meal right before weighing would be expected to make the body more dense, making it appear to have less fat. On the other hand, a gas-producing meal would make the body less dense, making it appear to have more fat. Does the pre-weighing meal really make a difference?

Ten subjects participated in a study to determine how food and fluid intake may affect hydrostatic weighing. On separate days, in random order, they ate one of the following meals:

- a salad and a can of soda
- two-and-a-half cans of soda
- two bean burritos, a bean tostada, and a can of soda

Subjects were weighed before the meal, and either immediately afterward (for the soda-only group), or 45 minutes afterwards (for the salad and bean groups).

A decrease in body density is interpreted as an increase in body fat. The salad and drink-only groups showed significant decreases in body density after the meals. Were it not known that the decreases were due only to the meals, it might appear that the subjects had suddenly increased their body fat by up to 3%.

Interestingly, the gas-producing bean group did not show decreases in density. This is probably because decreases in body density from intestinal gas production were offset by increases in body density from eating this heavy, dense meal.

This suggests that, although hydrostatic weighing has the potential to be accurate to within 0.4% body fat, measurements can be thrown off considerably by seemingly innocuous factors such as eating a salad beforehand. Athletes wanting to get the most accurate percentage body fat determination by hydrostatic weighing should probably not eat or drink for several hours before being weighed. ❏

Dietary Preparation and Percent Fat Measurement by Hydrostatic Weighing
T. R. Thomas. L. D. Crough and J. Araujo
British Journal of Sports Medicine
V 22 # 1: 9-11, March 1988

HEALTH

Various factors related to general health may affect or be affected by physical training. Ranging from pre-menstrual syndrome to frostbite, fetal health to tanning, the findings presented in this chapter are of value to any active person.

PHYSICAL EXERTION AND CARDIO-VASCULAR HEALTH

More good news for your heart. The Multiple Risk Factor Intervention Trial (MRFIT, or "Mr. Fit") is a study following over 12,000 middle-aged men at risk for heart disease. One of many factors looked into is exercise and its effects on coronary heart disease (disease of the coronary arteries, the vessels which supply blood to the heart tissue).

The participants filled out a questionnaire in which they detailed what kind of leisure-time physical activities they performed and for how long every day. Based on the questionnaire results, they were divided into three groups: low, moderate, and high exertion.

The subjects were followed for an average of seven years. There was little difference between the "moderate exertion" group and the "high exertion" group in terms of mortality rates or frequency of heart problems. However, both groups had less than two-thirds the number of deaths due to heart attacks, and only 70% as many deaths from all causes, as did the "low exertion" group.

The difference in energy expenditure between the "low exertion" group and the "moderate exertion" group was not much—only 160 calories per day (74 calories for the "low exertion" group versus 234 calories for the "moderate exertion" group). This difference is the number of calories burned by a 176 lb. man walking at a normal pace for 25 minutes.

The "high exertion" group averaged 638 calories burned in leisure-time physical activities daily. The extra 404 calories a day burned by the "high exertion" group did not result in any further reduction in problems from coronary heart disease.

So, leisure-time activities requiring moderate exertion appear to reduce the rate of heart attacks and death from coronary heart disease. High-exertion activities do not seem to provide any additional benefit, at least among middle-aged men at risk for heart disease. ❑

Leisure-Time Physical Activity Levels and Risk of
Coronary Heart Disease and Death
Arthur Leon, et al.
JAMA, V 258 #17: 2388-2395, November 6 1987

DECLINING FITNESS AMONG CHILDREN

Exercise has a number of benefits for adults, including decreased risk of heart disease, diabetes, obesity, and osteoporosis. For years schools have had programs of physical education for children, in part based on the thinking that the fitness activities of children influence their fitness activities as adults. With that in mind, how fit are our kids?

According to the recently completed National Children and Youth Fitness Study, not very. This two-part study looked at the fitness of American youth. Part I evaluated 10-to-18-year-olds, and found higher levels of body fat and lower levels of physical activity than in similar studies from the '50s and '70s.

Part II evaluated even younger children, 6- to 9-year-olds, with the thinking that perhaps fitness needs to begin at an earlier age. The researchers found:

Compared to a study from twenty years ago, today's 6- to 9-year-olds have more body fat, 54% more obesity, and 98% more superobesity. These changes were attributed to changes in both diet and physical activity.

Physical education does not seem to be a priority for schools. Thirty-seven percent of 6- to 9-year-olds have P.E. only once or twice a week; recess seems to substitute for physical education; only two-thirds of P.E. teachers have valid certification; and only 39% of children who take physical education do so in appropriate facilities, such as gymnasiums.

Schools are not promoting healthy exercise habits, concentrating instead on competitive team sports. This emphasis on competitive team sports starts as early as third or fourth grade.

Participation in a school physical education program does not seem to be much of a factor in how children perform in fitness tests.

Generally, parents are not serving as fitness role models. Fifty percent of parents fail to exercise vigorously even once a week. Parents average less than one day per week exercising with their children.

Six- to nine-year-olds spend an average of two hours per weekday and almost three-and-a-half hours per weekend day in front of the television.

Those children who participate in community fitness activities (such as YMCA programs), watch less television, and have physically more-active parents perform better on fitness tests.

The results of this two-part study suggest that the preparation America's youth receive for lifetime physical fitness is inadequate. James Ross and Russell Pate PhD, co-directors of the study, hope these findings will encourage schools to improve the quality of their physical education programs, and hope it will encourage parents to take a more active role in the early fitness of their children. According to Pate, "It is far more important that we develop positive attitudes and habits with regard to exercise in kids than it is to simply improve their fitness in the short term." ❏

Does Physical Fitness of Today's Children Foretell the Shape of Tomorrow's Adult America?
J. W. Zylke MD
Journal of the American Medical Association
V 259 #16; 2344-9, April 1988

EXERCISE AND AGING

Exercise can provide benefits both today and for years to come. There is increasing evidence supporting moderate, regular exercise for its long-term health benefits.

Aging can be looked at as a steady decline in functional aerobic capacity (the ability of the cardiovascular system to do work). The rate of decline in sedentary (inactive) men is *twice as great* as the rate of decline in active, healthy men. In a sense, inactive men are aging twice as fast as active men. A scary thought.

The much-publicized "risks" of aerobic training in older athletes are greatly reduced by maintaining a high level of fitness. On rare occasions, joggers *have* succumbed to heart attacks. However, this risk is ten times lower in the jogger accustomed to vigorous exercise than it is in the novice. ❏

Health Benefits of Exercise in an Aging Society
Archives of Internal Medecine
V 147: 353-356, 1987

AEROBIC ACTIVITY AND MENTAL ACUITY IN AGED PEOPLE

Aerobic exercise improves cardiovascular and respiratory fitness, overall muscle tone, and general sense of well-being. Now, new research indicates it may help older people think more clearly, as well.

Forty-three elderly patients were divided into three groups. The first performed aerobic exercise, maintaining a training heart rate of 80% of maximum heart rate. The second, the control group, performed exercises promoting strength and flexibility, but calling for little increase in heart rate. The third performed little or no exercise.

Before and after the training, all patients were given a series of mental acuity tests.

Results? The aerobic group showed improvement on all tests. The control group showed less improvement. And the non-exercising group showed no improvement.

The authors then performed a second study which compared mental acuity of sixty young and old volunteers. Participants were either out-of-shape or very fit, as indicated by their maximal oxygen uptake.

Again, the fit subjects showed a higher degree of mental acuity than the unfit subjects. Furthermore, the elderly fit subjects outperformed the young out-of-shape subjects.

The authors state that "there was a strong fitness effect on cognitive efficiency at all ages..."

Chalk up another plus for working out! ❑

Aerobic Fitness Can Improve Cognitive Efficiency in Aged
Internal Medicine News
V 20 #16: 57, August 15-31, 1987

AEROBIC QUALITIES OF PLAYING TENNIS

Some twelve million Americans (5% of the U.S. population) play tennis. For many of these, it is their sole aerobic activity, thus the only exercise that has the potential of improving their cardiovascular health. The American College of Sports Medicine advises that, for an aerobic activity to promote cardiovascular health, it should:

■ Raise heart rate to 60 to 90% of maximum heart rate reserve (see box)

■ Keep heart rate elevated for fifteen minutes to an hour

■ Be performed 3 to 5 days a week

CALCULATING YOUR MAXIMUM HEART RATE RESERVE

Intensity of exertion is inferred from *maximum heart rate reserve*, which is calculated by the Karvonen method. In the Karvonen method, exercise heart rate and maximum heart rate are compared, after correcting for resting heart rate.

Ann Med Exp Bio Fenn, 35: 307-315, 1957

Percentage of max heart rate reserve = (EHR - RHR)/(MHR - RHR) X 100

where:

EHR = measured exercise heart rate

RHR = measured resting heart rate

MHR = maximum heart rate, determined for each individual by a graded treadmill run to exhaustion

---

Does tennis meet these criteria?

To find out, seventeen male tennis players, average age thirty-one, were monitored during singles and doubles competition for heart rate and amount of time spent in actual exertion. They played hour-long matches against opponents of comparable ability (earlier studies have demonstrated the effect of competition on heart rate to be greatest when an individual's opponent is of comparable or better ability). All were experienced players, averaging about eight hours a week playing tennis.

The heart rates of the singles players averaged 61% of maximum heart rate reserve, barely meeting the American College of Sports Medicine recommendation. Even though the ball typically was in play only 31% of the time, and heart rate reserve fluctuated between 40% and 80%, the minimum criterion of 60% was met.

For doubles, heart rates averaged only 33% of maximum heart rate reserve, well below the ACSM recommendation. The ball was in play even less than in singles (only 25% of the time), and heart rate reserve fluctuated between 20% and 60%, never reaching a steady state.

Singles competition tennis meets the ACSM heart rate criterion for promoting cardiovascular fitness, and potentially can meet all three criteria if performed long enough and often enough. Doubles, however, fails to meet the heart rate criterion, thus is not the best form of exercise for improving cardiovascular health. ❑

Heart Rate Responses During Singles and Doubles Tennis Competition
L Morgans, PhD et al.
The Physician and Sportsmedicine
V 15 # 7: 67-74, July 1987

EXERCISE AND WOMEN'S HEALTH RISKS

Sometimes research reveals hidden connections between seemingly unrelated facts, often yielding surprising results. Rose Frisch, PhD, an associate professor at the Harvard School of Public Health, has recently proposed such a connection.

Frisch conducted a survey of 2,622 women who were former college athletes and 2,776 female non-athletes. She found two seemingly unrelated facts:

Former athletes had a significantly lower incidence of cancer of the breast and reproductive tract (uterus, ovary, cervix, and vagina), as well as a lower incidence of diabetes.

Females who exercised regularly during girlhood often had their first menstrual periods a year or more later than average.

Frisch thinks these two seemingly unrelated facts are related. She feels that a woman's risk of getting breast cancer, cancer of the reproductive tract, or diabetes is related to the total number of menstrual periods a woman has in her lifetime. The more menstrual periods, the greater the risk; the fewer periods, the less the risk.

Early and consistent strenuous exercise, Frisch reasons, delays a woman's first menstrual period and predisposes her to late and missed periods throughout her reproductive life. This lowers the total number of menstrual periods she has in her lifetime, in turn lowering her risk of these conditions, according to Frisch. Frisch therefore advocates early and consistent strenuous exercise for all females, with the intention of delaying first menstrual periods and causing late and missed periods.

Others disagree, and feel it's dangerous to "fool Mother Nature." Exercise-induced amenorrhea (lack of menstrual periods) is associated with decreased levels of estrogens, which in turn are associated with bone disorders such as osteoporosis. In addition, women with exercise-induced amenorrhea can have difficulty gaining enough fat to restart menstrual periods, even after they stop exercising. (Interestingly, low body fat from highly strenuous exercise programs can also interfere with fertility in men. Low body fat and high exercise load can lower testosterone levels and impair sperm production.)

Frisch counters such criticisms by pointing out that exercise actually strengthens bone, and that getting body fat up to 25% of total weight is sufficient to restart menstrual periods.

Frisch has made some controversial recommendations, and the debate will doubtlessly continue. Is it advisable for females to exercise with the intention of delaying their first menstrual periods and causing late and missed periods? Here, as is often the case with newly proposed connections, the information is probably too sketchy to say for certain. Until we know more about the effects of exercise on hormones and certain cancers, it is advisable to approach these recommendations with caution.

[Ed. note: Total body fat appears to be an important factor in breast cancer and cancer of the reproductive tract. Body fat affects metabolism of estrogen, which in turn may influence development of these cancers. Exercise, of course, lowers total body fat. It may be that the former athletes had lower incidences of these cancers because of lower body fat, independent of the total number of menstrual periods. Appropriate diet, too, lowers total body fat, and there is some suggestion that lower levels of dietary fat are associated with lower levels of breast cancer.

From all available evidence, a low-fat, high-carbohydrate diet coupled with regular exercise appears to be the most healthful overall approach for adults. However, the question of whether consistent strenuous exercise is advisable for pre-pubertal girls has yet to be answered.] ❏

Will Exercise Help Keep Women Away From Oncologists—or Obstetricians?
M. Goldsmith
Journal of the American Medical Association
V 259 # 12:1769-70, March 25 1988

EXERCISE AND PREMENSTRUAL SYNDROME

Athletic women may be less troubled with premenstrual syndrome than non-athletic women, suffering from fewer and less-severe premenstrual complaints.

That's the conclusion of a recent review article in the *Journal of Applied Sports Science Research*.

Premenstrual syndrome refers to a collection of symptoms experienced by women during the **luteal phase** of the menstrual cycle. (The *luteal phase* is the interval after ovulation but before menstruation.) These symptoms can include irritability, depression, tension, headache, bloating, increased appetite, breast tenderness, lethargy, constipation, and acne.

A number of factors have been considered as potential causes of PMS, including deficiencies of vitamins A, B1, B6, and E, and minerals magnesium and zinc; allergies to one's own hormones; impaired glucose metabolism; and psychological factors. Recent research has disproven most of these (for example, it appears PMS is *not* the result of vitamin or mineral deficiencies), and is now focusing on the most likely candidate, internal hormone imbalance.

A complicated series of hormonal changes occurs during the menstrual cycle. Three of the primary hormones involved are **estrogen**, **progesterone**, and **endorphins**. *Estrogen* and *progesterone* are female hormones released by the ovaries, and *endorphins* are "natural painkiller" hormones released by the brain.

One theory is that the "natural painkiller" hormones decline during the luteal phase, decreasing any "painkilling" effect and increasing tension and other symptoms. Indeed, women suffering from PMS have been shown to have lower levels of endorphins during the premenstrual phase than during the rest of the cycle, and lower levels of endorphins during the premenstrual phase than women not suffering from PMS.

Exercise affects release of all three of the primary hormones involved in the menstrual cycle. Exercise appears to increase release of estrogen, increase release of painkilling endorphins, and decrease release of progesterone. Any of these changes, or perhaps a combination of the three, may be responsible for the decrease in PMS seen in athletes.

PMS symptoms have been shown to decrease with exercise. Various studies have shown decreased premenstrual breast tenderness and fluid retention with three months of running; elimination of tension and headache with skiing, swimming, and cross-country track; and decreased depression with wrestling, jogging and tennis.

PMS responses to exercise are probably quite variable, depending on type and severity of symptoms, and type, intensity, duration, and frequency of exercise. Because of this, exercise prescriptions for PMS need to be tailored to the individual. For example, premenstrual breast tenderness may rule out premenstrual running for some women. For those women, swimming may be a better exercise. Knee injuries occur more frequently premenstrually, which again may affect choice of exercise.

Clearly, an athlete suffering from premenstrual tension, headache, and lethargy is likely neither to perform nor train at her peak. Those athletes who can determine what exercises can minimize their symptoms, and what alternative exercises can minimize the influence of PMS symptoms on their workout, will be the ones least troubled by the performance-robbing effects of premenstrual syndrome. ❑

Exercise and the Premenstrual Syndrome
G. Lambert
Journal of Applied Sports Science Research
V 2 # 1: 16-19, Feb 1988

Vitamin and Trace Element Status in Premenstrual Women
M. Mira et al.
American Journal of Clinical Nutrition
V 46: 636-41, 1988

HOW VIGOROUS EXERCISE MAY AFFECT FETAL HEALTH

Two research observations:

■ Vigorous exercise reduces blood flow to the internal organs in animals, including blood flow to the uterus of pregnant animals. The amount of the reduction is proportional to the duration and intensity of exercise.

■ Studies in humans have noted a drop in fetal heart rate immediately after exercise.

These two observations have raised concerns about whether vigorous exercise in pregnant women endangers fetal health. Anything that affects uterine blood flow or fetal heart rate can potentially affect fetal health.

To assess the effect of vigorous exercise on fetal heart rate, 45 pregnant women rode bicycle ergometers at four different levels of aerobic exertion, including cycling to exhaustion. Sixteen of the 45 women had been engaging in regular aerobic exercise during their pregnancy.

During exercise, fetal heart rate was found to be stable, regardless of the level of exertion. Immediately after exercise, however, fetal heart rate dropped significantly in 16% of exercise sessions. Ninety-four percent of the heart rate drops occurred after the most strenuous level of exercise, exercise to exhaustion.

Subjects who were able to achieve higher levels of aerobic output (higher VO_2 max) were more likely to have a drop in heart rate in their fetus. This suggests that women who regularly exercise may put their fetus at higher risk of a drop in heart rate after maximal exercise.

Since the drop in heart rate almost always occurred only with the most vigorous exercise, and only after stopping, the authors recommend that pregnant women should:

■ keep their heart rates below 150 beats per minute while exercising;

■ end all sessions of aerobic exercise with a gentle and gradual slowing of exertion, rather than abruptly stopping. ❏

Fetal Heart Rate Response to Maternal Exertion
M. Carpenter MD et al.
Journal of the American Medical Association
V 259 # 20: 3006-9, May 27 1988

EFFECTS OF EXERCISE ON FEMALE CANCER INCIDENCE

Some benefits of exercise, it appears, don't show up until well down the road.

Detailed medical, reproductive, diet, and exercise histories were obtained from almost 5,500 women aged 21 to 80. Half of these women had been college athletes; half had not.

Those who had not been college athletes had a 28% greater risk of benign breast disease, and a 45% greater risk of benign tumors of the reproductive system, than those who had been college athletes.

These findings are in line with a similar study by the same authors in 1985, which found female former college athletes to be at lower risk for malignant tumors of the breast and reproductive system than those who had not been college athletes.

Why these differences? It could be that exercise itself during the college years has a long-term protective effect; or that women who are athletically active in college tend to have differences in diet, physical activity, and total body leanness that persist throughout life. It could also be that the sex-hormone sensitive tumors of the breast and reproductive system (so-called because the tumors' aggressiveness is related to circulating levels of sex hormones) are exposed to lower levels of tumor-stimulating estrogens in female athletes.

More research needs to be done, but this relationship between college athletic activity and decreased life-long risk of both benign and malignant tumors of the breast and reproductive system is a promising one.

British Journal of Cancer
V 54:841-845, 1986

SWIMMING TO RETARD BONE MINERAL LOSS

Weightbearing exercises—for example, running or walking—have been recommended to help retard mineral (especially calcium) loss from bones. It had been assumed that non-weight-bearing exercises—such as swimming—were not effective in retarding mineral loss from bones because they did not provide sufficient "bone stress."

Now it appears that swimming does indeed retard mineral loss from bone.

Fifty-eight middle-aged male swimmers were compared with seventy-eight matched non-swimmers for bone mineral density. The mineral content of vertebrae averaged 12% higher in the swimmers than in the non-swimmers. This increase was unrelated to how long or how often they swam.

This suggests either that bone stress in swimming is greater than was previously thought, or that weight-bearing does not play as prominent a role in preventing bone mineral loss as was previously thought.

In any event, swimming appears to be a viable alternative for those at risk for bone mineral loss who are unable or unwilling to pursue running or other weight-bearing exercises. ❑

Swimming Can Have a Positive Effect on Bone Mineral Content
Internal Medicine News
V 20 # 7: 27, April 1987

CARING FOR SKIN ABRASIONS

An abrasion is a scraping away of skin as the result of friction. Abrasions are common in contact sports, indoors and out. Abrasions from indoor surfaces—mat and floor "burns"—are usually fairly superficial, while those from outdoor surfaces—for example, bare dirt for base sliding in baseball, or grass for football, soccer, and rugby—tend to be deeper. Among those at highest risk for abrasions are football players with exposed skin practicing on artificial turf.

The biggest problem with abrasions is that they frequently become infected. To minimize risk of infection, abrasions should be cleansed immediately. The deeper and dirtier the wound, the more likely infection will result and the more thoroughly the wound needs to be cleaned. Since the goal of cleansing is removal of bacteria, irrigating with a high-pressure stream of water is generally more effective than low-pressure rinsing.

After the wound has been irrigated, it should be washed with an antibacterial soap, such as Hibitane (containing chlorhexidine), Phisohex (containing hexachlorophene), or Betadine (containing povidone-iodine). If the abrasion is not too deep, a mild detergent (such as Johnson's Baby Shampoo) or hydrogen peroxide may suffice.

After washing, the wound should be dressed with a sterile dressing. Dressings should be changed frequently. If the athlete is re-entering the game, the wound needs to be protected against soiling and re-injury. Abraded areas tend to be subject to repeated trauma, which may delay healing.

The best protection against abrasion is appropriate clothing, such as long-sleeved shirts, protective stockings, sliding pads, and knee and elbow pads. Ill-fitting equipment may produce abrasions by repeatedly rubbing against the skin. If this occurs, a minor equipment adjustment or extra padding may alleviate the problem. ❑

Selected Cutaneous Disorders in Athletes
J. Walker MD
Canadian Family Physician
V 34: 169-172, January 1988

CARING FOR DRY SKIN

Skin normally has a certain amount of fat, helping to keep it soft and smooth. However, heavy sweating, frequent showering, and swimming can "de-fat" the skin, leaving it dry and rough.

Athletes are more susceptible to dry skin than non-athletes, because athletes tend to swim more often, sweat more heavily, and shower more frequently than non-athletes. Other predisposing factors include a history of allergic skin reactions, low humidity (as is common indoors in winter), heavy clothing, and irritating fabrics.

Dry skin (medically known as **xerosis**) can occur anywhere but usually is most pronounced on the back of the hands and arms. The skin typically has many fine wrinkles and redness. In more severe cases, it can progress to plaques of eczema, with breaks in the skin, small fluid-filled cysts, oozing, and crusting.

Xerosis can be controlled or prevented with the following steps:

- Keep showers short and not too hot.
- Use a high-fat soap, such as Dove, Oilatum, Lowilla, or Petrophylic Bar.
- Avoid antibacterial soaps and hard, highly alkaline soaps such as Irish Spring, Safeguard, and Zest.
- Pat skin dry after showering, and immediately apply a moisturizer/lubricant.
- Don't overdress.
- Wear cotton and soft synthetics.
- Avoid wearing wool next to the skin.
- Consider humidifying dry rooms.
- If dry skin persists despite these steps, see your doctor.

Selected Cutaneous Disorders in Athletes
J. Walker MD
Canadian Family Physician
V 34: 169-172, January 1988

SUNBURN

Some athletes spend a lot of time in the sun. While no one tries to get a sunburn, it's easy to overdo it. Not only can excess sun exposure cause the temporary discomfort of sunburn, but it can also cause permanent changes such as premature wrinkling and aging of the skin, DNA damage, cataracts, and certain types of skin cancer.

Fair-skinned people, of course, are the most susceptible to sunburn. Certain athletes may also be at higher risk because of the nature of their sports. Sports involving prolonged sun exposure (e.g. marathons), high altitude (mountain climbing, skiing), or lack of protective clothing (swimming, surfing, boardsailing) all increase exposure to ultraviolet light and increase risk of burning. Time factors contributing to sunburn include working out midday, and working out during the spring and summer months.

There are some less-obvious factors that increase risk of burning, too. Certain foods, such as limes, parsnips, celery, and figs, contain **psoralens**, chemicals that sensitize the skin to sunlight. If you eat psoralen-containing foods before spending the day in the sun, you are much more likely to get a severe sunburn.

Certain drugs sensitize the skin to sunlight, too. The most common of these is the antibiotic **tetracycline**, and closely-related drugs, such as **doxycycline**. Other drugs with the potential to cause sun sensitivity include certain diuretics and oral contraceptives.

The best thing to do about a sunburn is not to get one in the first place. When possible, the athlete should avoid midday sun exposure, especially in the spring and summer. Protective clothing, such as wide-brimmed hats, can help minimize exposure. If spending time in the sun is unavoidable, the athlete should use a good sunscreen.

Sunscreens with sun protective factor (SPF) of 15 or greater are best. Most burns are caused by ultraviolet B (UVB) rays, and the PABA-containing sunscreens protect well against UVB. However, some people are intolerant of PABA; for them, PABA-free sunscreens, containing benzophenones and cinnamates, work well. PABA does not protect against ultraviolet A (UVA) exposure, the kind of rays that cause skin reactions from psoralens or drugs. To protect against UVA burns, use a benzophenone sunscreen.

Sunscreens are most effective if applied at least one-half hour before sun exposure. This allows time for the active ingredients in the sunscreen to bind to the **stratum corneum** (one of the layers of the skin). After swimming or substantial sweating, the sunscreen should be reapplied.

Most sunscreens contain ingredients that can irritate the eyes. Because of this, extra care should be taken when applying sunscreens on the forehead and around the eyes. Athletes who perspire a lot are at higher risk for getting sunscreen in their eyes, and may need to forego sunscreen on the forehead in favor of a visored hat.

Common as it is, there are few satisfactory treatments for sunburn. Non-steroidal anti-inflammatory drugs, such as indomethacin (*Indocin*) and aspirin, can reduce redness if given in the first 24 hours. Cool-water compresses may help. Topical "caine" medications (*Solarcaine, Histocaine*) and antihistamines (*Phenergan cream*) may cause allergic sensitization, and should be avoided. In all cases, further sun exposure should be avoided. The best treatment may simply be time.

With a few simple precautions, the athlete can help prevent this summer's sunburn, and some more serious health problems down the road. ❏

Selected Cutaneous Disorders in Athletes
J. D. Walker MD
Canadian Family Physician
V 34: 169-172, Jan 1988

THE SAFETY RISKS OF ARTIFICIAL TANNING

Now that the sun has gone south for the winter, athletes and non-athletes alike are turning to indoor tanning booths to maintain their summer bronze. Bodybuilders, especially, make heavy winter use of these booths, hoping to improve their appearance and their chances of winning physique contests.

But are the booths safe?

Manufacturers promote the UV fluorescent tubes used in these devices as "safer than the sun" because they emit only ultraviolet A (UVA) radiation (wavelengths from 320 to 400 nanometers), and not ultraviolet B (UVB) radiation (290 to 320 nanometers). It's the UVB rays, found in sunlight, that cause sunburn.

In fact, many of these lamps emit UVB as well as UVA.

Also, although UVA exposure is less likely to cause sunburn than UVB, it is still associated with a number of serious health risks. Short—thirty minute—UVA exposure can suppress the immune system. Prolonged UVA exposure has been linked with skin aging, skin cancer, and eye damage.

Certain diseases that are aggravated by "regular" suntanning (such as systemic lupus erythematosus) may be aggravated by exposure to the rays in tanning booths.

And, contrary to popular belief, a tan gained as a result of UVA exposure will not protect against sunburn outdoors. It actually augments the sunburn reaction caused by UVB, and may promote a more serious burn.

If you use a tanning booth, be sure to wear opaque "tanning goggles" specifically designed for the purpose. Closing your eyes while in the booth does not protect the corneas and lenses of your eyes from being burnt by the UVA, which easily penetrates the eyelids. ❑

Health Club Tanning Booths: Risky Business
Valerie DeBenedette
The Physician and Sportsmedicine
V 15 #7: 59, July 1987

FROSTBITE

Frostbite is an actual freezing of the skin. Though serious, it is easily prevented with a few precautions and some common sense.

Frostbite can occur with any prolonged exposure to extreme cold, but is more likely under conditions of wetness, wind-chill, and tight or insufficient clothing. Conditions that may cause spasm of the arteries in the fingers and toes, such as nicotine exposure from smoking, can also predispose to frostbite.

Frostbitten skin looks white, waxy, and lacks sensation. Ironically, the loss of sensation may give relief from the pain of the extreme cold. Once the frostbitten tissue is warmed, the skin becomes red and very painful, and often blisters. If the freezing is deep enough, there may be not only significant tissue loss but also long-term complications such as abnormal nerve and artery function, arthritis, and bone tissue death.

The first line of protection is clothing. Dress in layers, and bring along extra clothes (including dry mitts and socks) on long outings. Garments made from polypropylene or Gortex are lightweight and non-absorbent, and allow sweat to evaporate or wick away from the body.

Shoes should be roomy. This not only provides space for an insulating layer of air but also prevents constriction of blood vessels in the foot from too-tight shoes. Since most of the heat leaves the foot through the sole, the sole should be thick and non-conductive. A felt-lined boot, accompanied by a thick wool sock, provides good protection for the foot.

Mitts with a leather shell and a wool lining provide good protection for the hands. Have a spare pair in case the wool lining gets wet.

Although the hands and (especially) the feet are most susceptible to frostbite, don't ignore the rest of the body. If the central body temperature drops, the blood vessels in the skin of the feet and hands constrict, increasing the risk of frostbite in these bodyparts.

Several other techniques can reduce risk of frostbite. A thick layer of zinc oxide over exposed skin may provide some protection. Aluminum chloride hexahydrate in ethanol (such as in the antiperspirant *Drysol*) applied to the hands and feet before prolonged exercise in the cold may reduce sweating and decrease risk of frostbite. Be aware that short bursts of exertion cause sweating, and sweating may predispose to frostbite.

Treatment calls for rapidly warming affected tissues in a 104° to 112°F bath (warm but not hot), *after protection from refreezing is certain*. Tissue damage from refreezing thawed skin is much greater than if the skin had remained frozen to begin with. Warming frozen skin is very painful, and pain medications should be given.

Gently clean with antibacterial soaps to reduce risk of infection. The damaged tissue should be protected from physical injury, as it is easy to bruise and slow to heal.

Use of tobacco products should be avoided, again because of the vasoconstricting effects of nicotine.

Above all, use common sense. Know the weather conditions, dangers, availability of assistance, and your own physical limitations for all cold weather sports. ❑

Selected Cutaneous Disorders in Athletes
J. Walker MD FRCP (C)
Canadian Family Physician
V 34 #1: 169-172, January 1988

ATHLETE'S FOOT

Despite the name, athlete's foot doesn't just affect athletes. In fact, the term really doesn't have anything to do with athletics—it was coined by an advertiser in the 1930s to promote a patent remedy for fungal infections of the feet. However, since athletes do get athlete's foot, it deserves discussion here.

Athlete's foot (medically speaking, *tinea pedis*) is a fungal infection of the skin of the toes and toe webs. In some circumstances the term may also be used to refer to contact allergy, psoriasis, hyperhidrosis (excessive sweating), or any of several other conditions involving the skin of the feet.

Ninety-five percent of people with fungal infections have very little in the way of symptoms, showing only slight and occasional peeling of the web of the little toes and sometimes adjacent webs. The other 5% have moderate to severe itching and burning, and can develop painful cracks (fissures) in the skin. If the athlete is hypersensitive to the fungus or to metabolic by-products of the fungus, blisters may occur.

Treatment is usually local, with any one of several over-the-counter or prescription products. These are usually soothing, antiseptic, and astringent wet dressings, and bland pastes and ointments. The best over-the-counter remedies include tolnaftate (*Tinactin*) and undecylenic acid (*Desenex*).

Specific antifungal medications may be indicated, but should be appropriate for the kind of fungus. Systemic oral medications are sometimes necessary. For these reasons, and because the wrong treatment can produce complications and prolong discomfort, a physician should be consulted before treatment is begun.

When using creams and ointments for athlete's foot, always apply them at least three inches beyond the edge of the visible infection. Massage them into the foot—don't just spread them on. Try not to make the areas between the toes too greasy.

Warm, moist skin encourages growth of all types of fungi. Thus, to facilitate healing and prevent reinfection, the skin should be kept as cool and dry as practical.

Socks that promote sweating, such as those made of wool or synthetic fibers such as Orlon, nylon, and Dacron, should be avoided. This is especially true for athletes who sweat excessively or live in humid climates. Socks made of 100% cotton are best. Shoes with rubber or synthetic soles can also encourage excessive warmth and moisture. Sandals or aerated shoes are better.

After bathing, the feet should be thoroughly dried and moist debris between the toes removed. After working out, it's best to remove shoes and socks as soon as possible, shower or at least wash feet, and change into fresh cotton socks and a different pair of shoes.

Contrary to popular belief, athlete's foot is not highly contagious. ❑

Skin Disorders in Athletes: Identification and Management
L. Stauffer MD
The Physician and Sportsmedicine
V 11 # 3: 101-121, March 1983

The AMA Book of Skin and Hair Care
L. Schoen, Ed.
J. B. Lippincott Co., New York
262-3, 1976

Home Skin Treatment
W. Dvorine MD
Charles Scribner's Sons, New York
60-1, 1983

SHARING WATER BOTTLES AND SPREADING VIRUSES

The polyethylene water bottle is a common sight on the sidelines of a football game. The nozzle-spouted bottle gets passed around to team members, who take a squirt to quench a hard-earned thirst.

Is this practice safe? Not really. Shared water bottles can spread enteroviruses, viruses that can cause outbreaks of pleurodynia (pain with breathing from an inflammation of the lining of the outside of the lungs) or meningitis. The Centers for Disease Control report that enterovirus outbreaks affecting ten or more football players occur about once a year in every state in the Union.

Although any group of athletes sharing a water bottle is at risk, football players seem to be at higher risk because the bottle gets passed around to more players.

Athletes tend to suck on the nozzle like a straw, rather than squirting the water into their mouths. This practice can contaminate both the nozzle and the water in the bottle. Outbreaks have occurred when a team shared just one or two cups as well.

Would it be safer to squirt the water in from a distance of a few inches? If all athletes followed this practice, yes. But it is unlikely all of them will. One athlete who sucks from the nozzle can contaminate the nozzle and the water. The next athlete who squirts water in may get enteroviruses from the water, or possibly aerosolize viruses from saliva on the nozzle. Aerosolized viruses can float to the back of the mouth and be breathed in, potentially causing respiratory tract infections or influenza.

The best way to avoid spreading enteroviruses among the team is to use disposable cups, or to have a separate water bottle for every player. ❑

Sharing a Water Bottle: a Dangerous Practice?
The Physician and Sportsmedicine
V 16 # 7: 29-30, July 1988

PSEUDO-HEPATITIS

Heavy endurance exercise causes a number of physiological effects. The signs of these effects sometimes mimic pathological (disease) conditions, and can result in medical misdiagnosis, unnecessary worry, and performance of unneeded, expensive tests.

One such condition is **pseudohepatitis**.

Pseudohepatitis involves elevations in the blood of certain enzymes found in the liver and muscles. Elevated levels of these enzymes in the blood usually suggests a problem with the patient's liver.

However, in runners, such elevations may not indicate liver problems, and instead may simply be a sign of temporary damage to muscle cells resulting from strenuous exercise. The author notes that, "Chronic elevations of serum enzymes such as SGOT [*serum glutamic oxaloacetic transaminase*] [and] LDH [*lactate dehydrogenase*]...are common in highly trained long-distance runners because of chronic muscle fiber injury and repair."

The author recommends that, for endurance athletes with elevations of the enzymes pointing to a liver condition, further tests be done. These tests should look for: (1) normal levels of enzymes found in liver but *not* in muscle (such as SGPT, *serum glutamic pyruvic transaminase*), and (2) elevated levels of enzymes found in muscle but *not* in liver (such as CK, *creatine kinase*).

These findings would point to muscle cell damage, rather than active liver disease. ❑

Gastrointestinal disorders in athletes
Arthur J. Siegel, MD
Your Patient & Fitness
V 1 # 2:10-15, March/April 1987

ABDOMINAL DISTRESS IN MARATHON RUNNERS

Many marathoners are familiar with the gastrointestinal disturbances associated with running. The most common of these, "Runner's Trots," is well-known. It refers to watery diarrhea that can occur during or immediately after running.

Other common gastrointestinal complaints include heartburn, nausea, abdominal pain, urge to have a bowel movement, and loss of appetite.

These maladies are more common in female than male runners, and more common in younger athletes. They are seen in triathletes, and are more common during the running phase than during cycling or swimming.

How common are these conditions? In a recent marathon, 83% of survey respondents said they occasionally or frequently experience gastrointestinal symptoms during or immediately after running. Urge to have a bowel movement (53%) and diarrhea (38%) were the most common symptoms, especially in women (74% and 68%, respectively). Athletes felt symptoms were more common after "hard" runs than after "easy" runs. Of those afflicted, 72% felt running was the cause, and almost one-third (29%) felt it worsened their performance.

These results may overstate the true incidence, because athletes who suffer from these problems are the most likely to respond to the questionnaire. However, similar studies have shown similar results. In any event, these results suggest that the incidence of gastrointestinal complaints in marathon runners is quite high.

As common as these conditions are, little is known about what causes them. One possible explanation is that the repeated pounding of running may alter intestinal function, perhaps even causing internal damage. Another possibility is that the psoas muscle, hypertrophied from exercise, may press on the colon, stimulating intestinal activity. A third possibility is that the working muscles draw so much blood away from the intestines that intestinal fluid absorption is impaired, causing diarrhea.

Yet another possibility is that these symptoms are hormonally caused. Exercise raises blood levels of certain hormones of the gastrointestinal tract, several of which cause diarrhea.

While little is known about what causes these symptoms, even less is known about how to prevent them. Many of the runners in this study had their own remedies, such as decreasing dietary fiber, eating slowly, relaxing, training on grass, wearing good shoes, or doing sit-ups. Success with these remedies is probably quite variable.

Since close to one-third of marathoners feel gastrointestinal disturbances impair their performance, learning more about cause and prevention of these problems may have a substantial impact on performance for many runners. ❏

Gastrointestinal Disturbances in Maratho Runners
C. Riddoch and T. Trinick
British Journal of Sports Medicine
V 22 # 2: 71-4, June 1988

SUDDEN DEATH IN ATHLETES

Over the last twenty-five years the popularity of regular exercise of all kinds has steadily increased. With increased participation in vigorous exercise, however, has been an increase in cases of exercise-related sudden death. Sudden death does not afflict only the out-of-shape; there have been reported cases of sudden death of well-conditioned athletes.

Coronary atherosclerosis ("hardening of the arteries") appears to be the culprit. Ninety-five percent of the victims of exercise-related sudden death, when evaluated at autopsy, had evidence of heart disease, including those under thirty.

Complete autopsies have been performed on 43 victims of exercise-related sudden death. These were experienced athletes; of those over thirty, most were runners, running 4 to 100 miles a week, with one to ten years of experience. Ninety-six percent died of atherosclerotic coronary heart disease. Over half had evidence of "clinically silent" heart attacks, meaning at some point they had experienced a heart attack without even knowing it. All had at least one major coronary artery more than 75% blocked off with atherosclerotic plaque. (A heart attack occurs when not enough blood can get through the coronary arteries to meet the oxygen demands of the heart.)

There have also been several reports of experienced athletes having non-fatal heart attacks during exercise. All of them developed new chest pain during vigorous exercise.

All of these athletes, those who experienced fatal and non-fatal heart events alike, had at least one coronary atherosclerotic risk factor: high blood pressure, high total serum cholesterol, or family history of coronary heart disease.

What does this mean? Exercise is not a panacea; it may significantly improve but does not guarantee cardiovascular health. The authors recommend that: 1) athletes should undergo medical screening of their cardiovascular systems, with this screening focusing on coronary atherosclerosis; and 2) attention should be paid to new symptoms. For middle-aged persons, new symptoms—especially those (such as chest pain) suggestive of heart origin—should be promptly evaluated, whether directly associated with exercise or not. ❏

Sudden Death in Middle-Aged Conditioned Subjects:
Coronary Atherosclerosis is the Culprit
Mayo Clinic Proceedings
V 62 # 7: 634-636, July 1987

WEIGHTLOSS FOR COMPETITION RISKS DEHYDRATION

Wrestling demands both strength and endurance. Since heavier wrestlers tend to be stronger than lighter ones, the rules require wrestlers to compete only against others in the same weight class.

Many wrestlers try to take advantage of these rules. They diet in an attempt to qualify for lower weight divisions, divisions in which they feel they can compete against smaller, weaker opponents. Wrestlers often lose enough weight during the first several weeks of the season to "make weight" one to three divisions below their normal weight. In addition, they may undergo 15 to 30 crash weight-loss episodes over the course of a four-month season, each a last-ditch attempt to make weight for the upcoming match.

In general, the dieting and crash weight loss programs undertaken by these athletes do not follow sound nutritional practices. Rather, the wrestlers resort to weight loss through dehydration. This can take the form of liquid intake restriction, sweating (often by running with heavy clothes on, or in saunas, steam baths, or rubber suits, all conditions that risk heat injury), laxatives, diuretics, induced vomiting, even spitting.

Acute food and fluid restriction causes a number of physiological changes, none of which are good for athletic performance. They include:

- decreased strength
- decreased endurance
- decreased work output
- lower blood volume
- reduced cardiac function during exercise, including increased heart rate, and decreased cardiac output
- decreased oxygen consumption
- impaired heat regulation
- decreased blood flow to the kidneys
- depletion of liver glycogen stores
- increased electrolyte loss

These physiologic changes translate directly into worsened performance. Loss of as little as 2% of body weight as fluid (three pounds for a 150-pound athlete) decreases endurance. Loss of 5% can cause heat exhaustion and heat stroke.

Consequently, wrestlers who dehydrate to make weight are competing under conditions that worsen performance and may threaten health.

Trying to replenish lost fluids after weighing in by gulping right before a match does little good—the fluids simply can't be replaced that quickly. For example, if weight loss is from 4% to 7.5%, rehydration can take from 24 to 36 hours. While gulping may decrease risk of overheating, it won't restore lost strength and endurance.

In one study, intercollegiate wrestlers dehydrated to make weight, losing an average of 4.8% of total weight over four days. All showed substantial decreases in strength output. The wrestlers then attempted to rehydrate after the weigh-in but before the match, rehydrating to 2.2% below original weight. The decrease in strength output persisted even after pre-match rehydration.

It is possible, on the other hand, to lose weight *without* losing strength and endurance if the weight loss comes from *excess fat*, instead of needed water. Some researchers have suggested that wrestlers should monitor their percentage body fat, striving for the optimal range of 7% to 10%. (Body fat should not fall below 5%.)

To lose fat, rather than body water, the athlete must lose weight gradually over a long period of time. This requires advance planning, often well before the season begins. The goal should be loss of not more than two to three pounds per week, since greater losses result in loss of muscle mass. Weight losses in the 2 to 3 lb./week range can be accomplished by increasing training while decreasing caloric intake; however, caloric intake should not fall below 1500 to 2000 calories per day. Decreasing caloric intake demands careful nutritional planning.

There is a second means of losing weight without losing strength and endurance: avoiding foods that make you retain water. Foods high in salt, such as most fast food and "junk food," cause retention of excess water, and thus excess weight. Avoiding these foods, and going easy on the salt shaker, decreases water retention without depriving your body of the water it needs for strength and endurance.

On any given day, most Americans eat ten to twenty times more salt than they need. Athletes get plenty of salt from the food they eat, and there is no physiologic reason to add salt to food. (Also, athletes should never take salt tablets unless prescribed by a doctor.) On the other hand, your body *does* need water, and athletes should drink at least eight glasses of water and other fluids a day.

Dehydrating to "make weight" has probably been around for as long as there have been weight divisions. No doubt the practice will continue. However, wrestlers armed with knowledge of the detrimental effects of dehydration and the beneficial effects of good nutrition have the potential to gain a competitive edge.

[Ed. note: This information applies not only to wrestling, but also to other activities—such as boxing, weightlifting, and bodybuilding— in which athletes may be tempted to dehydrate to make weight or (in the case of bodybuilding), improve physique.] ❏

Weight Loss Through Dehydration in Amateur Wrestling
S. Yarrows, RD
Journal of the American Dietetic Association
V 88 # 4: 491-493, April 1988

COSEQUENCES OF PASSIVE SMOKE INHALATION FOR PERFORMANCE

There is mounting evidence pointing to the negative effects of passive inhalation of someone else's cigarette smoke. Now there is evidence of the negative effects of "sidestream smoke" on athletic performance.

Eight women were tested on treadmills to determine to what degree maximal and submaximal exercise are affected by passive cigarette smoke inhalation. They were exposed to levels of smoke equivalent to breathing air from a smoke-filled room.

During maximal exercise, when compared to smoke-free trials, the subjects passively inhaling cigarette smoke exhibited significantly reduced maximal oxygen uptake, shorter time to exhaustion, increased blood lactate concentrations, increased ratings of perceived exertion, and increased R values (a measure of anaerobic metabolism). Similar results were seen during submaximal exercise.

The authors conclude that "the reduction in maximal performance is directly attributable to the carbon monoxide from the inhaled smoke binding with the hemoglobin (COHB) and reducing the oxygen carrying capacity." They go on to say that *any* reduction in oxygen carrying capacity reduces peak aerobic performance.

[Ed. note: While this study does not address the question, it would be interesting to know how long the reduced aerobic capacity from inhalation of sidestream smoke persists.] ❑

The Effects of Passive Inhalation of Cigarette Smoke on Exercise Performance
European Journal of Applied Physiology
V 54: 196-200, 1985

INJURIES

The risk of injury is present at any level of athletic participation. Sixteen recent studies have investigated the exact nature and cause of a number of sport-specific injuries, offering new insights into how they might be prevented.

FITNESS AND INJURY REDUCTION

Physical fitness appears to decrease the incidence of mild and moderate injuries.

One group particularly interested in this information is the U. S. Army, which puts upwards of 200,000 people through eight weeks of basic training every year. They've noted that about a quarter of the male recruits and half the female recruits sustain some type of injury requiring a clinic visit during basic training. Some 80% of these injuries are to the lower extremities, commonly stress fractures, tendinitis, and sprains.

The risk of injury during basic training is estimated to be similar to risk of injury during high school athletics.

Army researchers have identified some predictors of risk of injury. One of these is time in the mile run.

Median time for the mile run for male recruits was seven minutes; median time for female recruits was almost ten minutes. Those with mile run times considerably slower were at much greater risk of injury.

Another predictor of injury risk is the number of sit-ups a recruit can perform in two minutes.

Median number of sit-ups in two minutes for male recruits was 52; for female recruits it was 30. As with mile run times, those who were well below the median were at much greater risk of injury.

Over the eight weeks of training, the median number of sit-ups for female recruits increased from 30 to 51 (a 70% increase), whereas with male recruits it increased from 51 to 54 (only a 4% increase). The rapid improvement in sit-up ability in women, coupled with the much-higher rate of injury during basic training (50%, compared to 25% for men) suggests that female recruits are less physically fit than male recruits to begin with.

Thus, it seems that appropriate programs encouraging improved physical fitness in young men and especially young women have the potential to decrease the incidence of minor and moderate injuries. ❑

Adolescent Patients Pose Particular Problems;
Physical Fitness May Help Prevent Injuries
V. Cowart
Journal of the American Medical Association
V 259 # 23: 3380-3381, June 17, 1988

OVERUSE INJURIES

The bad news is that the upsurge of interest in fitness has caused a tremendous increase in sports-related injuries. The good news is that most of those injuries are caused by overuse, not accidents, and thus are potentially preventable.

A review of more than 1,000 patients seen at Lenox Hill Hospital sports medicine clinic in New York revealed fifty-four percent of the patients had soft tissue injuries, including a high incidence of overuse injuries—muscle strains, muscle spasms, and ligament strains. Forty-six percent had skeletal injuries, also with a high incidence of overuse injuries—chronic joint inflammation and stress fractures.

Running and jogging accounted for the largest group of injuries (one-third), followed by basketball, tennis, and dancing. Most common injury sites: knee, ankle, and shoulder.

Four factors were said to contribute most strongly to overuse syndromes:

Fatigue

Muscle becomes progressively more vulnerable to strain as fatigue sets in. Pulled hamstrings, for example, usually occur at the end of a training session when fatigue is high.

Biomechanical Variability

Differences in ankles and feet—varying degrees of pronation or supination, for example—may be associated with excessive wear and tear on joints.

Likewise, excess body weight can greatly increase intraarticular (inside joint) pressure. Although it is not clear whether this accelerates joint damage, it definitely contributes to joint pain.

Improper Training

Overuse injuries from improper training are usually the result of continuing to exercise without allowing sufficient recovery from injury, or exerting beyond accustomed levels. A typical example of the latter is the athlete who normally runs two to four miles at a time, then goes out and runs seven to ten miles.

Improper Equipment

The greatest offender here is shoes. Old, ill-fitting, or simply the wrong kind of shoes may contribute to many soft tissue problems, such as Achilles tendinitis.

Preventive measures associated with these factors are clear:

Exercise bearing in mind the fact that as you tire, risk of injury increases. Stop exercising when you "run out of gas."

Fatigue

Be open to the idea that your body may not be built for some sports. If you develop persistent pain from a particular form of exercise that doesn't resolve with appropriate treatment, consider switching to another kind of exercise.

Biomechanical variability

Warm up and warm down. Work on flexibility. Decrease exercise duration or severity when necessary to alleviate exercise-associated pain and discomfort. Increase workout intensity slowly. Don't overdo it.

Improper training

Make sure your shoes and other equipment are of good quality, in good repair, proper-fitting, and appropriate for the activity.

Improper equipment

These measures are not difficult, and suggest that some common-sense procedures can help prevent many sports-related problems.

[Ed. note: *Fatigue not only increases vulnerability to muscle strain but also may increase risk of joint stress. Muscles around joints often act as "shock absorbers," lessening the load a given joint is subjected to and helping to prevent joint injury. It may be that fatigued muscle doesn't make as good a "shock absorber," increasing risk of joint injury.*]❑

Internal Medicine News
Most Sports-Related Problems Caused
by Overuse
V 20 #13: 53, July 1-14, 1987

EMOTIONAL RESPONSES TO INJURY

An estimated 3.33 million professional, amateur, and recreational athletes are injured every year. Although injured athletes often get excellent help for medical recovery from doctors, nurses, physical therapists, and other medical personnel, psychological recovery is often neglected.

What are the emotional responses to injury?

Researchers at the Mayo Clinic evaluated 72 athletes who sustained sports-related injuries for type, magnitude, and time course of emotional response. Subjects were given two questionnaires: the Emotional Responses of Athletes to Injury questionnaire and the Profile of Mood States. The athletes were divided into three groups, based on length of time they were sidelined with the injury.

Compared to normal college-age controls, the injured athletes had significantly higher levels of depression and anger, but lower levels of fatigue and confusion. The group sidelined for the longest period of time (who tended to have the most severe injuries) had the highest levels of tension, depression, and anger, and lowest levels of vigor.

Athletes' moods improved as they recovered from their injuries. However, the more severely injured the subject, the slower the mood recovery. For the most severely injured athletes, mood disturbances persisted at least one month after injury.

There are many potential reasons for these mood disturbances. Frustration at interrupted training, potentially missing long-pursued goals, uncertainty, alienation from teammates, and loss of position and status can all contribute to feelings of depression, anger, and loss of vigor. Coaches, trainers, and others caring for athletes need to be aware of these emotional responses.

While medical therapy is often necessary to ensure full physical rehabilitation of the injured athlete, at times counseling may also be necessary to ensure full psychological rehabilitation as well. ❏

The Emotional Responses of Athletes to Injury
A. Smith, M. Young, and S. Scott
Canadian Journal of Sports Sciences
V 13 # 3: 84p-85p, September 1988

LOW BACK PAIN IN RETIRED ATHLETES

Athletes sustain a variety of injuries, both major and minor, in the course of their careers. In heavyweight lifters, low back injuries are among the most common. Wrestlers often complain of low back pain. How do injuries sustained while competing affect the athlete after retirement?

To find out, researchers looked at the prevalence of residual injuries among top-ranked weightlifters and wrestlers 20 years after retirement.

Seventy-one percent of wrestlers and 46% of weightlifters stated that they had residual physical problems from 20 years before. The higher incidence in wrestlers was mostly attributable to the higher number of neck injuries.

Low back pain was more common in wrestlers (59%) than in weightlifters (23%) and aged-matched non-athletes (31%). Wrestlers also showed impaired back mobility.

X-rays of the back showed a much higher-than-average frequency of old fractures in wrestlers. Wrestlers are thought to suffer frequent vertebral fractures, many of which go undiagnosed and untreated. These fractures seem to predispose wrestlers to low back pain later in life.

X-rays in weightlifters revealed significant decreases in intervertebral disc space. This is thought to result from the very high loads weightlifters put on their spines.

Wrestlers and weightlifters seem to have a higher-than-average pain tolerance. Since both groups frequently experience back pain while competing, this study suggests that perhaps these athletes should take minor back pain more seriously. ❑

Low Back Pain Among Retired Wrestlers and Heavyweight Lifters
H. Granhed MD and B. Morelli MD
American Journal of Sports Medicine
V 16 # 5: 530-3, 1988

INJURIES IN AEROBIC DANCE

TYPES OF INJURIES IN AEROBIC DANCE

Strain	25%
Tendinitis	21%
Shin splints	18%
Sprain	11%
Ligament	10%
Stress fracture	9%
Bursitis	4%
Fracture	3%
Other	15%

SITES OF INJURIES

Head	0.2%
Neck	4.4%
Shoulder	5.5%
Arm	1.0%
Elbow	0.6%
Wrist	1.4%
Hand	0.6%
Upper Back	2.5%
Lower Back	12.9%
Abdomen	1.5%
Hip	2.9%
Thigh	2.4%
Knee	9.2%
Calf	6.4%
Shin	24.5%
Ankle	12.2%
Foot	5.5%
Other	6.3%

Aerobic dance is a popular form of exercise. Its popularity is especially surprising in light of the fact that aerobic dance didn't exist before 1969. Participants dance for a variety of reasons, primarily for benefits of cardiovascular fitness, muscle tone, weight loss, and stress reduction. However, along with the health benefits has come increased incidence of aerobic dance injuries.

Those wanting to decrease risk of injury from aerobics are often told to wear special aerobics shoes, and to dance on resiliant surfaces (plywood, for example, rather than less-resilient surfaces such as carpeted cement). This sounds like reasonable advice. However, in a recent study, participants who took this advice actually experienced *more* injuries than those who didn't.

Seven hundred twenty-six aerobic dancers (610 women, 116 men) were surveyed by questionnaire to determine prevalence, type, and severity of aerobic dance injuries. In addition, they recorded where and how they exercised over a one-week period.

Almost half (49%) reported having suffered at least one aerobics injury in the past. Most of these involved the shin (24.5%), lower back (12.9%), and ankle (12.2%). Almost a quarter of those hurt had injuries severe enough to require a visit to their doctor's office (see box).

Resiliant floor surfaces, such as plywood, have been assumed (but never shown) to result in fewer injuries than less-resilient surfaces. In this study, however, aerobic dancers who exercised on plywood floors had a significantly greater prevalence of injuries (59%) than did those who exercised on carpeted cement (47%).

Subjects wearing shoes specifically designed for aerobic dance experienced significantly more injuries (63%) than those wearing jogging shoes (45%), tennis shoes (40%), or dancing barefoot (23%).

These findings need to be interpreted with caution. Other factors—for example, types of routines and quality of instruction, or condition of the shoes—were not controlled for and may have confounded the results. However, these findings do imply that there is more to preventing aerobic dance injuries than simply wearing special aerobics shoes and dancing on resiliant floors.

Other findings:

Risk of injury was associated with number of workouts per week. Most subjects worked out at least every other day. Those subjects working out more than four times a week showed the highest prevalence of injuries (66%). Those doing aerobics exactly four times a week showed a lower prevalence (60%), and those exercising three or fewer times a week showed the lowest (43%).

Subjects under 40 experienced the most injuries, but sought the least medical care. Those over 40 experienced the most back injuries.

Some subjects always did back-to-back aerobics classes; some never did. Dancers in both these groups experienced significantly fewer injuries than dancers who sporadically did back-to-back aerobics classes. This is probably because those who sporadically do double-length workouts are predisposing themselves to overuse injuries, whereas those who consistently do double-length workouts are more accustomed to that degree of exertion.

Type of warm-up was related to frequency of injury. Subjects who warmed up with ballistic (bouncing) stretches experienced significantly more injuries than those who warmed up with static (stretch-and-hold) stretches.

This information leads to several training recommendations for minimizing injuries in aerobic dance:

- Don't assume that special aerobics shoes are the best shoes for aerobic dance.

- Don't assume that more-resiliant floors are always better.

- Exercise caution if working out more than three times a week. Injury rate goes up significantly in people doing aerobic dance more than three times a week.

- Don't sporadically do back-to-back aerobics classes. If you want to do two-hour sessions, do them consistently.

- Static stretches are superior to ballistic stretches in preventing aerobic dance injuries. ❑

Prevalence and Types of Injuries in Aerobic Dancers
L. Rothenberger MA, J. Chang MD, T. Cable MD
American Journal of Sports Medicine
V 16 # 4: 403-407, July/August 1988

SHIN SPLINTS

Shin splints are among the most common overuse injuries. Rather than being one specific entity, the term **shin splints** refers to a variety of processes that cause shin pain as the result of exertion. These include inflammation of tendons, muscle tissue, or the fibrous membrane covering bone (periosteum), or insufficient blood to muscle and nerves as a result of muscles swelling within their membrane sheaths (compartment syndrome).

Whatever the cause, shin splints follow from repetitive contact of feet against hard surfaces, occur in specific locations in the leg, and have certain predisposing factors. Appropriate measures can help prevent their occurrence.

Anatomy

Anatomically speaking, the *leg* is that part of your body below the knee and above the ankle (not to be confused with the *thigh*, that part of your body below the hip and above the knee). The muscles of the leg are involved primarily with motions of the ankle and toes. These muscles are grouped, both functionally and anatomically, into four **compartments**: the **anterior tibial compartment**, the **deep posterior compartment**, the **lateral compartment**, and the **superficial posterior compartment**. Each compartment is covered with a tough membrane sheath.

Anterior tibial compartment

Anterior means "toward the front," and *tibial* means "relating to the **tibia**," or shin bone. The anterior tibial compartment contains that group of muscles in the front of the leg just to the outside of the shin bone. These muscles (the *tibialis anterior*, the *extensor digitorum longus*, and the *extensor hallucis longus*) are primarily responsible for bending the foot up at the ankle, bending the toes up, and stabilizing the foot from side to side.

Superficial posterior compartment

Superficial means "on the surface," and *posterior* means "in back of." The superficial posterior compartment contains the two muscles on the surface in the back of the leg. These muscles, the *gastrocnemius* and the *soleus*, are commonly referred to as the **calf muscles**. The calf muscles are primarily responsible for bending the foot down at the ankle.

The deep posterior compartment is located just underneath the superficial posterior compartment (that is, just underneath the calf muscles), and contains the *tibialis posterior*, the *flexor digitorum longus*, and the *flexor hallucis longus*. These muscles are primarily responsible for bending the toes down, assisting in bending the foot down, and rolling the foot inward at the ankle **(ankle inversion)**.

Lateral means "to the side." The lateral compartment contains those muscles located on the outer edge of the leg, the *peroneus longus* and *peroneus brevis*. These muscles are responsible for rolling the foot outward at the ankle **(ankle eversion)**, and assisting in bending the foot down.

Shin splints most commonly involve the muscles of the anterior tibial or deep posterior compartments; some researchers believe the superficial posterior compartment (calf muscles) may contribute as well. As it turns out, the muscles of all three of these compartments are important during the "shock absorption and distribution" phase of running.

The foot performs some remarkable feats during running. During the brief time the foot is in contact with the ground, it must absorb and distribute the force of gravity and forward momentum of the entire body. To do this, the foot must act as a relatively rigid, stable structure at the moment of heel impact. This requires stabilization primarily from the muscles of the anterior tibial compartment.

The foot then becomes a more flexible structure as it flattens out to spread the shock over the entire foot. This "flattening out" requires a controlled bending down at the ankle. Since the tendency at this point is for the foot to flop down on the ground, the control for slowly bending the ankle down is provided by the muscles that bend the ankle *up*. (The muscles that bend the ankle up are the same muscles that slow the rate at which the ankle bends down). This requires a "lengthening" contraction, or **eccentric contraction**, of the muscles of the front of the leg.

In addition, flattening out of the foot involves a rolling of the ankle to a temporarily more flat-footed position **(ankle pronation)**.

Deep posterior compartment

Lateral compartment

Biomechanics

Once the foot has absorbed the shock, the ankle rolls to a less flat-footed position (**ankle supination**) and the foot becomes a more rigid structure once more, providing the stability necessary for a solid push-off.

Eccentric contractions, the kind the muscles of the front of the leg undergo in absorbing the shock of running, tend to cause more muscle damage and muscle soreness than regular concentric contractions. In addition, the muscles of the anterior tibial compartment and the deep posterior compartment are usually smaller and weaker than the powerful calf muscles. This muscle imbalance, combined with impaired flexibility of the calf muscles and repeated eccentric contractions, can lead to shin splints.

Pain is the primary symptom of shin splints. Location of the pain varies, depending on which muscles are involved. Usually pain is located along the lower inner side of the shin bone, or in the muscles of the anterior tibial compartment in the front of the leg just to the outside of the shin bone. X-rays are usually normal, but shin splints can show up on bone scans.

The primary treatments are rest and rehabilitation. Rest eliminates the source of the stress, and allows the tissues time to heal. The amount of rest necessary depends on the severity of the shin splints: mild cases need only a few days' rest, severe cases may require several weeks' rest.

Ice applied to the involved area for ten to fifteen minutes two or three times a day may help reduce pain and inflammation. Anti-inflammatory medications, such as *aspirin* or *ibuprofen (Advil)*, may help as well. Rehabilitative exercises can be very beneficial (see box on next page), but ought not be attempted until after the initial pain and inflammation have subsided. If started before that, they can actually worsen the injury.

Prevention

The best treatment, of course, is prevention. Some 60% to 80% of lower extremity overuse injuries, including shin splints, are attributable to training errors. Typical training errors include sudden increases in total mileage, workout intensity, or workout frequency.

Another predisposing factor for shin splints is **hyperpronation,** excessive flattening out of the foot during the "shock absorption and distribution" phase of running. This is

EXERCISES FOR SHIN SPLINT REHABILITATION

Shin splints are often caused by a muscle imbalance between the powerful calf muscles (the *gastrocnemius* and *soleus*), and the generally weaker (and smaller) muscles that run along the front of the leg.

Lack of flexibility on the part of the calf muscles may contribute as well.

The goal of rehabilitative exercise, therefore, is to strengthen the muscles that run along the front of the leg, and also to increase flexibility of **all** muscles involved.

Neither flexibility nor strengthening exercises should be painful. In fact, the athlete should be aware improper performance of exercises may worsen the injury.

Flexibility. You can increase the flexibility of the large calf muscles by performing the following exercise: Stand about two to three feet from a wall. Step forward with your right foot, keeping your left foot in place. Support yourself against the wall with your hands, keeping your right knee bent, left leg straight, and left heel flat against the floor. Lean in toward the wall, keeping your left leg straight, your body upright, and your left heel against the floor. Feel for the stretch in the back of your left calf. Hold for about 20 seconds, then repeat with your left foot forward.

Anterior Compartment Strength. Secure a small weight to the instep of the foot of the injured leg. Sit on the edge of a table or high stool, knees bent, injured leg hanging straight down. Slowly bend up at the ankle as far as you can. Hold for a second, then lower back down. Use an amount of weight that allows you to do two sets of twenty-five reps (repetitions) without sharp pain. Rest no more than thirty seconds in between the two sets.

You can perform this exercise two or three times per day. Gradually increase the amount of weight. Ice applied to the affected area after the exercise may help reduce inflammation.

Posterior Compartment Strength. Secure a weight to the instep of the foot of the injured leg. Lie on your side on a table or exercise bench, injured leg down, with your foot off the edge of the table or bench. Roll the foot in at the ankle so the toes are pointing toward the ceiling. Hold for a second, then lower the foot. Repeat for a total of twenty-five reps. Do two sets with a thirty second rest in between.

a biomechanical problem that is best addressed in consultation with a doctor. He or she may prescribe an orthotic device designed to reduce pronation.

Choice of shoe can play a major role in the prevention of shin splints. Shoes designed for specific activities—running or aerobic dance, for example—are generally the best choices. For example, a good running shoe can reduce the likelihood of shin splints from running by providing adequate support and cushioning for the heel and the mid-sole.

Bear in mind, however, that materials used in making even the best sports shoes have finite lifespans. As the materials age, elasticity—and thus shock-absorbing ability—is lost. Most running shoes are good for about five hundred miles. Worn-out shoes transfer more of the shock-absorbing responsibility to the muscles, tendons, and bones of the feet and legs, increasing the risk of shin splints.

The flexibility and strength exercises described in the *Exercises for Shin Splint Rehabilitation* box are worthwhile not only for recovery from but also prevention of shin splints. By increasing the flexibility of the calf muscles and increasing the strength of the muscles of the anterior tibial and deep posterior compartments, two of the predisposing factors for shin splints can be minimized. ❑

Shin Splints: Diagnosis, Management,
Prevention
Michael P. Moore, MD
Postgraduate Medicine
V 83 # 1: 199- 210, Jan 1988

COMPARTMENT SYNDROME IN CROSS-COUNTRY SKIING

Cross-country skiing has enjoyed a burgeoning popularity in the past decade. Along with the increased interest have come improvements in both equipment and technique.

One improvement in technique that has caught on internationally since 1984 is the **Siitonen** step. In this maneuver, the rear leg pushes off to the side, rather than straight back, resulting in a kind of "skating" movement. The Siitonen step is so much more efficient than the classical cross-country ski step that it has almost completely replaced the latter in most national and international competitions since 1985.

Although thousands have safely used the Siitonen step at high levels of competition, the *American Journal of Sports Medicine* reports one case of Sittonen-induced **recurrent compartment syndrome**.

All muscles of the body are wrapped in tough, inelastic membranes called **fascial sheaths**. In the arms and legs, these fascial sheaths form **compartments** inside which the muscles go about their normal contraction.

If a muscle is consistently exercised, it will hypertrophy (get bigger) inside the compartment. Since the fascial sheaths are inelastic, if the muscle gets *too* big there is not enough room for it inside the sheath. Then, when it gets exercised, there is no room for the extra blood the muscle needs during exercise. Result: not enough blood gets to the muscle inside the compartment, causing pain and loss of strength in that muscle. This is recurrent compartment syndrome.

Although rare, compartment syndrome has been reported in runners, powerlifters, and bodybuilders.

The skier reported on in this study experienced recurrent compartment syndrome in the front part of his thigh when using the Siitonen step, but not when using the classical cross-country step. He was a member of the Swiss national cross-country ski team, but had to drop off the team once the more efficient Siitonen step was adopted by his competitors, as he could not keep up.

The treatment for recurrent compartment syndrome is surgical: by making an incision in the fascial sheath, pressure inside the compartment is lowered enough to make room for the extra blood the muscle needs during exercise.

This patient underwent the appropriate surgery with excellent results, subsequently using the Siitonen step successfully at high levels of competition. ❑

New Cross-Country Skiing Technique and
Compartment Syndrome
P. Gertsch MD et al.
American Journal of Sports Medicine
V 15 # 6: 612-3, Nov/Dec 1987

Sixty runners from two clubs in Sweden were evaluated for frequency, location, and severity of running injuries experienced during training and competing over the course of one year.

Thirty-nine (65%) of these runners experienced injuries. Almost half of those experiencing one injury experienced a second injury during the course of the year.

Frequency and location varied, depending on the type of running. Long-distance and marathon runners experienced fewer injuries per 1,000 hours of training, but tended to require a longer recovery period after an injury. In contrast, sprinters had over twice the number of injuries per 1,000 hours of training as did long-distance runners, but recovered more quickly. Long-distance runners tended to have more injuries of the feet; middle-distance runners tended to have more backache and hip problems; sprinters tended to have more tendonitis and injuries of the hamstrings.

There was no significant difference in injury rates between male and female athletes.

In examining the causes of these injuries, the authors conclude that potentially preventable causes contribute in 90% of cases. These include training errors, such as excessive distance or sudden changes in training routine, and other preventable causes, such as running on inappropriate surfaces or using poor shoes. Only 10% were the result of unpreventable anatomic factors, such as knee or foot misalignment, abnormal joint angles, or muscle stiffness.

Injuries in Runners
Jack Lysholm, et al.
American Journal of Sports Medicine
V 15 # 2 pp 168-171

INJURY VARIATION IN DIFFERENT TYPES OF RUNNERS

FOOT NERVE DAMAGE IN DISTANCE RUNNERS

Twenty-five long-distance runners underwent detailed neurologic testing to see if long-distance running damages nerves of the feet and legs. They were tested with a variety of standard neurologic measurements, including sensitivity to light touch, vibration, and temperature, and evaluation of motor nerve conduction.

All were healthy, and many had histories of minor running-related injuries. All used special running footwear.

When compared to controls, the long-distance runners had small but statistically significant decreases in vibratory sensation, and small but statistically significant changes in leg and foot nerve conduction characteristics.

These changes are thought to be the result of repeated minute injuries to the toes and feet, causing small, measurable differences in nerve function but not out-and-out neuropathy (nerve disease). While noting that this nerve damage does take place, the authors conclude, "the trivial subclinical neuropathic deficits we noted are readily offset by the assumed health and recreational benefits of running."

[Ed. note: It is likely that the degree to which these changes occur is related to the distance and intensity of the running. More good reasons to wear high-quality footwear, care for injuries promptly and appropriately, and not to overdo it.] ❑

Assessment of Nerve Damage in the Feet of Long-Distance Runners
Mayo Clinic Proceedings
V 62: 568-572, July 1987

MEDICAL CONSEQUENCES OF TRIATHLONS

An estimated one million Americans will participate in triathlons this year. These races, involving swimming, bicycling, and running, can last anywhere from tens of minutes to tens of hours. The medical consequences of such prolonged, grueling exercise are quite different from the consequences of shorter, less varied exercise.

Medical records of all triathletes seeking event-related medical care were examined in association with three different lengths of triathlons: a United States Triathlon Series race (finish times, 2 to 4 hours), an Ironman Qualifier race (finish times, 4 to 8 hours), and four Hawaii Ironman World Championships (finish times, 9 to 17 hours).

For the shortest triathlon, less than 2% required medical attention. These problems were relatively mild: abrasions and bruises, leg cramps, nausea and vomiting, weakness.

For the 4-to-8-hour triathlon, about 10% required medical attention. Again, most of the complaints were mild, but there were a number of more serious problems including heat exhaustion and trauma. Five percent of those seen required intravenous fluids.

For the Ironman, 17% required medical attention; 45% of these were for dehydration. Thirty-seven percent of those seen required IV fluids; 5% of these required hospitalization.

After the 1984 Ironman, a year when the competition was held in temperatures reaching 107 degrees, 25% of athletes not seeking treatment and 62% of those seeking treatment were hyponatremic (had abnormally low serum sodium concentrations) from salt losses in sweat.

This study clearly indicates the increasing problems seen with increasing race length—a fourfold increase in race time results in a tenfold increase in number of athletes seeking medical attention. The problems of dehydration and hyponatremia can be minimized with prerace education for competitors, "hyperhydration" the day before the race, three to four pints of fluid per hour, electrolyte solution for races lasting more than four hours, and periodic "head douses" to cool off.

Following these simple guidelines will not only keep you out of the medical tent but will improve performance as well. ❑

Medical and Physiological Considerations in Triathlons
American Journal of Sports Medicine
V 15 # 2: 164-167, 1987

MARTIAL ARTS INJURIES

Martial arts is a general term for a group of sports and recreational activities involving fighting techniques. "Weapons" for martial arts can be either body parts—hands, elbows, feet—or hand-held devices, such as dull-bladed knives or rattan sticks. Different styles of martial arts, such as karate, kendo, tae kwon do, and kung fu, emphasize different fighting techniques.

There are an estimated one million participants in martial arts nationwide. Despite this popularity, until now little research has been done looking into the incidence and severity of martial arts injuries. Recently, the *American Journal of Sports Medicine* reported on the results of a 5-year study of martial arts injuries.

Data relating to these injuries were collected from 1980 to 1984 from a sampling of hospital emergency rooms across the country. Severity of injuries was rated on a scale from one (mild) to six (most severe).

The survey recorded almost 2,000 injuries, translating into a national estimate of 105,000 martial arts injuries requiring emergency room visits from 1980 to 1984. Most were minor, occurred during sparring, and involved the extremities. Almost half involved thigh, leg, or foot. Head and neck injuries were less common, but tended to be more severe. Slightly under 1% required hospitalization; there were no deaths.

Injuries were more common in unsupervised situations, and when protective gear was not used. Injuries involving hand-held weapons were remarkably infrequent, and none were severe.

In general, the martial arts are relatively safe, especially when performed with protective gear and under adequate supervision. Based on the low incidence of weapons-related injuries, practicing with hand-held weapons is probably safer than many people believe. Compared to other contact sports, risk of injury in martial arts is considerably lower (see box at left).

INCIDENCE OF INJURY IN VARIOUS SPORTS*

Basketball	188
Football	167
Aquatic Activities	46
Lacrosse	39.5
Wrestling	26
Sledding	24.6
Gymnastics	23
Dancing	18.8
Martial Arts	16.9

Figures are estimates of number of injuries resulting in hospital emergency room visits per 100,000 population per year.

TYPES OF MARTIAL ARTS INJURIES

Contusions/abrasions	35.6%
Lacerations	14.2%
Strains/sprains	27.7%
Fractures/dislocations	15.3%
Miscellaneous	7.2%

[Ed. note: This study dealt only with injuries severe enough to re-quire an emergency room visit. A significant number of injuries—30% to 60% by some estimates—receive no medical attention at all. Thus the true incidence of injury is likely to be somewhat higher than reported here.] ❑

Martial Arts Injuries: Results of a Five Year National Survey
R. Birrer MD MPH and S. Halbrook PhD
American Journal of Sports Medicine
V 16 # 4: 408-10, July-August 1988

TAE KWON DO INJURIES

Tae kwon do is a Korean fighting art, characterized by greater reliance on kicking (as opposed to punching) than many other martial arts. In tae kwon do competitions, points are awarded for the correct delivery of powerful blows to head, solar plexus, and flanks. Contestants may not deliver punches to the head, but are allowed to deliver direct kicks to the head.

Although contestants wear protective padding on the trunk and groin, no head protection (with the exception of an optional mouthguard) is worn.

In a recent tae kwon do competition (the 6th Tae kwon do World Championship, held in Denmark), more than 4% of the competitors were injured severely enough to require hospitalization. Sixty percent of these injuries were to the head and neck, including several fractures of facial bones; all of these fractures were the result of direct kicks to the face.

By comparison, in the 1978 European Knock-down Karate Championships, most of the injuries were to the trunk and limbs. No fractures were reported.

The more-serious injuries noted from the tae kwon do championships, as opposed to the karate championships, are probably attributable to the underlying differences in technique.

To reduce the frequency and severity of injuries in tae kwon do, the authors favor changing the rules to outlaw direct kicks to the face or, at least, requiring use of increased protective padding, mouthguards, and face shields. ❑

Injuries in taekwondo
J. E. Siana MD et al.
British Journal of Sports Medicine
V 20 # 4: 165-166, December 1986

Of football, women's gymnastics, and wrestling, which one do you think has the highest rate of injury at the NCAA level?

Most people would guess football. Surprisingly, wrestling has the highest rate of injury, according to a survey of injury rates in seven NCAA sports for the 1985-86 school year. Women's gymnastics was second, and football was third. An injury was defined as any athletically related condition that prevented participation in at least one game or practice.

In fact, wrestling has topped the injury list since these statistics started being tabulated in 1983. In 1985-86, the injury rate for wrestling was 10.84 injuries per 1,000 athletic exposures. (An athletic exposure is defined as one practice session or one game.) For women's gymnastics the rate was 9.38 injuries per exposure, and for football the rate was 6.81 injuries per exposure.

Fourth through seventh on the list of the seven sports the survey looked at were (in order) men's lacrosse, women's volleyball, baseball, and women's lacrosse.

Football *does* have the highest rate of injuries suffered during games, as opposed to injuries suffered in games and practices combined. ❑

NCAA Survey Shows Injury Trends
Marty Duda
The Physician and Sportsmedicine
V 15 # 2: 30, Feb 1987

NCAA INJURY SURVEY, 1987

RISK FACTORS FOR FOOTBALL INJURIES

A number of studies have investigated football injuries among children and adolescents, and the findings have been remarkably consistent. About 40% of all football injuries are from sprains and strains, 25% from contusions (bruises), 10% from fractures, and the remainder primarily from concussions and dislocations. These percentages are fairly constant throughout a variety of age ranges.

In addition, their distribution tends to be quite consistent: about 50% involve lower extremities, and 30% involve upper extremities.

The consistency of these observations from study to study, across differing age groups and differing study methods suggests that some similar risk factors may be operative.

What are these risk factors? This investigation identifies four: *type of shoe, condition of the playing field, type of practice sessions, injury-prone preseason practices.*

Type of Shoe

Knee, ankle, and foot injuries account for 25% of all football injuries, and 33% of all football-injury medical costs. Many of these injuries occur in non-contact circumstances, implicating the type of shoe as a risk factor.

Most football players wear one of two types of shoes: "football-style" shoes, which have long cleats, or "soccer-style" shoes, which have short cleats. Long-cleat football shoes are associated with a greatly increased incidence and severity of knee and ankle injuries when compared to soccer-style shoes. This is thought to be due to the fact that football-style shoes make the foot temporarily stationary in the turf, and therefore unyielding to any internally or externally applied forces.

Condition of the Playing Field

Investigators compared rates of knee and ankle injuries for athletes playing on resurfaced fields to rates of knee and ankle injuries for athletes playing on unresurfaced fields. Those playing on resurfaced fields suffered 22.3% fewer knee and ankle injuries; those playing on resurfaced fields *and* wearing soccer-style shoes suffered 46% fewer such injuries.

Type of Practice Sessions

Some activities during football practice place the player at significantly higher risk than other activities. In general, practice games are associated with the greatest risk of injury, followed by contact two-person drills, contact three-person drills, and scrimmage drills. Less injury-prone activities include non-contact drills and individual activities, such as calisthenics, agility drills, and individual skill drills.

Compared to individual activities, non-contact drills are four times more likely per player-hour to cause injury; contact drills are twenty-two times more likely to cause injury; and practice games are seventy-five times more likely to cause injury.

Preseason practice is over five times as likely to cause injury as inseason practice. This is at least in part attributable to two factors: individual players practicing risk-prone techniques not yet identified and stopped by coaches, and coaches employing different training activities when no games are imminent.

Given these four risk factors, several preventive measures follow:

- Players should wear short-cleat, soccer-style shoes.
- Schools should resurface fields regularly and strive to keep them as well-maintained as possible.
- It is estimated that these two changes alone, if uniformly adopted, would reduce the incidence of football knee and ankle injuries by well over 40%.

In addition:

- Coaches should emphasize individual exercises and non-contact drills over practice games and contact drills whenever possible.
- Coaches should be vigilant of individual players practicing high-risk techniques, especially during preseason.
- Efforts should be made to identify high-risk coaching techniques used during preseason practice that differ from coaching techniques used during inseason practice.

Among children and adolescents, 20% of sports injuries requiring emergency room visits are from football. These preventive measures can help reduce that number. ❑

High School Football Injuries: Identifying the Risk Factors
B. Halpern, MD et al., American Journal of Sports Medicine
V 15 # 4: 316-320, Jul/Aug 1987

Injury-prone Preseason Practices

PUSH-UP INDUCED NERVE DAMAGE

Push-ups have been a standby exercise for years. They're simple, they're a good upper body exercise, and they can be done almost anywhere. They can also cause nerve damage to the hand.

The *Journal of the American Medical Association* reports a case of a 38-year-old male who began a program of push-ups. After several weeks of doing push-ups on a hard floor, he developed pain at the base of his left hand, followed by progressive weakness and wasting of the muscles of that hand. He stopped doing the push-ups, but four weeks later the weakness still persisted. At the end of three months he was almost, but not completely, recovered.

His doctors concluded that he had put excessive pressure on his hands by doing push-ups on a hard floor. This pressure damaged his ulnar nerve (the nerve serving the little finger side of the hand), leading to pain, weakness, and muscle wasting. Other activities that put a lot of pressure on the hand, such as bicycle riding, grasping crutch handles, and striking jammed window frames, have also been shown to cause ulnar nerve damage.

If athletes are going to do push-ups over a prolonged period of time, they should avoid doing them on hard surfaces. If hand pain or weakness develops, the push-ups should be discontinued immediately. ❏

Push-Up Palmer Palsy
F. Walker MD & B. Troost MD
Journal of the American Medical Association
V 259 # 1: 45-6, Jan 1988

COLD THERAPY FOR SPRAINS

A long-held approach to the treatment of sprains has been ice for the first 24 to 48 hours, followed by heat three to four times a day.

However, recent research suggests that treatment only with cold (ice packs, cold packs, or cold-water immersion) is preferable to cold-followed-by-heat. Externally applied cold penetrates to deep tissues, such as ligaments, more effectively than does heat. Cold increases circulation in the deep tissues, thereby reducing muscle spasm, pain, and swelling. Heat, on the other hand, decreases circulation in the deep tissues, and may consequently increase swelling. ❑

Journal of the American Medical Association
V 257 # 22: 3132, June 12, 1987

ULTRASOUND THERAPY FOR TENDON INJURIES

Achilles tendon ruptures are relatively common, but can require prolonged recovery periods—usually 8 to 12 weeks of immobilization. During that time both muscle strength and limb range of motion greatly decline. The injury can be treated surgically or non-surgically, but surgical complications are frequent, and in either case full restoration of function cannot be assured.

A recent study in rats reveals that it might be possible to accelerate recovery from tendon injuries by using therapeutic ultrasound. Rats, who had partial Achilles tendon ruptures, received either ultrasound therapy to the tendon or no therapy over the course of three weeks.

Those receiving ultrasound therapy showed microscopic changes suggesting faster healing. They also tended to have greater tendon tensile strength than those who did not receive ultrasound therapy.

Why ultrasound therapy may accelerate healing is poorly understood. It may be that ultrasound changes cell membrane permeability in a way that promotes collagen synthesis, or it may be that it provides a "micro-massage" to damaged tissues that facilitates repair.

Regardless of the mechanism, ultrasound therapy appears to accelerate tendon repair in rats. Though some years down the road, this treatment may eventually prove useful for tendon injuries in humans, as well. ❑

A Pilot Study: The Therapeutic Effect of Ultrasound Following Partial Rupture of Achilles Tendons in Male Rats
S. Friefer PhD PT et al.
Journal of Orthopaedic and Sports Physical Therapy
V 10 # 2: 39-46, August 1988

DRUGS

Nowhere are the dangers of misinformation greater than in the area of drug use. Driven by the pressure to compete, a growing number of athletes experiment with performance-enhancing drugs—the risks of which far outweigh any possible benefits. This chapter reports on recent studies of athletic drug use and its effects, exploring the benefits and hazards of some common ergogenic substances.

ADVERSE CONSEQUENCES OF STEROID USE

Most studies of anabolic steroids have involved doses far below what bodybuilders and other athletes take. Also, bodybuilders and other athletes who use steroids tend to engage in "stacking"—they take several different kinds of anabolic steroids simultaneously. Even at lower doses and without stacking, very serious side effects have been reported. This study is one of the few to look at a large group of steroid users and follow them as they self-administered the drugs with their usual high doses and stacking.

Fifty-eight amateur male bodybuilders, average age 28, participated in this study. Forty-five were regular steroid users. Thirteen had never used steroids, and served as controls. The 45 regular users were followed over the course of a self-directed 8-week stacking regimen, using both oral and injectable steroids (readily available on the black market or from countries where steroids are legal). All athletes were evaluated for blood pressure, heart rate, cholesterol levels, and liver function. In addition, several subjects subsequently quit steroid use; they were evaluated again five months after quitting.

The steroid group had HDL levels 50% lower and LDL levels 57% higher than the non-steroid group. (HDL's, or high-density lipoproteins, are the "good" cholesterol, associated with lower levels of heart disease. Lower HDL levels, as seen in the steroid group, are associated with greater risk for heart disease. LDL's, or low-density lipoproteins, are the "bad" cholesterol. Higher levels, as seen in the steroid group, are associated with higher levels of heart disease.) Five months after quitting, HDL levels were almost back to normal, but LDL levels remained 20% higher than normal. ApoA-1/ApoB ratios, another strong indicator of risk of coronary artery disease, also showed adverse changes despite discontinued steroid use.

The steroid group also had significantly higher systolic blood pressures, which may further increase the risk of heart problems. Steroids have been shown to cause structural changes in heart muscle cells of animals, changes which are probably deleterious to the health of the animal.

Still more problems: the steroid users' liver enzymes were elevated, indicating inflammation and damage to liver cells. Enzymes remained significantly elevated five months after stopping steroid use.

These findings suggest that the adverse effects of steroids on blood cholesterol, blood pressure, and liver enzymes are only partly reversed even as much as five months after stopping steroid use. ❑

Deleterious Effects of Anabolic Steroids on Serum Lipids, Blood Pressure, and Liver Function in Amateur Bodybuilders
J. W. M. Lenders et al.
International Journal of Sports Medicine
V 9: 19-23, 1988

STEROID ADDICTION

The *New England Journal of Medicine* reports a case of a bodybuilder who developed an addiction to steroids. The unusual feature of this case was that his addiction bore an uncanny resemblance to addiction to opioids, even though he was not taking any opioids. (Opioids are synthetic morphine-related narcotics, such as heroin).

A 23-year-old bodybuilder had been using steroids for three years. His regimen for the preceding two months involved injecting 75 mg of *Dianabol (methandrostenolone)* and 150 mg *Primobolan (methenolone)* every other day, and taking 20 mg *Anavar (oxandrolone)* and 100 mg *Anadrol (oxymetholone)* by mouth every day. He complained of not being able to stop his steroids without experiencing opioid-like withdrawal symptoms, including depression and disabling fatigue. At times he felt uncontrollably violent, paranoid, and suicidal.

On physical examination he was found to have muscle hypertrophy, but was also found to have an enlarged liver, shrunken testicles, acne, abnormal sweating, and dilated pupils.

His physician, in an attempt to get him off the steroids, treated him with a medication *(clonidine)* often used to ease opioid withdrawal. Each day for six days the bodybuilder had decreased withdrawal symptoms, attaining normal blood pressure, normal heart rate, normal pupil size, and no abnormal sweating by the end of six days. On the seventh day of treatment, however, the bodybuilder decided he could no longer stand the depression, fatigue, and craving for steroids, and told his doctor he was going back on the steroids.

This indicates that steroids not only have negative physiological effects, but can be powerfully addicting, as well. ❑

Anabolic Steroid Dependence With
Opioid-Type Features
F. Tennent MD DrPH, D. L. Black PhD,
R. O. Vov MD
New England Journal of Medicine
V 319 # 9: 578, Sept 1 1988

STEROIDS AND TENDON DETERIORATION

Anabolic steroids have been associated with a number of adverse side effects, including an increased incidence of tendon and ligament damage. A recent study from the American Journal of Sports Medicine sheds light on why steroids may make these injuries more likely.

Tendons are made, in part, of fibrous strands of collagen called **collagen fibrils.** The fibrils don't run straight, but rather in a zig-zag pattern. This gives the tendon elasticity: the zig-zags open up when the tendon is stretched, and return to their original position when the tendon is relaxed. Once the zig-zags have opened up all the way, the tendon becomes much less elastic; any further stretching will stretch the fibrils to the breaking point, causing injury.

Researchers from the Comparative Orthopaedic Group at the University of Bristol (England) examined the effects of steroids and exercise on the zig-zag pattern in rats. They found:

Tendons of the steroid-treated rats were less stiff. Tendon strength is thought to be proportional to stiffness, so a less-stiff tendon means less strength and greater risk of injury.

Exercise usually increases tendon strength. However, when steroids were given to exercising rats, there was a *decrease* in tendon strength.

Tendons of the steroid-treated rats were more elongated at a given stress, suggesting that they would reach their breaking point earlier, with lower stresses.

Tendons of the steroid-treated rats showed a tighter zig-zag pattern than tendons in the rats not given steroids. Tighter zig-zagging consumes more energy on a stretch than normal zig-zagging, and is thus less efficient.

Steroids seem to impair the tendon repair mechanisms.

These changes in tendon stiffness, strength, and zig-zagging lead not only to increased risk of injury, but also a change in tendon biomechanics. This can impair performance.

Injuries to tendons and ligaments can take a long time to heal. Exercise increases tendon mass, stiffness, and load capabilities, decreasing risk of tendon injury. Steroids seem to have the opposite effect. ❏

The Effect of Exercise and Anabolic Steroids on the Mechanical Properties and Crimp Morphology of the Rat Tendon
T. O. Wood et al.
American Journal of Sports Medicine
V 16 # 2: 153-158, Mar-Apr 1988

DRUG TESTING AND COMPETITIVE WEIGHTLIFTING RECORDS

Performance standards for most sports increase over time. Winning figure skating routines now require triple and quadruple spins, whereas twenty years ago double and triple spins were sufficient to win. Winning times for the mile and the marathon drop, jumping heights for pole vault and high jump increase, throwing distances for javelin and shot put increase, and on and on. Most of these improvements are attributable to athletes' having started younger, trained harder and longer, and having access to improved coaching.

For weightlifting, though, it is possible that some of the improvements in performance in recent years are attributable to steroid use, rather than to athletes' having started younger, trained harder and longer, or having had improved coaching.

Steroids are the most commonly taken banned drug used by weightlifters, but the introduction of urine testing for steroid use is thought to have discouraged their use. One might expect to see a falling-off in the rate of improvement of weightlifting performance since drug testing was introduced in 1984. Has there been?

Results of the eighty top performers (eight in each of ten weight categories) in the 1978, 1981, and 1984 Junior World Weightlifting Championships were compared. From 1978 to 1981, performances improved in nine of ten weight divisions for the snatch, in nine of ten weight divisions for the clean and jerk, and in all ten weight divisions overall. From 1981 to 1984, there was no significant improvement in *any* weight division. In fact, performances were *worse* in four weight divisions for the snatch, in four weight divisions for the clean and jerk, and in five weight divisions overall.

A similar trend was seen in top performers in the Senior World Championships for 1979, 1982, and 1985. Furthermore, from 1984 to 1985, world records fell abruptly for both the Junior and Senior men.

There is no evidence for any changes in coaching or diet that may account for these findings. Nor are these changes attributable to differences in countries that participated, since the same countries participated. There may be some other, as-yet-unidentified factors responsible for these changes, but the only identified common factor operating for all these competitions is the introduction of drug testing.

This strongly suggests that a decrease in steroid use, as the result of drug testing, may have limited the improvements in weightlifting performance. ❑

Effect of Doping Control on
Weightlifting Performance
K. Virvidakis et al.
International Journal of Sports Medicine
V 8 # 6: 397-400, Dec 1987

STEROID USE AND STROKE RISK

Chalk up two more probable side effects from steroids: cardiomyopathy and stroke.

The Physician and Sportsmedicine reports a case of a 32-year old bodybuilder who had two strokes over a four-month period. An echocardiogram done at the time of the second stroke showed severely impaired functioning of the left ventricle of the heart, indicating disease of the heart muscle (**cardiomyopathy**).

The bodybuilder was in otherwise perfect health, with no risk factors for stroke or cardiomyopathy (he was young, didn't smoke or drink, and had no family history of either disease).

However, he had used oral and injectable steroids off and on for 16 years, and had competed in two bodybuilding contests in the previous year. He admitted to having used about 15 different kinds of steroids, in various combinations ("stacking") and in high doses. Oral steroids included *methandrostenolone* (trade name *Dianabol*), *oxandrolone* (*Anavar*), and *stanozolol* (*Winstrol*). Injectable steroids included *nandrolone decanoate* (*Deca-Durabolin*), and nandrolone phenpropionate (*Durabolin*). In addition, he admitted to using *human chorionic gonadotropin (HCG)* and *tamoxifen*, an anti-estrogen compound used by steroid-taking bodybuilders to decrease the estrogen effects of steroids.

He stopped taking steroids after his first stroke, but continued to lift weights. His second stroke occurred while he was lifting weights.

He was treated and underwent comprehensive rehabilitation. Six months after finishing therapy his heart size had returned to normal, but he still had spastic left-sided weakness from the second stroke.

Most of the side effects of steroids affect the liver (liver disease, liver tumor, jaundice) and reproductive systems (shrunken testes, enlarged clitoris, enlarged prostate, reversible sterility, impotence, sexual problems). However, there is mounting evidence for adverse effects on the cardiovascular system as well. Increased LDL's (the "bad" cholesterol), decreased HDL's (the "good" cholesterol), heart attacks, and atherosclerosis have all been associated with steroid use.

Other studies have shown associations between androgen use and abnormal clot formation. Most strokes are due to **atherosclerotic thrombosis**, that is, clot formation at the site of atherosclerosis in an artery supplying the brain. Since steroids appear to increase risk of both atherosclerosis and clot formation, it is not surprising that a long-time steroid user might experience a stroke.

This doesn't prove that this bodybuilder's strokes and cardiomyopathy were caused by steroid use, but in an otherwise healthy 32-year-old with no risk factors, the steroids become strongly suspect. ❑

Case Report: Cardiomyopathy and Cerebrovascular Accident Associated with Anabolic-Androgenic Steroid Use
R. Mochizuki MD and K. Richter DO
The Physician and Sports Medicine
V 16 # 11: 109-114, November 1988

STEROID USE IN HIGH SCHOOL

A 1975 study of high schools in Arizona estimated that 0.7% of all students, and 4% of athletes, had used anabolic steroids. Since then, steroid use has steadily risen, and is thought by many in the media, in sports medicine, and in athletics to have reached epidemic proportions.

How widespread is steroid use in high school today?

To answer that question, researchers surveyed male high school seniors from 46 schools across the United States. The questionnaire was answered by 3403 students. Results were evaluated to determine overall steroid use and characteristics of users and non-users.

6.6%—one in fifteen—of all male high school seniors stated they use or have used anabolic steroids. Over one-third of users started before they were 16 years old, and two-thirds started before age 17.

Users were more likely to be involved in sports, especially football and wrestling. They tended to be older than non-users, and were more likely to be minority students. Non-users were more likely to have had a parent finish high school.

Almost half said they were taking the steroids "to improve athletic performance." Over one-quarter took them for "appearance." And even though it is not accepted medical practice in the U.S., ten percent took them for injury prevention or treatment.

Sixty percent claimed to have gotten their steroids on the black market, 20% from a health professional (physician, pharmacist, veterinarian), and 10% from mail order.

The most disturbing finding from this study is the large number of steroid users who started before age 16. One of the permanent effects of steroids is premature sealing of the growing plate of the bones, resulting in permanent shortness. Students under 16 are still growing, and if they take steroids they may never reach their full height. Steroids also have effects on the pituitary gland, effects with potentially severe consequences in growing bodies.

The figure of 6.6% of male high school seniors translates into as many as a half-million adolescent users nationwide. This suggests a definite place for educational intervention in the schools. Since over one-third of users were not in school sports, and one-third started before age 16, education needs to address non-athletes as well as athletes, and junior high as well as high school students.

Educational programs need to be done carefully, however. In one study, students were given a lecture about the dangers of steroids. A survey of attitudes about steroids was taken before and after the lecture. After the lecture, students indicated an *increased* willingness to take steroids, compared to their attitudes before the lecture. This is probably because students often feel immune from health problems, and the lecture made them more aware of how steroids are used by athletes and others.

[Ed. note: Education, whether from the student's coach, classroom teacher, physical education teacher, or physician, has the best chance of decreasing steroid use and preventing its myriad health problems. With estimated school-age use up almost tenfold since 1975, the time for intervention is now.] ❑

Estimated Prevalence of Anabolic Steroid Use Among Male High School Seniors
W. Buckley PhD et al.
Journal of the American Medical Association
V 260 # 23: 3441-5, December 16 1988

COUNTERFEIT HCG

The Commissioner of the Food and Drug Administration recently warned that a contaminated counterfeit hormone is being sold on the black market to bodybuilders, weightlifters, and other athletes.

The contaminated product is a black market version of the hormone **human chorionic gonadotropin**, or **HCG**. HCG is made from human placenta, and is being sold to athletes to counter some of the side effects, such as enlarged breasts, that can occur in athletes taking anabolic steroids. The counterfeit product does not contain HCG, but rather some other, yet-to-be-identified substance. The counterfeit product is both non-sterile and pyrogenic, meaning it can cause infections and fever.

The FDA, in cooperation with the Department of Justice, seized a certain amount of the illegally produced drug, but an unknown amount may already be in underground circulation. The product is labelled:

Pregnyl Chorionic Gonadotropin for Injection
10,000 units/vial, 10ml Multiple Dose Co-Vial
Organon Labs, Cambridge, England

Organon Laboratories is a drug company with manufacturing facilities in the U.S. and in England. Although the counterfeit product bears the Organon label, it was not manufactured by Organon, and is available only through the black market. Athletes, coaches, and physicians treating athletes need to be on the lookout for this contaminated counterfeit drug. ❑

FDA Consumer
Feb 1988

GROWTH HORMONE IN ATHLETICS

In recent years there has been a marked increase in the use of drugs, especially steroids, among athletes. With the advent of sophisticated tests for detecting use of steroids, however, athletes have turned to other substances in their quest for the competitive edge. One of the substances that has been getting increasing attention is **growth hormone**.

Growth hormone, also called **somatotropin**, is a hormone produced by the **pituitary gland**, a pea-sized organ located at the base of the brain. Since growth hormone is naturally produced by the body, detecting supplementation is difficult. Growth hormone has a number of effects, including stimulation of muscle growth. It is its effect on muscle growth, as well as its lack of detectability, that has sparked so much interest from certain segments of the athletic community.

Where Growth Hormone Comes From

There are two ways of increasing growth hormone levels in the body: injecting growth hormone that has been produced outside the body, or increasing release of growth hormone produced inside the body.

Until recently, the only human growth hormone that was available for injection was from the pituitary glands of human cadavers. It was expensive and in very short supply. Its medical use was for children with pituitary failure and growth retardation, but some found its way into the hands of athletes. Use of cadaveric human growth hormone has since been discontinued amid fears of potential transmission of a virus that produces an Alzheimer's-like dementia.

New recombinant DNA technology has resulted in development of a synthetic injectable growth hormone. However, it is not an exact duplicate of human growth hormone. It is different enough that about 30% of the children who have taken it have developed antibodies to it. This may cause those who take it to develop antibodies not only to the synthetic growth hormone, but to their *own* growth hormone as well. Although not a problem for children with pituitary failure, who have no growth hormone of their own to start with, developing antibodies is a major concern to athletes taking synthetic growth hormone. These antibodies could well attack and destroy an athlete's own internal supply of growth hormone, making him dependent on growth hormone injections for the rest of his life.

An exact duplicate of human growth hormone may be available in the near future, one that ought not have the problems of antibody development. However, any injected substance, if injected using shared needles and non-sterile techniques, carries with it risks of AIDS, hepatitis, and other infections.

Some athletes take what is referred to as "gorilla juice," said to be growth hormone from primate sources. Some samples of this product are not primate growth hormone at all but rather an anabolic steroid.

Using injectable growth hormone is not the only way to increase blood levels of growth hormone. It is also possible to increase release of growth hormone produced inside the body.

Production and control of growth hormone release from the pituitary is a very complicated and poorly understood process. Blood levels of growth hormone vary considerably through the course of the day, and are affected by a number of factors including exercise, sleep, stress, alterations in blood sugar levels, drugs, and amino acids (see chart, next page).

The physiological significance of the changes in growth hormone caused by exercise, sleep, stress, and alterations in blood sugar levels are as yet unknown. Better known are the effects resulting from drugs and amino acids.

There are several drugs commonly taken to elevate blood growth hormone levels, including *propranolol (trade name Inderal), vasopressin (Pitressin), clonidine (Catapres),* and *levadopa (Larodopa).* However, the most commonly taken and readily available substances, easily purchased in the United States through health food stores and mail order outfits, are single amino acids.

The amino acids arginine, lysine, ornithine, and tryptophan, alone or in combination, are touted as growth hormone releasing substances in books, magazine articles, and advertisements. In fact, there does seem to be some truth to these claims. Studies have demonstrated that certain amino acids are effective growth hormone releasing agents, taken orally as simple amino acids or in protein-rich drinks, or taken intravenously.

In one study, blood growth hormone levels increased by seven times after ingestion of 1.2 grams of arginine and 1.2 grams of lysine; there was no response to either amino acid alone at that dose. In another study, arginine taken at the very high dose of 250mg/kg (20 grams for a 176 lb. person)

FACTORS AFFECTING
GROWTH HORMONE RELEASE

Many factors affect the release of growth hormone from the pituitary gland. The mechanisms by which these factors act are not well understood. Although there is some disagreement among studies, the effect of the following factors on growth hormone are generally accepted.

GROWTH HORMONE RELEASE IS INCREASED IN OR BY:

ADOLESCENTS

FEMALES
- women not only have higher levels of growth hormone than men but also release more growth hormone given the same stimulus as men

SLEEP
- HGH surge sixty to ninety minutes into sleep
- sleep surge increased in trained athletes with increased activity

PSYCHOLOGICAL STRESS

LOW BLOOD SUGAR

RAPID DROP IN BLOOD SUGAR

EXERCISE
- exercise-induced HGH release varies with type of exercise
  - *intermittant exercise produces higher levels than constant exercise*
  - *arm work produces higher levels than leg work*
- exercise-induced HGH release varies with intensity of exercise
  - *earlier spurt with higher-intensity exercise*
  - *release proportional to intensity of cycle ergometry*
- exercise-induced HGH release varies with physical characteristics
  - *less in older athletes*
  - *less in males*
  - *less in obese*
  - *less in more-fit*
- exercise-induced HGH release varies with environment
  - *more in hot weather*
  - *less in cold weather*
- exercise-induced HGH release is decreased with glucose ingestion

AMINO ACIDS
- arginine, lysine (see text)

DRUGS
- propranolol, vasopressin, clonidine, levadopa (see text)

resulted in an immediate increase in blood growth hormone levels.

Amino acids are not without side effects, especially when taken in high doses. Mounting concern about increased use of high doses of single amino acid supplements, in the face of little knowledge of their potential adverse effects, has prompted the Health Protection Branch of the Canadian Government to reclassify the single amino acids as new drugs, and to suspend their distribution until more is known about their adverse effects.

Does Growth Hormone Work?

Most of the claims supporting growth hormone supplementation are anecdotal. There is no published evidence showing improvements in performance from either externally or internally supplemented growth hormone. However, some of the anecdotal reports (mostly from weightlifters and bodybuilders) are quite striking, telling of thirty-to-forty-pound gains in lean body mass. Others report disappointing results. This may be due in part to instances of injectable anabolic steroids being passed off as growth hormone, in which the steroids may be responsible for the more-spectacular gains.

It is clear, however, that growth hormone does affect muscle growth, a change that does not appear to translate into improvements in performance. Although it may increase muscle size and definition, *growth hormone does not increase muscle strength*. It seems to increase the amount of connective tissue in muscle with no increase in actual muscle fibers. This results in muscles that are bigger-appearing, *but functionally weaker*.

Continued growth hormone excess produces a disease called **acromegaly**, characterized by muscles that appear well-developed but are actually quite weak and easily fatigable; thickening of certain bones leading to deformities of the face, skull, hands, and feet; diabetes, high blood pressure, heart disease, and nerve disease. Most of these changes are irreversible, and half of all people with acromegaly die by age fifty. Some athletes using growth hormone have shown early signs of acromegaly.

Despite these serious documented side effects, and the lack of evidence of any improvements in performance, abuse of growth hormone in the athletic community appears to be on the rise. Attempts to curtail athletic abuse of anabolic steroids, another class of substances with serious documented side effects, have met with decidedly mixed results. Attempts to curtail athletic abuse of growth hormone is likely to meet with similarly limited success, for now and probably well into the future, as some athletes continue their quest for the competitive edge no matter what the cost.

Growth Hormone and Athletes
J. G. Macintyre
Sports Medicine
V 4 # 2: 129-142, Mar/Apr 1987

NEGATIVE EFFECTS OF COCAINE USE ON ATHLETIC PERFORMANCE

Cocaine is a popular drug of abuse, and some well-publicized cocaine-related deaths (most notably basketball star Len Bias) have focused attention on cocaine use in athletes. However, cocaine use by some athletes goes beyond recreational purposes; some athletes take cocaine specifically to improve performance.

Cocaine decreases fatigue, and provides a sense of euphoria and well-being. Some feel these properties give cocaine the potential to enhance athletic ability, especially endurance ability. However, whether cocaine does in fact improve athletic performance has not been well-documented.

In an attempt to shed some light on the subject, researchers from the Exercise Biochemistry Laboratory in Provo, Utah tested the effects of cocaine injection on endurance in rats.

Rats were injected with either a cocaine solution or with saline, rested for twenty minutes (to allow the cocaine to circulate through the bloodstream and take effect), and then run uphill at a constant rate on a treadmill to exhaustion. Run times were recorded, and tissue samples were taken to measure muscle glycogen levels. (Glycogen is a form of carbohydrate fuel stored in the muscles and liver. Endurance is related to how long muscle glycogen stores last.)

The saline-treated rats ran an average of two-and-a-half times longer than the cocaine-treated rats (an hour and fifteen minutes for the saline-treated rats, compared to twenty-nine minutes for the cocaine-treated rats). However, at exhaustion, glycogen content of the vastus lateralis (one of the quadriceps muscles) was the *same* in both groups. Since the saline-treated rats ran for a much longer period of time, this suggests that the cocaine-treated rats were depleting their glycogen stores at a much faster rate. By the calculations of the authors, the cocaine-treated rats were depleting their glycogen stores *four times faster* than the saline-treated rats. Once glycogen stores are depleted, extreme fatigue sets in.

Although cocaine had no effect on blood lactic acid levels at rest, during exercise blood lactic acid levels were almost two-and-a-half times greater in the cocaine-treated rats. This suggests that the cocaine-treated rats were not using their internal fuel supplies efficiently. The cocaine-treated rats were burning their internal fuel supplies much faster using inefficient anaerobic energy production, rather than the much more efficient aerobic energy production.

Curiously, twenty minutes after cocaine administration, the soleus muscle (one of the calf muscles) showed a 30% decrease in glycogen content *before exercise even began*. This decrease was not seen in the vastus lateralis muscle. It may be that cocaine preferentially depletes glycogen stores in certain muscles, giving the athlete a disadvantage from the start.

This experiment demonstrates that, in contrast to what some athletes may believe, cocaine significantly *reduces* endurance (at least in rats). This fact, coupled with the fact that cocaine does not increase strength, does not increase coordination, and has significant side effects, makes cocaine a poor choice for athletes who want to improve performance. ❑

Effect of Cocaine on Exercise Endurance and
Glycogen Use in Rats
M. Bracken et al.
Journal of Applied Physiology
V 64 # 2: 884-7, Feb 1988

DELAYING MUSCLE SORENESS WITH ANTI-INFLAMMATORY DRUGS

Most athletes are familiar with delayed muscle soreness, the vague muscular discomfort that peaks about 24-48 hours after exercise. It has been associated with increases in serum activity of the enzymes creatine kinase (CK), lactate dehydrogenase (LDH), and aspartate aminotransferase (AST), all pointing to muscle fiber damage. This damage provokes an inflammatory response, which in turn is thought to be responsible for the soreness.

If delayed muscle soreness is indeed the result of an inflammatory response, can it be prevented or treated with anti-inflammatory medications?

In this study, researchers from the Dept. of Environmental and Occupational Medicine at the University Medical School in Aberdeen looked at the effects of the non-steroidal anti-inflammatory drug *diclofenac* (trade name *Voltaren*) on muscle soreness and muscle fiber enzyme release.

Twenty men were run downhill on a treadmill for 45 minutes to induce muscle soreness. (Running downhill requires use of the quadriceps and other muscles to slow down and control body motion. The muscles are thus forced into a series of "slowing-down" movements, or **eccentric contractions**. Eccentric contractions produce significantly more muscle soreness than concentric contractions.)

The subjects received either *diclofenac* or placebo before and 72 hours after the run. The experiment was repeated ten days later, with subjects receiving whichever drug (placebo or diclofenac) they didn't get the first time. Participants were evaluated for delayed muscle soreness and serum enzyme levels.

The *diclofenac*-treated subjects showed no higher enzyme levels than did the placebo-treated subjects, indicating that the diclofenac did not protect against muscle fiber damage.

Diclofenac did reduce muscle soreness in some individuals, but the result was not consistent. Thus it appears that diclofenac does not have a significant effect on muscle fiber damage, but may reduce inflammation and delayed-onset muscle soreness in some athletes.

Besides the primary conclusion, the researchers observed an interesting secondary phenomenon in this experiment. Subjects showed significantly higher enzyme levels on the first run compared to the second, regardless of whether they took the anti-inflammatory drug or placebo. In other words, even though they did two runs of equal intensity, they showed much greater muscle fiber damage on the first run than on the second.

This has been observed before, and is poorly understood. Somehow, a single episode of 45 minutes of downhill running produces a "protective effect," reducing muscle fiber damage and muscle enzyme release from subsequent exercise bouts for at least ten days. Other studies have shown the protective effect to last as long as ten weeks.

Diclofenac is just one of many non-steroidal anti-inflammatory drugs available. Others, such as i*ndomethacin* (trade name *Indocin*), have shown promise in reducing exercise-induced muscle inflammation in mice. Another *(aspirin)* has been shown to reduce soreness in humans. However, a drug that consistently reduces both muscle fiber damage and delayed-onset muscle soreness has yet to be found.

[Ed. note: Diclofenac, the most widely prescribed arthritis drug in the world, is just now being released for the U.S. market. One of the patients who has received diclofenac experimentally with good result is Mickey Mantle, who was treated for osteoarthritis.] ❑

Effects of a Non-Steroidal Anti-Inflammatory Drug on Delayed Onset Muscle Soreness and Indices of Damage
British Journal of Sports Medicine
V 22 # 1: 35-38, March 1988

ANTI-INFLAMMATORY DRUGS AND SPRAINED ANKLES

There are two classes of anti-inflammatory medications: steroidal and **non-steroidal**.

Non-steroidal anti-inflammatory drugs (NSAID's), of which aspirin is the best-known example, are commonly used for reducing the pain and recovery time of musculoskeletal injuries.

This study examined the effectiveness of one NSAID, *ibuprofen* (also called *Motrin, Advil, Nuprin,* and *Trendar*) on the pain and recovery time of patients with sprained ankles.

Those taking ibuprofen reported less subjective pain, exhibited less objective pain to palpation (touch) and passive movement, less swelling, less functional impairment, and faster recovery times than did those taking placebo. While these data show a definite trend, none of these differences achieved statistical significance.

The authors speculate that the reason statistical significance was not achieved is that non-steroidal anti-inflammatory drugs may not have much benefit after the first few hours following an injury. Once an appropriate treatment program is begun (taping, ice, rest), the further benefit gained from NSAID's may be slight.

The patients with more-severely injured ankles seemed to benefit more from NSAID's than did those with less-severely injured ankles. This suggests that NSAID's may be indicated in more-severe injuries; however, this remains to be more conclusively demonstrated. ❏

The Efficacy of Anti-Inflammatory Medication in the Treatment of the Acutely Sprained Ankle
American Journal of Sports Medicine
V 15 # 1: 41-45, 1987

POSSIBLE MUSCLE INJURY PREVENTION WITH INDOMETHACIN

While we're on the topic of non-steroidal anti-inflammatory drugs, there has recently been some interesting research on *indomethacin* (trade name *Indocin*), a commonly-prescribed NSAID for acute bursitis and tendinitis.

NSAID's, such as *indomethacin*, block the production of **prostaglandins**, a family of chemicals which produce a whole host of localized responses. *[For example, the familiar bodybuilder's "pump" is at least partially caused by release of prostaglandins— Ed.]* Prostaglandins may also play a role in muscle soreness and stiffness after exercise, and swelling after injury.

Since prostaglandins play a role in injury, it was reasoned that perhaps extent of injury could be modified by drugs that affect prostaglandins. Mice were vigorously exercised, then examined for evidence of exercise-induced muscle damage. Those given *indomethacin* before, during, and after exercising showed a considerable reduction in the severity and extent of muscle injury when compared with controls. Those given *indomethacin* before and during but not after showed only a slight reduction in injuries.

These data suggest that reduction of prostaglandin synthesis through use of NSAID's can reduce the extent and severity of exercise-induced muscle injuries, especially when administered immediately after exercise (at least in mice). Since there is much inter-species variation in prostaglandin response, it is unclear what the implications of these findings are for human athletes, but it does suggest some directions for future research.

Protective Effect of Indomethacin Against Exercise-Induced Injuries in Mouse Skeletal Muscle Fibers
International Journal of Sports Medicine
V 8 # 1:46-49, 1987

PERFORMANCE ENHANCEMENT QUALITIES OF ANTI-ASTHMATIC DRUGS

At the 1972 Olympics in Munich, asthmatic swimmer Rick De Mont won a gold medal in the 400 meter free-style. Before the event, he took the anti-asthma medication *ephedrine sulfate*, as prescribed by his doctor. Unfortunately, neither he nor his doctor was aware that ephedrine was on the Olympic list of banned drugs. *Ephedrine* was banned because it was thought not only to reverse asthmatic attacks but also artificially to enhance performance. Sixteen-year-old Rick De Mont had his gold medal taken away.

Ephedrine sulfate is still banned. One of the allowable anti-asthma drugs is *albuterol* (trade names *Ventolin* and *Proventil*). Albuterol is thought to prevent and reverse asthma attacks while having no effect on performance. However, a recent study published in the *Canadian Journal of Sports Sciences* suggests that *albuterol* may indeed enhance performance. Furthermore, it seems to enhance performance artificially in *non*-asthmatics who use it.

Exercise-induced asthma is common, even at top levels of competition. At the 1984 Summer Olympics in Los Angeles, 67 out of 597 athletes (11%) reported having exercise-induced asthma. Asthmatics have won Olympic medals at every Olympics for the past 28 years (mostly in swimming).

When these athletes exercise, the smooth muscle in their bronchial walls goes into spasm. The spasming muscles restrict airway diameter, preventing adequate air from entering the lungs and impairing performance. *Albuterol* relaxes the bronchial smooth muscle, preventing the spasm and thus preventing exercise-induced asthma attacks.

Fifteen experienced cyclists participated in a placebo-controlled double-blind cross-over study examining the effects of *albuterol* on performance. None were asthmatic. They inhaled either an aerosol placebo or a 180 microgram dose of *albuterol* 30 minutes before the start of a simulated race. All subjects pedalled for one hour on stationary bicycles at 70-75% of their maximum work output, then did a final sprint to exhaustion. Metabolic measurements were made at several points during the cycling, and pulmonary function tests were determined before and after the race.

Subjects given *albuterol* showed small but significant increases in airway diameter, as reflected in pulmonary function tests. They also lasted significantly longer on the final sprint to exhaustion than did the placebo group, and were able to achieve higher levels of fatigue, indicating improved performance with *albuterol*.

This all suggests that non-asthmatics may artificially improve their performance by inhaling *albuterol*.

[Ed. note: If albuterol and other beta-adrenergic bronchodilators do indeed enhance performance, as this study suggests, their status as allowable drugs for competition needs to be re-evaluated. Unfortunately, a ban on all such bronchodilators may eliminate asthmatics from competition altogether. These findings need to be evaluated further, under conditions closer to actual competition, to see if these drugs do in fact need to be banned.] ❏

Enhancement of Exercise Performance with Inhaled Albuterol
J. F. Bedi et al.
Canadian Journal of Sports Sciences
V 13 # 2: 144-148, March-April 1988

PERFORMANCE AND TOBACCO CHEWING

Smokeless tobacco is popular among some athletes, especially baseball players. Forty percent of male college baseball players use smokeless tobacco regularly; only 3% smoke.

Many use smokeless tobacco in the mistaken impression that smokeless tobacco is a safe alternative to cigarettes. It isn't; it has been shown to cause cancer of the mouth and receding gums, and can lead to nicotine dependence. Babe Ruth, a heavy snuff "dipper," tobacco chewer, and cigar smoker, died of oropharyngeal cancer (cancer of the back of the mouth) at age 52.

Nor does it improve performance. A group of smokeless tobacco users were evaluated for muscular and cardiovascular endurance. The longer they had used "dip" or "chaw," the worse their performance.

In another study, professional baseball players were asked why they used smokeless tobacco. Almost four out of five said "for something to do." Other common responses were "it's a habit" (60%); "it helps me relax" (52%); "can't stop" or "am hooked" (28%); "it's a ritual" (23%); and "it's part of the game" (19%). Only 11% said it helped them concentrate, and no players claimed that smokeless tobacco sharpened their reflexes or improved their game. Indeed, a recent study showed that smokeless tobacco does not improve reaction time, movement time, or total response time in athletes.

The combination of health hazards, addictive potential, and detrimental effects on performance make smokeless tobacco a bad habit for young (or old) athletes to get into.

Performance of Habitual Smokeless Tobacco Users on the
U.S. Army Physical Fitness Test
M. Bahrke, T. Baur, and D. Poland
Journal of Applied Sports Science Research
V 2 # 3: 53, August- September 1988

Use of Smokeless Tobacco in Major-League Baseball
G. Connolly DMD MPH et al.
New England Journal of Medicine
V 318 # 19: 1281-5, May 12 1988

NUTRITION

Good nutrition is fundamental to peak athletic performance, though just what constitutes "good nutrition" has always been an area of controversy. Nevertheless, certain aspects are becoming better understood. In particular, a number of recent studies have enlarged our understanding of the importance of carbohydrate, and shed new light on the effects of physical activity on vitamin and mineral requirements.

THE NUTRITIONAL DEMANDS OF ATHLETIC TRAINING

From time to time a paper appears whose information is so applicable and whose points are so clearly made that it justifies reprinting in full. This article, from the Journal of the American Dietetic Association, is such a paper. Reprinted with permission from the July, 1987 issue....

A proper, well-balanced diet is an essential component of any fitness or sports program. As more persons assume responsibility for their own health and fitness and engage in a variety of sports and exercise programs, it is essential that they have access to appropriate and accurate nutrition information. Those involved in more intense athletic activity require more specific information and education. This article addresses the needs of both groups and makes specific recommendations on how best to achieve their unique nutrition and fitness goals.

It is the position of The American Dietetic Association to support the need for accurate and appropriate nutrition education to promote optimum fitness and well-being. The American Dietetic Association also recognizes the need for more specific nutrition recommendations for those individuals involved in more intense athletic activity.

Taking personal responsibility for one's health is a major force behind the fitness movement. Participants in exercise programs range from school-age children to adults of all ages, from elite competitors to weekend golfers. Although all these persons consider themselves athletes, their interests, skills, and training needs are varied. Messages from the marketplace on how best to achieve each of their unique nutrition and fitness goals can confuse the consumer.

There are several factors to consider when discussing appropriate nutrition for the athlete. Specific athletic events require different body composition for maximal performance. Body composition can be estimated indirectly by several methods, including anthropometric measurements, hydrostatic weighing, multiple isotope dilution, and electrical impedance units.

Energy demands are based on individual basal metabolic rate plus the intensity, duration, frequency, and type of activity involved. For weight reduction, a calorically prudent diet combined with appropriate exercise will increase the body's muscle mass while reducing body fat stores. Individuals engaged in vigorous exercise training programs may have energy needs ranging from 3,000 to 6,000 kcal [kilocalories] per day or more. Weight management, whether weight loss, gain, or maintenance, may be difficult to achieve without a well-planned dietary program.

Complex carbohydrates should account for at least 50% to 55% of total calories for the athlete. Carbohydrate loading will be beneficial only to athletes participating in long duration endurance or multiple-event competitions. It is now recommended that athletes follow a high-carbohydrate diet throughout training and begin a tapered rest approximately 7 days prior to the event, with complete rest the day before the event.

The current Recommended Dietary Allowance (RDA) of 0.8 gm protein per kilogram per day may be inadequate for endurance athletes. An intake of 1 gm/kg/day is advised, which is more than adequately met by the typical American

Position

DIETARY RECOMMENDATIONS FOR ADULT ATHLETES

CARBOHYDRATES

Current Average:	*45% of all calories*
Recommended Intake for Non-Athletes:	*50-60% of all calories (40-50% from complex carbs)*
Recommended Intake for Athletes:	*60-65% of all calories (50-55% from complex carbs)*
Recommended Intake for Endurance Athletes:	*65-70% of all calories (60-65% from complex carbs)*

PROTEIN

Current Average:	*1.5 grams/kilogram body weight per day*
Recommended Intake for Non-Athletes:	*0.8 gm/kg/day*
Recommended Intake for Athletes:	*1.0 gm/kg/day (12-15% of all calories)*
Recommended Intake for Endurance Athletes:	*1.0 gm/kg/day (12-15% of all calories)*

VITAMINS

VITAMINS	USRDA	RECOMMENDATION FOR ATHLETES
Vitamin A, IU*:	*5000*	*same*
Vitamin B_1 (thiamine), mg**:	*1.5*	*same*
Vitamin B_2 (riboflavin), mg:	*1.7*	*about 3.1*
Vitamin B_3 (niacin), mg:	*20*	*same*
Vitamin B_6 (pyridoxine), mg:	*2.0*	*same*
Vitamin B_{12} (cyanocobalamine), µg***:	*6.0*	*same*
Folic acid, mg:	*0.4*	*same*
Biotin, mg:	*0.3*	*same*
Pantothenic acid, mg:	*10*	*same*
Vitamin C (ascorbic acid), mg:	*60*	*same*
Vitamin D, IU:	*400*	*same*
Vitamin E, IU:	*30*	*same*

MINERALS

MINERALS	USRDA	RECOMMENDATION FOR ATHLETES
Calcium, mg:	*1000*	*if amenorrheic, may need 1500*
Chromium, µg:	*50-200*	*same*
Copper, mg:	*2*	*same*
Magnesium, mg:	*400*	*same*
Iron, mg:	*18*	*same*
Zinc, mg:	*15*	*same*
Selenium, µg:	*50-200*	*same*

* International Units   **milligrams   ***micrograms

diet. Excessive protein consumption has not been demonstrated to enhance athletic performance.

Extended physical activity may increase the need for some vitamins and minerals, which can easily be met by consuming a balanced diet in accordance with the extra caloric requirement. Although a nutritional deficiency can impair physical performance and cause several other detrimental effects, there is no conclusive evidence of performance enhancement with intakes in excess of the RDA. Consuming the RDA's for iron and calcium requires special attention by female athletes. Amenorrheic athletes may require additional calcium for calcium balance to accommodate both their lower estrogen levels and the decreased intestinal calcium absorption related to their prolonged training. Athletes may be at extra risk for developing iron deficiency because of sweat and intestinal losses, hematuria [blood in the urine], increased demands for total body hemoglobin, and poor dietary intakes. However, iron deficiency should not be confused with sports anemia, a condition defined as the increased destruction of erythrocytes [red blood cells] and a transient drop in hemoglobin as a result of an acute stress response to exercise; generally no supplement is required.

Proper hydration is essential for athletic performance. Dehydration can cause a reduction in maximal oxygen consumption and can compromise heat dissipation, which increases body temperature and results in a loss of coordination. Vigorous exercise blunts the thirst mechanism, making it difficult to replace fluid loss without a plan for periodic consumption. An adequate quantity of plain cool water will meet the fluid needs of most persons exercising in moderate climatic conditions. Extreme exercise levels and/or certain environmental conditions may warrant a low-dose supplemental electrolyte replacement beverage during endurance competitions to guard against electrolyte disturbances experienced as a result of excessive sweat loss.

Ergogenic aids are reputed to enhance performance above the levels anticipated under normal conditions. In most cases, they are without validation and are, in effect, more expensive forms of protein, sugars, or vitamins that provide psychological rather than proven physiological benefits. Alcohol has been shown to have no beneficial effect on exercise performance and, in fact, is more likely to impede performance. Caffeine, theorized to have a glycogen-sparing action during exercise, may offset fatigue, but its negative side effects may outweigh possible benefits.

What an athlete eats before competition makes a difference, both physically and psychologically. The pre-competition meal should be individualized to reflect different transit times, personal food preferences, and the scheduling of events to ensure gastric emptying and avoid discomfort or cramping. The meal should consist primarily of foods high in complex carbohydrates; foods high in fats and proteins that may require more time to digest should be avoided. The precompetition meal ought to be eaten 3-1/2 to 4 hours prior to competition. A well-planned, balanced program is the basis for good health and enhanced athletic performance.

[Ed. note: There is evidence that additional calcium alone for amenorrheic athletes is not sufficient to prevent osteoporosis; rather, it must be taken with supplemental estrogen to be effective.] ❑

Journal of the American Dietetic Association
V 87 # 7: 933-9, July 1987

CARBOHYDRATE FOR OPTIMUM PERFORMANCE

Carbohydrate is a vital fuel for athletic performance. The kind of carbohydrate the athlete eats, and when he or she eats it, can exert a strong influence on performance.

Glucose and Glycogen

At the cellular level, muscle movement is powered by **adenosine triphosphate**, also called **ATP**. Supplies of ATP must be continually regenerated. ATP is regenerated primarily from energy supplied by the breakdown of **glucose** and **glycogen**, two forms of carbohydrate.

Glucose, also called **blood sugar**, is a carbohydrate that naturally circulates in the blood. *Glycogen* is a storage form of carbohydrate found in the liver and muscles. Glycogen gets broken down into glucose, and the glucose either gets released into the bloodstream (if it's from liver glycogen) or used locally for energy production (if it's from muscle glycogen).

Fat and protein contribute to energy production during exercise, too. However, they cannot sustain energy production without the presence of sufficient glycogen and glucose. When glycogen and glucose become depleted, muscle cells cannot synthesize enough ATP to meet the muscular metabolic demands of intense exercise.

It has been estimated that in running a marathon, a runner's muscle and liver glycogen stores are totally depleted, while less than 1% of the body's fat and protein stores are used.

Muscle Glycogen Stores

Once muscle glycogen stores are depleted, extreme fatigue sets in. How long the muscle glycogen stores last depends on a number of factors.

Exercise intensity

Higher-intensity exercise increases the demand for glycogen. This is a direct consequence of an increased demand for oxygen.

The more intense the exercise, the greater the demand for oxygen. If muscles require oxygen faster than the heart and lungs can supply it, a greater proportion of energy production (ATP regeneration) will come from anaerobic metabolism. Compared to aerobic metabolism, anaerobic metabolism uses fourteen times as much glycogen to produce the same amount of ATP.

For example, in one study, two hours of cycling at 30% of maximal work effort (low intensity) was compared to two hours of cycling at 75% of maximal work effort (high intensity). At the lower intensity, muscle glycogen was only about 20% depleted after two hours. At the higher intensity, muscle glycogen was almost totally depleted.

In another experiment, it was determined that light walking (20%-30% of maximal work effort) uses glycogen up at the rate of 0.3 mmol/kg/min. Repeated maximal contractions can use up glycogen at 40 mmol/kg/min, a 133-fold increase in the rate of glycogen use compared to light walking.

Type of exercise

Rate of glycogen depletion within a given muscle depends on how strenuously that muscle is exercised. Running, for example, places heavy demands on the calf muscles. Cycling, on the other hand, places heaviest demands on the thigh muscles. Different types of exercise involving the same muscle groups will cause proportionately different rates of glycogen depletion in those muscles.

How much glycogen is stored to begin with depends on **conditioning level** and **diet**.

Conditioning level

Trained endurance athletes have been shown to have muscle glycogen stores roughly twice the size of those of untrained subjects, and liver glycogen stores about 70% higher than untrained subjects. These increased glycogen stores are independent of diet.

Diet

Unlike some animals, who can replenish their glycogen stores from internal sources such as glycerol (from fat breakdown) and lactic acid (from glucose breakdown), humans can only replenish their glycogen stores from dietary carbohydrate. When humans don't get dietary carbohydrate, glycogen stores can easily be depleted.

In one experiment, liver glycogen stores were shown to decrease rapidly, even without exercise, in subjects deprived of carbohydrate for 24 hours. When combined with strenuous exercise, a low-carbohydrate diet can quickly deplete liver glycogen stores. On the other hand, a single high-carbohydrate meal can quickly replenish liver glycogen stores.

Exercising in hot weather increases rate of glycogen depletion, probably due to changes in muscle blood flow. Exercising at 106 °F has been shown to increase muscle glycogen use by 76% compared to exercising at 48 °F.

Besides muscle glycogen stores, the other major carbohydrate source for exercise is **circulating glucose**. Circulating glucose becomes an increasingly important source of fuel as muscle glycogen stores become depleted. For example, in later stages of exercise up to 90% of the carbohydrate fuel burned by muscles comes from circulating glucose.

If the liver can't supply glucose into the bloodstream as fast as the muscles are burning it for fuel, the blood sugar level will steadily drop and **low blood sugar**, or **hypoglycemia**, will set in. Hypoglycemia can produce fatigue, worsening performance. Hypoglycemia can easily be prevented, though, and is discussed under *Carbohydrate During Exercise*.

What do athletes eat?

Dietary intakes were determined for a group of twenty-two runners who were training for a marathon. The group included both international-level runners and recreational runners.

The runners came very close to meeting the Recommended Dietary Allowance (RDA) for most nutrients. Although the specific choices of foods varied considerably from athlete to athlete and from day to day, when analyzed for percentages of fats, proteins, and carbohydrates, and vitamin and mineral content, the diets were nutritionally quite similar. Interestingly, there was little difference between the diets of the elite runners and the diets of the recreational runners, suggesting that the differences in performance between elite and recreational runners are due to training and genetics rather than nutrition.

These runners received 50% of their calories from carbohydrates. Many nutritionists recommend diets containing at least 60% carbohydrate, making the diets of these runners seem low by comparison. However, the athletes in this study were eating very large quantities of food (almost 50% more calories than comparably sized sedentary individuals). So while the *percentage* of carbohydrate in their diets might be a bit low, the *amount* of carbohydrate is still quite high. These runners probably ate more than enough carbohydrate to meet the energy needs of their training.

Even though most of these runners did not take supplemental vitamins or minerals, vitamin and mineral intake came very close to or exceeded the RDA.

Dietary intakes were also determined for the same runners for the three days immediately prior to a marathon. During this period the runners changed both their dietary and training patterns. Mileage dropped from an average of 8.5 to 2.3 miles per day, a 73% decrease. This corresponds to a decrease in caloric expenditure of almost 500 calories per day.

In an attempt to load glycogen stores, the athletes increased their daily caloric intake from 3012 calories to 3730, a 24% increase. Some athletes increased caloric intake to over 5000 calories. This means the runners were eating a daily surplus of over 1200 calories. Those taking in over 5000 calories were eating *over twice* the number of calories they needed.

In so doing, they did load their glycogen stores but also risked gaining fat. However, this seems a reasonable risk. It is probably better to eat too many carbohydrate calories and risk having too much fat than to eat too few and risk having too little glycogen.

Absorption of Carbohydrates

The four most common carbohydrates used in solutions consumed during exercise are *glucose*, *sucrose* (table sugar), *fructose* (fruit sugar), and *glucose polymers* (long chains of glucose molecules hooked together).

Despite many studies investigating various types of carbohydrate solutions, confusion remains concerning the best fluid to drink during exercise.

Early studies suggested that any carbohydrate in a solution consumed during exercise slows the passage of water from the stomach, potentially causing gastric distress and bloating. However, more recent research has failed to confirm this. It is likely that transit of carbohydrate solutions out of the stomach is not as big a problem as once believed.

Carbohydrate Loading

Carbohydrate loading (**carbo-loading**) can double the glycogen content of muscles, substantially prolonging time to glycogen depletion and improving endurance.

For years it was thought that the best way to carbo-load was to do exhaustive exercise one week before the event, followed by three days of a low-carbohydrate, high-fat, high-protein diet. Then, the athlete was to stay on a high-carbohydrate diet until the event. The idea was to deplete glycogen stores as much as possible through both diet and exhaustive exercise, then reload muscle stores through diet. It worked, but was not always in the athletes' best interest. The exhaustive exercise probably caused microscopic muscle damage, interfering with carbo-loading and putting the athlete at risk for overuse injuries. The low-carbohydrate, high-fat, high-protein diet tended to make athletes irritable, hypoglycemic, and unable to train.

Recent studies have shown that neither the glycogen-depletion exercise nor the three days of low-carbohydrate diet is necessary. Athletes can amass sufficient glycogen reserves simply by resting for two to three days while eating a diet rich in carbohydrates.

Each gram of glycogen stores with it 2.6 grams of water. This can produce a weight gain of two to five pounds for an athlete who has carbo-loaded. Some researchers have suggested that bodyweight, measured before breakfast but after emptying the bladder, can be used to monitor total glycogen storage during carbo-loading.

Appropriate consumption of carbohydrates can significantly influence exercise performance, particularly endurance exercise. Carbohydrates are clearly necessary for optimal performance, but should be just a part of a well-balanced diet and training regimen. As research continues in this fast-evolving field, we are bound to learn more about the ergogenic properties of this vital nutrient.

Carbohydrates Immediately Before Exercise

Many athletes try to get some "quick energy" by eating a candy bar or other sugary snack before an event. Does this work?

It depends on how long before the event. As shown in the table, if carbohydrates are taken three to four hours before an event, performance is improved compared to not eating. If carbohydrates are taken 30 to 45 minutes before an event, performance is the same or worsened. If taken within five minutes of an event, performance is improved.

These effects are probably associated with changes in blood sugar. Eating carbohydrates, such as a sugary snack, causes blood sugar (glucose) levels to rise. This stimulates release of insulin, which brings blood sugar levels back down (sometimes to below normal levels). This whole process takes an hour or so, so carbohydrates eaten within one hour of exercising may cause low blood sugar at the start of exercise. The insulin may also decrease fat breakdown, causing a greater reliance on glucose and glycogen stores.

Fructose generally does not cause the same insulin response as other carbohydrates, and so has been recommended by some as a better "pre-exercise carbohydrate." However, fructose has its own problems. It can produce diarrhea, and is absorbed less completely than other carbohydrates. In addition, it has been shown to elevate blood lactic acid levels, perhaps causing premature fatigue.

Carbohydrates During Exercise

Consuming carbohydrate during prolonged exercise can prolong glycogen stores and prevent exercise-induced hypoglycemia. Both of these functions have the potential to improve performance, particularly in exercise of an hour or more. For example, in one study subjects who ate 33 grams of carbohydrate (equal to the carbohydrate in a Snickers bar) every hour during two hours of intermittent exercise showed improved sprint performance at the end of the two hours. Amounts smaller than 21 grams per hour have generally failed to improve performance, and may be the minimum necessary to promote an improvement.

Both solid carbohydrates, such as candy bars, and liquid carbohydrates, such as glucose solutions, appear to be equally well-tolerated and absorbed. As with the carbohydrates before exercising, no carbohydrate (glucose, sucrose, fructose, or glucose polymer) appears to hold any advantage over any other.

Glycogen Replenishment After Exercise

The rate of glycogen replenishment after exercise depends on, among other things, intake of carbohydrate after exercise and degree of microscopic damage to muscle tissue.

EFFECTS OF CARBOHYDRATE FEEDINGS ON BLOOD GLUCOSE, MUSCLE GLYCOGEN, AND PERFORMANCE

CONDITION	BLOOD GLUCOSE	MUSCLE GLYCOGEN	PERFORMANCE
Glucose 30-45 min before exercise	decreased	unchanged	worsened
Fructose 30-45 min before exercise	unchanged	unchanged	unchanged or worsened
Glucose, fructose, or carb. snack 0-5 min before exercise	unchanged or increased	unchanged	improved
Glucose or carb. meal 3-4 hours before exercise	unchanged or increased	unchanged	improved

If a low-carbohydrate diet is eaten after glycogen depletion, no glycogen storage occurs, because there is insufficient dietary carbohydrate to store.

Microscopic damage to muscle tissue interferes with glycogen storage, too. For example, after a marathon, during which considerable microscopic muscle damage occurs, muscle glycogen can only be replenished to levels approximating 50% of pre-race levels. This inability to replenish fully persists for a week following the marathon. After cycling, however, during which little microscopic muscle damage occurs, muscle glycogen can be fully replenished.

It must be noted that a high carbohydrate intake causes an increase in blood triglycerides (fats), which is associated with a higher risk of heart disease. However, it appears that, in endurance runners, dietary carbohydrate tends to be stored as glycogen rather than as fats. Also, there is some evidence that simple carbohydrates, such as table sugar and honey, are more likely to be converted into fats, whereas complex carbohydrates, such as starch, are more likely to be converted into glycogen. More research needs to be done in these areas.
❏

Carbohydrates for Exercise: Dietary Demands for Optimal Performance
D. L. Costill
International Journal of Sports Medicine
V 9: 1-18, 1988

PROTEIN UTILIZATION FOR ENERGY PRODUCTION

Athletes usually associate protein with building muscle. However, protein also functions within muscle in another way: as a fuel for muscular energy production.

Many chemical reactions in the body—including those involved in muscular energy production—are initiated and controlled by substances called **enzymes**. By observing the level of activity of these enzymes, researchers can track the degree to which certain reactions take place.

An enzyme called **keto acid dehydrogenase** is an essential ingredient when leucine, one of the branched-chain amino acids, is used as fuel for muscular energy production.

The activity of keto acid dehydrogenase greatly increases as intensity and duration of exercise increase. This suggests that the longer and harder you exercise, the more protein is used to produce muscular energy.

Fasting before exercise seems to increase protein utilization for energy even more. In this study, muscular keto acid dehydrogenase activity during exercise rose by over 300% when exercise was preceeded by a twenty-four hour fast.

These results have important implications for athletes. Protein is an essential element for muscle growth, and is also involved in maintenance and repair throughout the body. An excessive demand on the body's protein "stores" (muscle tissue) to provide fuel for energy production can actually lead to a loss of lean muscle tissue. Consequently, it's important for athletes to limit, as much as possible, the use of protein for energy production. This can be accomplished by consuming adequate supplies of carbohydrates, a practice which has been shown to have a protein-sparing effect. ❏

Effects of Exercise Intensity and Starvation on Activation of Branched-Chain Keto Acid Dehydrogenase by Exercise
George J. Kasperek and Rebecca D. Snider
American Journal of Physiology
252: E33-E37, 1987

UNDERSTANDING THE TECHNIQUES OF CARBOHYDRATE LOADING

Glycogen, a carbohydrate, is the form in which glucose is stored in the muscles and liver. Whenever you engage in strenuous exercise, you call on your glycogen stores to some degree.

For prolonged endurance events, such as marathons, the ability to keep going after two hours or so is limited by the amount of glycogen stored. The more glycogen you have stored, the longer you can continue exercising. Once you run out of glycogen, extreme fatigue sets in. (This is known as "hitting the wall").

Carbohydrate loading (carbo-loading) increases liver and muscle glycogen stores, and is a proven technique for enhancing performance of prolonged endurance events.

It involves a series of dietary and exercise manipulations done during the several days prior to an endurance event.

The classical carbo-loading technique uses four days of glycogen depletion followed by three days of glycogen replenishment. During depletion, the athlete eats a low carbohydrate diet and exercises heavily. During replenishment, he or she eats a high carbohydrate diet (at least 70 to 80% of calories coming from carbohydrate) and exercises lightly or not at all. This technique can double an athlete's glycogen stores.

Carbo-loading is quite common among endurance athletes, especially marathon runners. To do it correctly, the athlete must not only know the time course of depletion and replenishment, he or she must also be able to choose appropriate low-carbohydrate and high-carbohydrate foods.

What percentage of athletes who direct their own carbo-loading programs do so correctly?

Seventy-six participants in a Nike marathon, all of whom planned to carbo-load before the event, filled out questionnaires providing day-by-day summaries of their intended diet and training program for the week prior to the marathon. The questionnaires were designed so that the participants did not know they were being evaluated for their knowledge of carbo-loading.

Most runners exercised during the depletion phase, but more than half continued to train strenuously during the replenishment phase when carbo-loading calls for exercising lightly or not at all. Many failed to taper their workouts at all.

The average carbohydrate intake during the high-carbohydrate phase was 53% of all calories, only slightly above the average American intake of 40% and well below the 70 to 80% level recommended for the high-carbohydrate phase.

Although athletes who carbo-load with moderate carbohydrate intake (50% of all calories) show a small increase in muscle glycogen, that increase is not nearly as large as the increase that can be achieved with a high carbohydrate intake. So, while the athletes in this study doubtlessly received *some* benefit from their individual carbo-loading regimens, clearly they did not receive as great a benefit as they could have. This is partly due to some athletes' having incorrectly identified relatively high-*fat* foods, such as ice cream and chocolate, as high-*carbohydrate* foods.

In summary, most of these athletes practicing self-directed techniques for carbo-loading did not carbo-load as effectively as they might have. Most did not consume enough carbohydrate during the replenishment phase, in some instances due to incomplete nutritional knowledge. If athletes are going to pursue carbo-loading as a means of improving performance, it is important that they understand nutrition well enough to ensure correct application of the technique. ❏

A Study of Carbohydrate Loading Techniques Used by Marathon Runners
L. Burke and R. Read
Canadian Journal of Sports Sciences
V 12 # 1: 6-10, Mar 1987

THE POSSIBLE SIDE EFFECTS OF CARBO-LOADING

Carbo-loading is a technique for enhancing endurance performance. It involves a set of dietary and exercise manipulations, and appears to work by increasing the stores of glycogen in muscle tissue. When carbo-loading is recommended, it is often accompanied by a warning about its potential side effects. These include weight gain due to increased muscle water storage, muscle damage, and electrocardiogram (EKG, or heart tracing) abnormalities. Although increased muscle water storage and muscle damage can be a minor problem, EKG abnormalities have the potential to be much more serious. What are the EKG abnormalities seen with carbo-loading, and how worrisome are they?

It turns out that all the warnings about the relationship between carbo-loading and EKG abnormalities are based on one study of one forty-year-old marathoner. To re-evaluate this relationship with younger athletes, and to see if the EKG results with the forty-year-old marathoner are indeed representative, a similar experiment was performed with six younger subjects. These six, average age 24, underwent a standard carbo-loading regimen: five days of a mixed diet (17% protein, 44% carbohydrate, and 39% fat), three days of a high-fat/high-protein diet (25% protein, 15% carbs, and 60% fat), and three days of a high-carbohydrate diet (16% protein, 75% carbs, and 9% fat), accompanied by appropriate exercise. At the end of each dietary phase, each subject ran on a treadmill to exhaustion, while being evaluated for EKG response before, during, and after exercise.

A few EKG abnormalities were noted after the mixed diet phase, but were of a type generally thought of as benign, transient, and of limited medical consequence, especially in young healthy adults. Indeed, these abnormalities subsequently disappeared, and were not noted after the high-fat/high-protein or high-carbohydrate diet phases. No medically significant EKG changes were noted after either the high-fat/high-protein or high-carbohydrate diet phases.

While carbo-loading as done in this experiment did not cause any medically significant changes in EKG readings, it did result in significant improvements in exercise time to exhaustion. Treadmill exercise times to exhaustion after mixed diet and high-fat/high-protein diet were not significantly different from each other: an average of 61.3 and 62.8 minutes, respectively. After three days of the high-carbohydrate diet, however, the average time to exhaustion increased by over 50% to 94.8 minutes.

One of the other side effects of carbo-loading, increased muscle water storage, may actually enhance performance under conditions of extensive sweat loss. This stored water is released as muscle glycogen is used up, and may help prevent dehydration.

This study demonstrates that carbo-loading significantly improves exhaustive aerobic performance with no apparent detrimental effect on heart function as reflected on EKG. However, this study only tested the effects of one-time carbo-loading; the cardiac effects of repeated carbo-loading have yet to be tested. ❑

The Effects of Glycogen Supercompensation On the Electrocardiographic
Response During Exercise
F. L. Goss and C. Karam
Research Quarterly for Exercise and Sport
V 58 # 1: 41-46, March 1987

Glycogen is a carbohydrate stored in the liver and muscles. It is a source of fuel for the exercising body, particularly during prolonged exercise. There is generally enough stored glycogen to last for about two hours of submaximal exercise. Once glycogen stores run out, extreme fatigue sets in.

Delaying glycogen depletion delays fatigue and improves performance in prolonged exercise. There are several ways to delay glycogen depletion. One is to start with larger glycogen stores; the most common way to do this is by carbo-loading. A second way is to increase reliance on fat stores, decreasing reliance on glycogen stores; this can be accomplished (not without risk) with drugs such as caffeine. A third method is to take some form of carbohydrate *during* exercise, thereby getting an outside source of fuel and decreasing reliance on glycogen stores.

This last method is the subject of a recent study out of the Sport Science Centre, University of Cape Town Medical School. Eighteen experienced university marathoners underwent a standard carbo-loading regimen (a low carbohydrate diet for three days with exercise, followed by a high carbohydrate diet for three days with no exercise), then ran a 26-mile marathon. During the marathon they drank one of three carbohydrate solutions—a 2% glucose solution, an 8% fructose solution, or an 8% glucose polymer solution.

In a second study, another group of eighteen subjects underwent the same carbo-loading regimen as the first group, then ran a 35-mile ultramarathon. During the ultramarathon they drank either a 4% glucose solution, or a 10% glucose polymer solution.

All subjects were unaware of the carbohydrate content of the solutions they were drinking. Muscle tissue samples were taken from all athletes immediately before and immediately after running, and blood samples were taken at intervals during running.

The overall volume of fluid ingested was approximately the same for all groups. As a result, the athletes drinking the more concentrated solutions ingested significantly more carbohydrate than those drinking the less concentrated solutions.

Despite the differences in carbohydrate ingestion over the course of the race, there were no differences in blood glucose levels, blood free fatty acid levels (a measure of rate of burning fat as fuel), or serum insulin levels among any of the

CARBOHYDRATE REPLACEMENT DURING PROLONGED DISTANCE RUNNING

athletes. Muscle tissue samples showed no differences in glycogen content, regardless of amount of carbohydrate ingested. Most importantly, the type and amount of carbohydrate ingested during the race did not affect performance.

Other studies have reported a fairly high incidence of marathon-induced hypoglycemia (low blood sugar) among runners who do not ingest any form of carbohydrate during a marathon. Runners probably need to ingest a minimum amount of carbohydrate during a marathon to ward off hypoglycemia. Since hypoglycemia clearly worsens performance, the runner can improve performance by ingesting the minimum amount.

However, this study demonstrates that amounts above that minimum do not appear to cause any further improvements in performance. The minimum amount of carbohydrate needed to ward off hypoglycemia can be provided by a 2% glucose solution. The type of carbohydrate appears to make no difference. ❑

Carbohydrate Ingestion and Muscle Glycogen Depletion During Marathon and Ultramarathon Racing
T. D. Noakes et al.
European Journal of Applied Physiology
V 57 # 4: 482-489, March 1988

Many athletes eat a meal high in carbohydrates before prolonged exercise. Other athletes ingest caffeine in the form of coffee, tea, or caffeine tablets before prolonged exercise. Caffeine has been shown to increase blood levels of free-fatty acids, the form of fat used by the body for fuel. Use of free-fatty acids for fuel has a "glycogen-sparing" effect; that is, it helps to preserve muscle glycogen stores for later use. This can help enhance endurance performance.

Hoping to receive the benefits of both techniques, some athletes eat a meal high in carbohydrates *and* ingest caffeine before prolonged exercise.

It turns out that the high carbohydrate meal blocks the effects of the caffeine! In other words, the increase in blood free-fatty acid levels usually seen when caffeine is taken alone is not seen when the caffeine is taken along with a high-carbohydrate meal. Athletes who take caffeine along with a high-carbohydrate meal lose the potential positive ergogenic effect of caffeine, while maintaining caffeine's potential negative effects—for example, increased risk of dehydration from the diuretic action of caffeine. ❏

A High Carbohydrate Diet Negates the Metabolic Effects of Caffeine During Exercise
J. Weir et al.
Medicine and Science in Sports and Exercise
V 19 # 2: 100-105, 1987

COMBINING CAFFEINE AND CARBOS

FASTING AND PHYSICAL ACTIVITY

Most athletes would assert that missing even one meal soon before an event will markedly worsen athletic performance. Not necessarily so, according to a recent study on the effect of fasting on physical performance.

For four days, eight male U.S. Army soldiers, average age 22.5 years, were placed on a balanced diet providing 12% protein calories, 53% carbohydrate calories, and 34% fat calories. Subjects were then tested for muscular strength, muscular endurance, and aerobic capacity.

After testing, all subjects underwent a three-and-a-half day fast. They consumed only water and selected herbal teas during the fasting period.

At the end of the three-and-a-half days, the tests were repeated.

The authors noted no change in muscular endurance or aerobic capacity. This was unexpected, because fasting both increases breakdown of muscle protein and decreases stores of muscle glycogen, a "reserve energy" fuel. However, fasting also increases blood concentrations of free fatty acids, an alternative fuel source from fat. It may be that fasting increased free fatty acids, and the improved endurance seen from increased free fatty acids compensated for the decreased muscle protein and muscle glycogen.

Muscular strength, which was tested both isometrically (holding a weight suspended without moving) and isokinetically (moving a weight through a muscle's range of motion at constant velocity), showed mixed results: no change in strength measured isometrically, but a small (10%) yet significant decrease in strength measured isokinetically.

Why a difference was seen with isokinetic measurement but not isometric measurement is not clear; it may be related to the fact that isokinetic maneuvers test a muscle's strength over its full range of motion, whereas isometric maneuvers test a muscle's strength at only one angle.

The authors concluded that "the absence of food for a period of a few days would seem to have little impact on the voluntary functional capacities measured here."

[Ed. note: After a three-and-a-half day fast, the energy for performance is clearly coming from energy stores rather than from recent pre-event meals. The body appears to have compensatory mechanisms for energy production during times of fasting, so that

*pre-event meals, at least in terms of supplying energy for perfor-
mance, are probably not as crucial as is commonly believed.]* ❏

*Influence of a 3.5 Day Fast on Physical
Performance
Joseph Knapik et al.
European Journal of Applied Physiology
V 56; 428-432, July 1987*

VITAMIN AND MINERAL SUPPLEMEN- TATION

In a nine-month placebo-controlled double-blind study, thirty experienced runners were given either multivitamin/multimineral supplements or placebo for three months. For the next three months, neither group received either supplements or placebo. During the final three months, the group that initially received placebo received supplements, and the group that initially received supplements received placebo.

Result: no significant differences between the vitamin-and-mineral-supplemented group and the placebo group in any of the standard fitness performance parameters measured (peak treadmill speed, maximal oxygen uptake, maximal heart rate, peak blood lactic acid concentration, and 15 kilometer race time). This indicates that young, healthy athletes who take vitamin and mineral supplements are not receiving athletic performance benefits beyond those available from taking placebo.

Now, the same researchers have released the results of a companion study done at the same time. The subjects were not only tested for physical performance, as mentioned above, but also for blood levels of the vitamins and minerals they were taking.

The amounts of the vitamin and minerals the athletes were given are listed in the table at right.

Blood levels of the minerals copper, zinc, magnesium, and iron were the same before the experiment, during supplementation, and during placebo ingestion. In other words, blood levels of these minerals were completely unchanged by supplementation. Among vitamins, supplementation resulted in a significant rise in only two: riboflavin (vitamin B-2) and pyridoxine (vitamin B-6). Blood concentrations of thiamine (B-1), niacin (B-3), ascorbic acid (C), and tocopherol (E) did not change significantly. Blood levels of retinol (vitamin A) actually fell after supplementation, probably because vitamin E interferes with the absorption of vitamin A.

An evaluation of the diets of these athletes showed that, even without supplements, average daily intake of all vitamins and minerals was above the RDA.

This study strongly supports the contention that athletes who get sufficient vitamins and minerals from a balanced diet do not require supplementation. Furthermore, with the exception of riboflavin and pyridoxine, supplementation did not increase blood levels of vitamins and minerals.

Why not? Probably because of the variable interactions of vitamins and minerals when taken together as supplements. For example, high doses of vitamin C (more than 50 mg) can decrease absorption of B-12. Vitamins A and E mutually interfere with each other's absorption. Iron, vitamin C, copper, and zinc have complex interactions that affect their absorption. Calcium and phosphorus may combine to inhibit absorption of iron. All of these nutrients taken together as supplements cause complex interactions resulting in variable

NUTRIENTS GIVEN TO TEST SUBJECTS IN VITAMIN / MINERAL SUPPLEMENTATION EXPERIMENT

NUTRIENT	CAPSULE DOSE	RDA	% OF RDA
Vitamin A	3 mg	1.5 mg	200%
Vitamin D	10 µg	10 µg	100%
Vitamin E	516 mg	15.1 mg	3000%
Thiamine (B1)	60 mg	1.4 mg	4300%
Riboflavin (B2)	60 mg	1.6 mg	3750%
Nicotinic acid (B3)	70 mg	18 mg	380%
Pyridoxine (B6)	60 mg	2 mg	3000%
Cyanocobalamin (B12)	60 µg	3 µg	2000%
Pantothenic acid	70 µg	4-17 µg	1000%
Folic acid	500 µg	400 µg	130%
Vitamin C	850 mg	60 mg	1400%
Selenium	50 µg	50 µg	100%
Iodine	150 µg	130 µg	115%
Calcium	230 mg	800 mg	29%
Magnesium	116 mg	350 mg	33%
Phosphorus	116 mg	800 mg	14.5%
Iron	13.4 mg	10 mg	134%
Zinc	5.2 µg	15 µg	35%
Copper	584 µg	2 mg	29%
Potassium	32 mg	—	—
Manganese	300 mg	—	—

Supplementation with these nutrients in these amounts for three months resulted in no improvement in athletic performance, and (with the exception of B2 and B6) no increase in blood levels of these nutrients. However, supplementation with these amounts resulted in no measurable toxicity, either. (mg = milligrams; µg = micrograms) absorption of every nutrient, in this case resulting in blood levels no higher than if no supplement were taken at all.

Vitamin and mineral supplementation with the amounts listed in the table on the previous page did not result in toxic levels. Even the fat-soluble vitamins A and E, taken at high doses for three months, did not show blood levels in the toxic range. This suggests that vitamins and minerals, when taken as multivitamin/multimineral supplements in amounts close to those used here, while not improving performance, are fairly safe.

[Ed. note: The athletes in this study ate well-balanced diets; not all athletes do. These subjects were not deficient in iron or copper; many athletes are. Supplementation with certain nutrients can enhance the performance of athletes deficient in those nutrients, but, supplementation for athletes who are not deficient in any nutrient does not improve performance.

[This study also points out the difficulty of supplementing with a multivitamin/ multimineral product, and running afoul of multiple absorption interactions. For this reason, it is probably not enough to take a supplement in the morning and assume your nutritional requirements are taken care of for the rest of the day. It is still the best advice to eat a varied diet throughout the day, although, as this study also points out, with low toxicity a supplement probably wouldn't hurt.] ❏

Vitamin and Mineral Status of Trained Athletes
Including the Effects of Supplementation
L. Wright et al.
American Journal of Clinical Nutrition
V 47: 186-91, 1988

AVERAGE VITAMIN AND MINERAL INTAKES

Who should take vitamin and mineral supplements? You've heard the recommendation from respected nutritionists countless times: vitamin and mineral supplements are unnecessary for people who eat a balanced diet.

Unfortunately, "a balanced diet" is often defined as a diet providing all the necessary nutrients in adequate amounts. This leads to a circular argument: vitamin and mineral supplements are unnecessary for those who don't need vitamin and mineral supplements—those with a balanced diet. The real question is, how balanced is the American diet?

To find out, researchers from the Consumer Nutrition Center of the U.S. Department of Agriculture collected dietary reports from 37,785 people. Subjects were requested to keep a 3-day dietary diary, and were given verbal instructions, pamphlets, and measuring devices to help them estimate intake. Results were tabulated for males and females in 11 different age groups. Results are for food intake only, and did not include any vitamin or mineral supplements that the subjects might be taking.

All groups showed intakes in excess of the RDA for protein, riboflavin (B-3), niacin (B-2), B-12, and vitamin C. All groups were over 100% of the RDA (except one or two groups which were under 100% but over 90%) for phosphorus, vitamin A, and thiamine (B-1).

Some nutrients, however, came in at under 70% of the RDA for several age/sex groups.

- **Calcium** intake averaged under 76% of the RDA in women of all age groups, and only 63-69% in women 15-18 and 35-64.

- **Iron** intake averaged 59-65% of the RDA in women aged 12-50.

- **Magnesium** intake averaged 71-80% of the RDA in women over 12, and only 65-69% in women 15-22. Men averaged a bit higher (77-88%), but still below the RDA.

- **Vitamin B-6** intake ranged from 58-63% of the RDA in women over 14, and 71-81% in men 19-74.

When the data was interpreted another way, looking at the percentage of all subjects below 70% of the RDA, the same vitamins and minerals surfaced as problem nutrients. Calcium, iron, magnesium and vitamin B-6 intakes were low in the diets of 42, 32, 39, and 51% of all subjects.

Women consistently showed lower nutrient intakes than men, even though their RDA's are similar for most nutrients. The reason is simple: men tend to eat more food than women, so men get more nutrients.

How do athletes compare to the rest of the population? Athletes tend to have better nutrition than non-athletes. They eat more than non-athletes, so they get more nutrients overall.

It is not true that athletes need a great deal more vitamins and minerals than non-athletes. Exercise increases the requirement for a few nutrients—vitamin B-3, copper, zinc, chromium—but athletes often make up for the increased need by eating more food. Indeed, athletes are *less* likely to need vitamin and mineral supplementation because they are *more* likely to get full nutrition from their food. A recent study looked at the diets of 30 well-trained athletes and found they were getting above the RDA for all vitamins and minerals.

So who *should* take vitamin and mineral supplements? The real problem nutrients appear to be calcium, iron, magnesium, and vitamin B-6. Ideally, practically no healthy persons should need these supplements, as everyone *should* be eating enough of the right foods. (The "right" foods are those low in calories and high in nutrients—low-fat or non-fat dairy products; lean meat, poultry, and fish; whole grain breads; fresh fruits and vegetables. The "wrong" foods are high in calories and low in nutrients—sodas, chips, pastries, candy).

However, not everyone eats enough of the right foods. For those who don't, an RDA-level multivitamin-multimineral supplement can help to ensure that they get enough of these nutrients. Some RDA-level supplements are listed in the table.

Since nutrient deficiencies can impair performance, athletes who are unsure about the adequacy of their diets may want to consider modest vitamin and mineral supplementation, even though they are less likely than non-athletes to have a deficiency. ❑

Problem Nutrients in the United States
E. Pao and S. Mickle
Food Technology
58-79, September 1981

Vitamin and Mineral Status of Trained Athletes
Including the Effects of Supplementation
L. Weight et al.
American Journal of Clinical Nutrition
V 47: 186-91, 1988

Vitamin B-6, pyrodoxine, is important in a number of physiologic processes, including synthesis of hemoglobin, myoglobin, epinephrine (adrenaline), and various proteins. It is also involved in breaking down amino acids, forming one amino acid from another, and in breaking down glycogen into glucose. All of these functions are necessary for high-intensity muscular activity.

The U.S. RDA for vitamin B-6 is 2.2 mg for men, 2.0 mg for women, and 2.4 mg for women during pregnancy and lactation. However, the diets of most Americans fall short of the U.S. RDA.

Women aged 19 to 50 typically consume only 58% of the RDA, and men in the same age range consume an average of only 78 to 81% of the RDA. A high protein intake increases the requirement for vitamin B-6; people eating the typical Western high-protein diet are thus more likely to be B-6 deficient.

Research has shown that a severe dietary B-6 deficiency clearly interferes with protein synthesis. This is not surprising given the central role B-6 plays in protein synthesis and metabolism. However, a recent study demonstrates that, in rats, the deficiency need not be all that severe to interfere with protein synthesis. Rats fed diets marginal in B-6 (20% of RDA for rats) showed alterations in synthesis of liver, kidney, and muscle proteins.

With men and women averaging well below the RDA, it is likely that some subpopulations have diets low enough in B-6 to interfere with protein synthesis and other functions affecting high-intensity muscular activity.

If too little vitamin B-6 is bad, should the athlete take large B-6 supplements? Alas, with vitamin B-6, too much can be almost as bad as too little.

Rats were given either the rat RDA or supplemented with 100 times the RDA for B-6, and placed on a short-term high-intensity resistance exercise program. The rats receiving high levels of B-6 showed lower food intake, lower weight gain, lower muscle weight, and lower strength than those receiving only the RDA. This suggests that supplementation with high levels of vitamin B-6 has an adverse affect on muscle growth and strength.

To be sure, most athletes who supplement with B-6 do so in amounts less than 100 times the RDA. However, this

HEALTHY NUTRITIONAL LEVELS OF VITAMIN B-6

demonstrates that it is indeed possible to get either too little or too much of a good thing.

Incidentally, in humans, supplementation with vitamin B-6 does not improve athletic performance.

[Ed. note: Good dietary sources of vitamin B-6 include liver, meat, whole grain cereals, green leafy vegetables, and nuts. Given the low average intake of vitamin B-6 among Americans, it is reasonable to recommend that athletes, especially those with high protein intakes or eating protein or amino acid supplements, increase their intake of these foods. Supplementation with RDA-levels of vitamin B-6 is probably not a bad idea either, to ensure the RDA is met. Excessively large doses appear to interfere with muscle growth and strength, so megadosing is not recommended.] ❏

Marginal Intake of Vitamin B-6: Effects on
Protein Synthesis in Liver, Kidney, and Muscle of the Rat
D. Sampson PhD, L. Young PhD, and M. Kretsch PhD
Nutrition Research
V 8: 309-319, 1988

Problem Nutrients in the United States
E. Pao and S. Mickie
Food Technology
35: 58-79, Sept 1981

Nutritional Biochemistry and Metabolism
M. Linder, ed.
Elsevier Publications, New York
1985, 82-89

Exercise appears to increase production of free radicals, a form of oxygen that is highly toxic to cells. Some researchers think that cell damage from free radicals may worsen athletic performance, especially at high altitudes. Vitamin E, an antioxidant, can help protect cell membranes against the damaging effects of free radicals. Can vitamin E then improve athletic performance, by decreasing exercise-induced cell damage from free radicals?

Investigators from the Sportmedizinisches Untersuchungszentrum des Bayerischen Landessportverbandes Grünwald, in Munich, tested high altitude mountain climbers to find out. They chose mountain climbers because the oxygen demands of exercise at high altitude are much more pronounced than oxygen demands at sea level, making any changes from vitamin E supplementation more likely to show up.

Twelve climbers were divided into two groups. One group was given 200 mg of vitamin E twice a day; the other group was given a placebo. All were evaluated while riding bicycle ergometers to exhaustion, once at 2500 meters (8200 feet) and three times at 5000 meters (16,400 feet).

Both groups showed improvements in endurance after two weeks of acclimatization to the higher altitude. After four weeks, the endurance of the vitamin E group continued to improve. The endurance of the placebo group, however, significantly declined. Furthermore, pentane exhalation, a measure of free-radical cell damage, showed no change in the vitamin E group but doubled in the placebo group.

This indicates that the vitamin E group was somehow protected from free-radical cell damage, and suffered little such damage, while the placebo group was not protected, and suffered measurable damage. Protection from cell damage provided by vitamin E may have been the reason that those taking vitamin E exhibited better endurance than those taking placebo.

Vitamin E probably works by stabilizing several components of the energy production chain, including membranes and enzymes in energy-producing cells. This effect is most pronounced under conditions of high oxygen demand, such as aerobic exercise, and low oxygen supply, such as high altitude.

Does exercise-induced free radical cell damage occur at sea level? Probably. However, a number of recent studies investigating the effect of vitamin E on athletic performance

LIMITING FREE RADICAL DAMAGE WITH VITAMIN E

have shown no improvement with vitamin E supplementation. It may be that the damage occurring at sea level is not great enough to affect performance appreciably. At higher altitudes, however, cell damage from the combination of high oxygen demand and low oxygen supply is great enough that vitamin E supplementation does make a difference. ❑

Influence of Vitamin E on Physical Performance
I. Simon-Schnass & H. Pabst
International Journal of Vitamin and Nutrition Research
V 58: 49-54, 1988

EXERCISE AND TRACE MINERALS

Trace minerals are directly involved in many physiological processes in the body, including a number that directly relate to protein, fat, and carbohydrate metabolism, and the formation of ATP. Exercise can affect the mobilization, storage, utilization, and excretion of trace minerals. This article examines the effects of exercise on several trace minerals.

Zinc

Zinc plays an important role in more than 100 enzymes, helping to maintain normal protein, fat, and carbohydrate metabolism. The RDA (Recommended Daily Allowance) for adults is 15 mg/day, but by some estimates much of the U. S. population is getting one-half that amount or less. Zinc deficiency manifests as decreased taste sensation, loss of appetite, delayed wound healing, impaired cell growth, and impaired immune defenses.

Good dietary sources of zinc include beef, liver, oysters, and turkey and chicken dark meat. Although some vegetable sources such as whole grains and cereals, nuts, and legumes (such as peanuts) contain zinc as well, they also contain phytate and certain types of dietary fiber that may interfere with the absorption of zinc from the intestines.

Exercise affects blood zinc levels. There is some variability among studies, but most show that blood zinc levels increase with exercise, then decline to resting levels shortly thereafter.

Exercise does increase urinary zinc losses, however; estimates run from as low as 12% to as high as 79% of the absorbed average daily intake can be excreted in the urine on an exercise day. Losses in sweat can be significant, as well. Heavy sweating can contribute to zinc deficiency, although these losses abate with acclimatization.

Exercise decreases resting serum zinc levels, as well. In a recent study, 23% of male athletes and 43% of female athletes were found to be "hypozincaemic" (having abnormally low zinc levels in their blood); however, none of these athletes was noted to have any clinical signs of zinc deficiency. Why they should be zinc-deficient and not show signs is unclear; it may be that these subjects are zinc-deficient but not to the point of exhibiting outward signs of deficiency, or it may be that athletes, with all the other changes in zinc metabolism that they undergo, develop an altered "metabolic profile" for zinc. In that case, the normal values for zinc deficiency in non-athletes wouldn't apply.

The authors state that this information on zinc "...may lead many to think zinc supplementation is the key to offsetting any possible problems with zinc status due to exercise and endurance training. This belief must be viewed with caution." While safe in amounts near the RDA, levels more than ten times the RDA have been shown to be detrimental to health. Symptoms of zinc toxicity include nausea, vomiting, anemia, gastric (stomach) bleeding, abdominal pain, and fever. They continue, "...it is very important to overall health to take in zinc at physiologic levels near the RDA. Drastically altering the relative quantities of zinc consumed or supplementing with non-physiological amounts is unwise and should be avoided."

[Ed. note: The fact that a large segment of the U. S. population may be consuming only one-half of the RDA or less indicates that 15 mg/day may be a difficult amount to get in the average American diet. This suggests that supplementation may be necessary to obtain the recommended dietary levels. As with chromium, a general multi-vitamin, multimineral supplement that contains nutrients in amounts close to the RDA may be advisable, but, as pointed out, taking in excess of the RDA is not a good idea.]

Chromium

The physiologic role of chromium has yet to be fully elucidated; however, chromium clearly has a role in the regulation of carbohydrate and lipid (fat) metabolism, primarily by affecting the action of insulin.

Aerobic exercise significantly increases serum chromium levels, by mobilizing it out of body stores. This mobilization probably enables the chromium to be transported from the body stores to where it is needed. However, mobilization also increases chromium excretion in the urine (almost fivefold after intense exercise).

Athletes appear to compensate at least some for the increased urinary losses. Physically fit rats have higher heart and kidney chromium levels than do sedentary rats. Trained runners excrete significantly less chromium on non-exercise days than do sedentary controls, suggesting an increased ability to conserve chromium. This increased ability to conserve chromium occurs either as an attempt to increase tissue stores or as an attempt to replace stores that have been depleted from increased excretion on exercise days.

The Recommended Daily Adult requirement for chromium is 0.050 to 0.200 mg/day. However, up to 90% of Americans may be getting less than this amount. In addition, diets high in simple sugars, as are most American diets, can increase urinary chromium losses by as much as 300%. Low dietary intake, coupled with increased losses from exercise and a high simple sugar diet, can make athletes deficient in chromium. This has the potential of causing abnormal carbohydrate and lipid metabolism, impaired glucose tolerance, elevated serum insulin, and elevated cholesterol and triglycerides. Theoretically, any of these changes may affect athletic performance; however, no cause-and-effect relationship between marginal chromium status and athletic performance has yet been demonstrated.

Foods high in chromium include mushrooms, oysters, black pepper, brewers' yeast, apples with skins, wine, and beer. Highly processed foods lose much of their chromium .

The authors contend that "it may be difficult to consume adequate trace minerals strictly from dietary food sources; supplementation may be necessary to obtain the recommended dietary levels." They recommend a general multivitamin, multimineral supplement that contains from 1 to 2 times the RDA, but state there is no evidence that "megadosing" with chromium, or indeed any trace mineral, provides any additional benefit.

[Ed. note: While the authors point out that chromium deficiency may result in abnormal carbohydrate and lipid metabolism, impaired glucose tolerance, elevated serum insulin, and elevated cholesterol and triglycerides, it is not clear how severe a deficiency over how long a time is necessary to produce clinical findings.]

Copper

Copper plays a key role in a number of processes in the body, including energy production, fat metabolism, red blood cell formation, and connective tissue formation. The recommended safe and adequate copper intake is 2 to 3 milligrams/day; the typical American diet contains only about one-half that amount. Prolonged marginal intake may cause anemia, loss of tendon and artery elasticity, and bone demineralization.

Good dietary sources of copper include shellfish, nuts, liver, kidneys, dried beans, and potatoes. Refined foods such as white flour and white sugar have had whatever traces of copper that might have been in them removed. In fact, high intakes of simple sugars (including honey) impair copper metabolism and may worsen health problems stemming from marginal copper intake.

Exercise increases serum levels of copper, more so in trained subjects than in untrained subjects. This is probably due to mobilization of copper from tissue stores to facilitate energy production and fat metabolism.

Exercise increases copper *loss* in stool, sweat, and urine. Losses in sweat can be considerable, especially in hot and humid climates. In an earlier experiment, men kept in a controlled hot and humid environment (99 °F, 50% humidity) lost almost *half* of their daily copper intake through their sweat, and had a negative copper balance overall (had daily copper losses exceeding intake), even though their intake at 3.5 mg/day was greater than the recommended intake.

The increase in serum copper levels with exercise may persist even during rest. This increase is thought to be due to increased levels of copper-containing proteins including **cytochrome oxidase**, the enzyme responsible for one of the last steps in the energy production process.

Increased copper losses, coupled with inadequate intake, may result in marginal serum copper levels. This may alter the pathways of fat metabolism and energy production, possibly affecting performance. However, no cause-and-effect relationship between marginal serum copper levels and athletic performance has yet been demonstrated.

Nonetheless, it makes sense to ensure adequate copper intake, indeed adequate intake of all necessary nutrients, so that nutritional factors don't become the limiting factors of athletic performance. As with zinc, copper is toxic in amounts much above the recommended levels, so "megadosing" is clearly inadvisable. However, since the typical American diet contains only half the recommended amount, supplementation with a general multimineral supplement containing no more than 1 to 2 times the RDA is reasonable. ❏

Effects of Aerobic Exercise and Training on the Trace Minerals
Chromium, Zinc, and Copper
W. W. Campbell and R. A. Anderson
Sports Medicine
V 4 # 2: 9-17, March/April 1987

MAGNESIUM DEFICIENCY AND DECREASED PERFORMANCE

The mineral **magnesium** plays a variety of physiologic roles. It is necessary for strong bones, helps release energy from food and muscle glycogen, facilitates transmission of nerve impulses to muscle, and assists in protein synthesis.

The RDA for magnesium is 350 mg/day for males, and 300 mg/day for females. It has been estimated that well over half of all Americans have diets that do not meet the RDA for magnesium. Many consume diets with less than 70% of the RDA.

Is a marginal magnesium intake dangerous? The answer isn't clear. Some researchers feel that the U.S. RDA is higher than necessary: the Canadian Recommended Nutrient Intake for magnesium, for example, is only 200 mg/day. However, markedly low magnesium intake has been associated with heart disease and high blood pressure.

More recently, low magnesium intake has also been associated with reduced endurance.

Researchers at the University of California at Davis have been studying the effects of magnesium-deficient diets on exercise capacity in rats. They found that rats fed diets low in magnesium showed a 50% reduction in endurance capacity compared to rats fed normal diets.

What accounts for the decrease in endurance capacity? The magnesium-deficient rats were also noted to have a macrocytic anemia—a drop in red blood cell concentration accompanied by an increase in average red blood cell size. This may partially account for the worsening in performance, but there are probably some other, poorly understood ways in which low magnesium affects performance as well.

[Ed. note: Since over half the population is getting less than the RDA of magnesium—including, presumably, many athletes—and since magnesium deficiency appears to reduce endurance (at least in rats), it would be prudent for athletes to make sure they consume the RDA for magnesium. This would include eating foods rich in magnesium, such as raw green leafy vegetables, whole grains, nuts, soybeans, seeds, cocoa, and high-magnesium mineral water. Magnesium supplementation might also be considered, which could be done with a magnesium supplement or a multimineral supplement. There is no evidence that magnesium supplementation will improve endurance in athletes whose magnesium status is normal to begin with.] ❏

The Effect of Variable Magnesium Intake on Potential Factors Influencing En-
durance
Capacity
P. Lowney et al.
Biological Trace Element Research
V 16 # 1: 1-18, June 1988

Dietary Magnesium Intake Influences Exercise Capacity and Hematologic
Parameters in Rats
C. L. Keen et al.
Metabolism
V 36 # 8: 788-793, Aug 1987

Nutrition plays a major role in the training strategy of every serious athlete. However, many athletes are uncertain about the adequacy of their own nutrition. This uncertainty, coupled with the relentless search for the "competitive edge," has made many athletes easy targets for charlatans peddling bogus nutrition.

Bogus nutrition can take many forms, from questionable diagnostic tests to unnecessary supplements. One example of a questionable diagnostic test is **hair analysis**.

Hair analysis is a procedure in which an investigator takes a length of hair, analyses it, and returns a report quantifying minerals said to be detected in the sample. Often the report takes the form of a computerized interpretation, listing "mineral imbalances" in the body.

There are several problems with this.

Mineral content of hair varies enormously, depending on choice of shampoos, hair bleaches and dyes, occupational exposure, geographic location, hair growth rate, medication use, age, sex, season of the year, natural hair color, and hair diameter.

Normal quantities of most minerals in hair have not been established, making determination of levels above or below normal difficult at best.

Analysis techniques are not standardized, and many sample preparation methods produce errors.

Since hair grows at a rate of only about one centimeter (0.39 inches) a month, the inch- or inch-and-a-half-long sample needed for analysis may not be an indication of current health status.

In a recent study, identical hair samples were sent on two occasions to thirteen hair analysis laboratories. The resultant reports varied widely even for identical samples at the same lab. Some labs reported mineral levels more than ten times greater than levels for the same mineral from other labs. There was no agreement from lab to lab on what constituted low, normal, or high levels of any mineral.

On the basis of their hair analysis findings, several of these labs suggested the presence of vague health problems ("malaise," "depression," "fatigue," "generalized aches and pains"). Many recommended supplements, but with no agreement on which supplements and how much of each.

PROBLEMS OF USING HAIR ANALYSIS TO EVALUATE NUTRITION

The Federal Trade Commission subsequently served an injunction against one of the hair analysis labs used in this study, barring it from "making false claims to the public about its testing services." The study concludes that hair analysis for evaluation of overall nutritional status is "unscientific, economically wasteful, and probably illegal."

[Ed. note: Hair analysis does have legitimate medical uses, primarily in the detection of poisoning with heavy metals such as lead and mercury. Well-meaning athletes can easily fall prey to a misuse of this test, leading them to dietary practices that may not be compatible with either good health or peak performance. Athletes are warned to be skeptical about **any** single test purporting to provide a broad evaluation of nutritional status.] ❑

Commercial Hair Analysis: Science or Scam?
S. Barrett MD
Journal of the American Medical Association
V 254 # 8: 1041-1045, Aug 1985
Misuse of Hair Analysis as a Diagnostic Tool
Archives of Dermatology
V 121: 1504-5, Dec 1985

SUPPLEMENTS

The sheer number of nutritional supplements marketed to the athlete today largely precludes their being tested in reliable, double-blind studies. Nevertheless, research has emerged involving vitamins, amino acids, and several popular supplements, offering new evidence concerning their ergogenic value.

THE LIMITED BENEFIT OF VITAMIN SUPPLEMENTS FOR PERFORMANCE

Some 40% of the U.S. population takes supplementary vitamins. Among Olympic athletes, the figure is 84%. Clearly, vitamin supplementation is a very common practice, despite the lack of firm evidence supporting it.

Most people who take supplementary vitamins do so in the belief that the extra vitamins are necessary for optimal health and peak performance. Others take vitamins just to be sure they get enough. While it is true that vitamin deficiencies impair overall health and athletic performance, and that correction of deficiencies improves health and performance over what it would have been in a deficient state, vitamin deficiencies severe enough to impair health and performance are rare in the U.S.

As for those who take vitamins "just to be sure they get enough," there is no evidence that vitamin supplementation improves performance in people who do *not* have symptoms of deficiency—even in athletes with low blood levels of those vitamins.

This study is one of the first placebo-controlled, double-blind, cross-over studies to look at effects of long-term multivitamin and multimineral supplementation on athletic performance.

Thirty experienced male runners, recruited from a local running club, participated in this experiment. The nine-month study was divided into 3 three-month periods. During the first three months, fifteen runners received daily vitamin and mineral supplements, and fifteen received placebo. During the second three months (the "washout period"), neither group received either supplements or placebo. During the final three months, the experiment was reversed: the group that initially received placebo received supplements, and the group that initially received supplements received placebo. At no time did either the researchers or the subjects know who was getting vitamins and who was getting placebo.

All subjects continued their regular training throughout. At zero, three, six, and nine months (that is, at the beginning of the study and at the end of every three-month period) subjects were tested on treadmills.

There were no significant differences between the vitamin- and mineral-supplemented group and the placebo group in any of the parameters measured, including peak treadmill speed, oxygen uptake, maximal heart rate, peak blood lactic acid concentration, or time in a 15 kilometer race.

Thus, three months of multivitamin and multimineral supplementation did not cause any significant changes in the physical performance values measured. This suggests that young, healthy athletes who take vitamin and mineral supplements are not receiving benefits beyond those available from taking placebo. ❑

Vitamin and Mineral Supplementation: Effect on the Running Performance of Trained Athletes
Lindsay M. Weight MSc et al.
American Journal of Clinical Nutrition
V 47: 192-5, Jan 1988

QUESTIONING THE BENEFIT OF AMINO ACID SUPPLEMENTS

If you are an athlete or bodybuilder in good health and eating a balanced diet, which of the following statements about amino acid supplements are true?

1) *They help you build muscle*
2) *They increase your endurance*
3) *They promote fat loss*
4) *They facilitate muscle repair*
5) *They are necessary to prevent dietary amino acid deficiencies*

If you believe the advertisements and promotional material of supplement manufacturers and promoters, you might think that all of the above statements are true. In fact, every one of these statements is *false*.

Amino acid supplements have never been shown to benefit endurance athletes or bodybuilders who are in good health and eat balanced diets.

Protein and Amino Acids

Dietary amino acids come from dietary protein. Protein molecules are, in fact, nothing more than long strings of amino acids linked together end-to-end, like beads on a necklace.

But the athlete's body doesn't need protein per se. Rather, it needs the amino acids that constitute the protein. So the daily protein requirement is, in fact, a daily amino acid requirement.

Dietary protein is broken down into component amino acids by stomach and intestinal enzymes. These component amino acids are absorbed through the intestinal lining, then travel to liver, muscle, and other organs where they are reassembled into new proteins. Excess amino acids are metabolized and stored as glycogen or fat.

There are approximately 20 amino acids thought to be of biologic importance (*approximately* because the importance of some amino acids is still a matter of scientific debate). The human body can manufacture all but nine of these. These nine—histidine, isoleucine, leucine, lysine, methionine, phenylalanine, threonine, tryptophan, and valine—are termed *essential* amino acids. (Histidine, an essential amino acid for infants, may or may not be essential for adults.) Since the essential amino acids cannot be synthesized by humans, they must come from dietary sources. Estimated requirements for the eight amino acids known to be essential for adults is shown in the box on page 272.

Exercise *does* increase the body's demand for protein (that is, increases its demand for amino acids), in several different ways. Exercise causes a breakdown of muscle protein, resulting in a slight increase in amino acid requirements. The increase is slight because most of the amino acids released from exercise induced protein breakdown are quickly recycled to make new protein.

Exercise also stimulates new muscle growth. New muscle requires new amino acids, increasing the total daily requirement.

Lastly, amino acids serve as a source of fuel. During endurance exercise, some amino acids are metabolized into glucose (blood sugar). The glucose, in turn, is taken up by the muscles and used to power muscle contraction. Amino acids probably provide about five percent of the total energy for exercise. Most of the amino acids metabolized for fuel are **branched-chain** amino acids—**leucine, isoleucine,** and **valine.** These branched-chain amino acids come primarily from breakdown of liver proteins (not muscle proteins, as is commonly believed).

While the use of branched-chain amino acids as fuel might lead one to think that endurance athletes need more branched-chain amino acids in particular, this doesn't appear to be true. There is no evidence that endurance athletes need significantly more branched-chain amino acids than non-athletes.

Amino Acids as Fuel

The combination of these three uses of amino acids with exercise-increased muscle protein breakdown, increased muscle growth, and protein as fuel—leads to the conclusion that athletes have somewhat higher protein requirements than non-athletes. How much higher is a matter of some debate.

The Food and Nutrition Board of the National Academy of Sciences/National Research Council has established the Recommended Daily Dietary Allowance for protein at 0.8 g/kg/day for adults. The American Dietetic Association recommendation for athletes is slightly higher—1.0 g/kg/day. That means, for example, that an adult male athlete weighing 176 pounds (80 kg) needs to eat about 80 grams of protein per day.

Others, however, place the recommended intake somewhat higher. One researcher has recommended 1.0 to 1.2 g/kg/day

Protein Requirements

for male endurance athletes, and 1.3 to 1.6 g/kg/day for strength and power athletes. Another has recommended values as high as 2.0 g/kg/day.

How does this compare to the amount of protein athletes normally get?

In one study of university football players, dietary protein intakes exceeded even the highest recommended levels. In addition, 18% took protein supplements *on top* of their already high dietary intakes. Similar results were found for members of a university track team.

This strongly suggests that athletes are not protein deficient. Even taking into account their increased metabolic demands, they appear to be consuming protein well in excess of their dietary requirements.

Growth Hormone

Clearly, athletes do not need to take amino acid supplements to make up for any dietary deficiencies.

However, there are other reasons athletes take amino acid supplements. One of these is for presumed effects on human growth hormone.

Human growth hormone, also called **HGH** and **somatostatin,** is a hormone produced by the pituitary gland, a pea-sized organ located at the base of the brain. Growth hormone has a number of effects, including stimulation of muscle growth (see human growth hormone article on page 211 in the *Drugs* chapter). Although growth hormone increases muscle size and definition, it does not increase muscle strength. Rather, it seems to increase the amount of connective tissue in muscle with no increase in muscle fiber size. The result is muscles that are bigger-appearing, but functionally weaker.

There are several factors that increase release of growth hormone from the pituitary gland, including sleep, stress, exercise, certain drugs, and certain amino acids. The amino acids marketed as "growth hormone releasers" are usually combinations of arginine and ornithine.

There is in fact some evidence to support amino acids as growth hormone releasers. In one study, blood growth hormone levels increased sevenfold after ingestion of 1.2 grams of arginine and 1.2 grams of ornithine. There was no response to either amino acid alone. In another study, an immediate increase in growth hormone release was seen in a subject who took very high doses of arginine (250 mg/kg, or 20 grams for a 176 lb. person).

However, there is no evidence that the temporary increase in blood growth hormone levels caused by the amino acid ingestion resulted in any increase in muscle mass.

Most of the other studies that show amino acids having an effect on growth hormone levels have required either intravenous administration of amino acids, or whopping oral doses.

Side Effects of Amino Acid Supplements

Excess protein—and, by the same token, amino acid supplements—can cause dehydration and calcium loss. It can also strain the liver and kidneys, which must get rid of the excess.

Large doses of single amino acids can cause amino acid imbalances and toxicities. As far back as 1944 it was recognized that feeding excessive amounts of certain single amino acids to rats with otherwise balanced diets resulted in decreased growth. Phenylalanine, tyrosine, tryptophan, cystine, methionine, homocystine, histidine, threonine, glycine, and serine have all been shown to have toxic effects when taken in disproportionately large amounts. Recently, there is some data suggesting that large amounts of ornithine increase risk of cancer in mice.

In essence, taking large doses of single amino acids for their pharmacological effects (for example, increasing growth hormone release) is taking drugs. Recognizing this, the Health Protection Branch of the Canadian Government has reclassified single amino acid supplements as new drugs, and has suspended their distribution until more is known about their effects and side effects.

If amino acid supplements do indeed cause a physiologically significant increase in growth hormone release, athletes who take them may be at risk for developing **acromegaly.** Acromegaly is a disease of excess growth hormone production, in which muscles appear well-developed but are actually quite weak and easily fatigable. Other changes with acromegaly include thickening of certain bones leading to deformities of the face, skull, hands, and feet; diabetes; high blood pressure; heart disease; and nerve disease. Most acromegalic changes are irreversible, and half of all people with acromegaly die by age fifty.

Finally, amino acid supplements are expensive.

ESTIMATED DAILY ESSENTIAL AMINO ACID
REQUIREMENTS IN ADULTS (IN MG)

	ISOLEU.	LEUCINE	LYSINE	MET/CYS*	PHE/TYR*	THREON.	TRYPT.	VALINE
In mg/kg/day	12	16	12	10	16	8	3	14
For a 176 lb. (80 kg.) adult	960	1280	960	800	1280	640	240	1120

SOME SOURCES OF ESSENTIAL AMINO ACIDS (MG)

FOOD	ISOLEU.	LEUCINE	LYSINE	MET/CYS*	PHE/TYR*	THREON.	TRYPT.	VALINE	COST
Skim milk (2 cups)	1010	1636	1326	574	1612	754	236	1118	$0.20
2 eggs	756	1062	816	678	1184	594	194	870	$0.20
1/2 chicken breast; skinless, roasted	1409	2002	2266	1080	1959	1127	311	1324	$1.20
Amino acid supplement A (6 pills)	900	900	900	900	900	900	900	900	$2.00
Amino acid supplement B (20 pills)	800	1240	1080	1200	1240	650	0	320	$3.20

A 176 lb. adult can get just about all the essential amino acids he or she needs for one day from two cups of skim milk, from two eggs, or from half a chicken breast. To get roughly the same amount of essential amino acids from two commercial supplements, you would have to take six pills of one supplement ($2.00) or *twenty* pills of another ($3.20). In addition to costing less and testing better, the food gives you vitamins and minerals the supplements don't.

Adapted from Amino Acid Supplements: Beneficial or Risky? / J. Slavin PhD et al. / Physician and Sportsmedicine / V 16 #3:221-224, March 1988; and Food Values of Portions Commonly Used, 14th ed. / Pennington and Church / Harper and Row /167-196, 1985

Methionine and cysteine do not have individual daily requirements because cysteine can be synthesized from methionine in the human body. You can get by with no cysteine and a lot of methionine, or some cysteine and less methionine. The total requirement, however, remains the same. Consequently, the requirement is given as the total amount of methionine and cysteine needed. Similarly, pheylalanine and tyrosine do not have separate requirements, as tyrosine can be synthesized from phenylalanine. The requirement is given as the total amount of phenylalanine and tyrosine needed.

Amino acid supplements have never been shown to be of any benefit to athletes, are unnecessary from a nutritional standpoint, are potentially dangerous, and are expensive. At the moment, athletes are poorly informed about the questionable value of these products. However, until athletes become better informed, or until the U.S. Government makes moves similar to those of the Canadian Government, amino acid supplements will continue to be marketed as a shortcut to title winning athletic performance and physique. In the meantime, *caveat athleta* (let the athlete beware) for both pocketbook and health. ❏

Amino Acid Supplements: Beneficial or Risky?
J. Slavin PhD RD et al.
Physician and Sportsmedicine
V 16 # 3: 221-224, March 1988

Protein as a Fuel for Endurance Exercise
G. Lynis Dohm PhD
Exercise and Sports Science Review
14: 143-73, 1986

Effects of Ingestion of Disproportionate Amounts of Amino Acids
A. Harper, N. Benevenga, R. Wohlhueter
Physiological Reviews
V 50 # 3: 428-558, July 1970

Growth Hormone and Athletes
J. Macintyre
Sports Medicine
V 4 # 2: 129-142, March-April 1987

SUCCINATES

Succinates, according to the advertisements, are dietary supplements that can "supercharge" your workout. Supposedly, they give you extra energy, allowing you to do longer, more intense workouts.

Succinates are involved in the body's energy-producing process. One way the body gets energy is by breaking down glucose into carbon dioxide and water. At one point in the process, glucose is temporarily converted into succinate. Moments later, this succinate is converted into another substance, and continues on the pathway to becoming carbon dioxide and glucose.

In this sense, succinates are "partially broken-down" glucose.

But is there any real evidence that succinate supplements increase energy?

It turns out there is essentially no published data on humans to back up the claims for "supercharging" your workout. One ad for succinate supplements cites two studies—a 1970 study in *Biochemistry Journal*, and a 1986 study in *Experimental Biology*—as evidence. However, these studies were done in oxygen-starved rat and cat heart tissue, not in exercising humans. Furthermore, neither study supported the use of succinate supplements because neither study even *looked* at the ergogenic effects of succinate.

A recent study in the *Journal of Applied Sports Science Research*, however, *did* look at the ergogenic effects of oral succinates. Fasted mice were given either large doses of succinate or salt water, then swum to exhaustion. The mice given succinate swam about 15% longer, but only when they received the succinate in a single large dose two hours before exercise. Smaller doses of succinate made no difference in swim times, nor did large doses given less than two hours before exercise.

This experiment indicates that, while small doses don't seem to be effective, a large single dose of succinate (much larger than found in most supplements) may enhance endurance in fasted mice when given two hours before exercise.

And in humans? The authors conclude that "applicability of these results in humans is unknown at present." Further research may eventually prove succinate supplements to be effective in humans, but at the moment there is no evidence that it is. ❏

Anaerobic Rat Heart: Effects of Glucose and Tricarboxylic Acid-Cycle Metabolites on Metabolism and Physiological Performance
D. Penney and J. Cascarano
Biochemistry Journal
V 118: 221-7, 1970

The Anaerobic Heart: Succinate Formation and Mechanical Performance of Cat Papillary Muscle
R. Wiesner, J. Ruegg, and M. Grieshaber
Experimental Biology
V 45: 55-64, 1986

Succinate Effect on Mouse Swimming Performance
M. White and L. Bucci
Journal of Applied Sports Science Research
V 2 # 3: 52-59, August/September 1988

FALSE VIEWS ABOUT BORON AS A TESTOSTERONE STIMULANT

Boron is a trace element. It is required for the healthy growth of certain higher plants, but its role in animal nutrition is unknown. It does not appear to be a necessary nutrient for humans.

A recent article in a popular muscle magazine stated that boron supplements are "a safe, natural way to increase testosterone levels." The article went on to note that "this supplement is now available in health food stores all around the country. For those inclined to experiment, it [taking boron supplements to increase testosterone] seems a workable idea."

The article was referring to a 1987 study appearing in the *FASEB (Federation of American Societies for Experimental Biology) Journal.* That study examined the effects of aluminum, magnesium, and boron on calcium metabolism in postmenopausal women. It seems dietary boron supplementation not only may help decrease bone calcium loss in postmenopausal women, it also increases blood levels of testosterone.

However, the blood chemistry of postmenopausal women and the blood chemistry of healthy young male bodybuilders are not at all the same, especially when it comes to male hormone levels. The fact that boron supplementation increases testosterone levels in postmenopausal women sheds no light on what boron does in healthy young males.

What's more, there's evidence that boron supplementation adversely affects the male reproductive system. In high concentrations, boron suppresses growth, causes skin and hair changes, decreases weight of testes and ovaries, and alters testicular cellular structure in rats. At very high concentrations it interferes with sperm production. These changes in the male reproductive system are thought to be caused by a boron-induced *decrease* in the activity of testosterone and other androgens.

Boron is found in certain fruits and vegetables. Supplementation with amounts common to diets high in fruits and vegetables may prove to be a reasonable way for postmenopausal women to decrease risk of osteoporosis. However, there is no evidence that boron is a "testosterone releaser" for healthy young male or female athletes. ❑

Effect of Dietary Boron on Mineral, Estrogen, and Testosterone Metabolism in Postmenopausal Women
F. Nielsen PhD et al
FASEB Journal, V 1: 394-7, 1987

THE LIMITED BENEFIT OF CARNITINE SUPPLEMENTS

Muscles can use several different substances as fuel for energy production. One of these, **free fatty acid** (which comes from fat), becomes the primary fuel during prolonged submaximal exercise, such as running a marathon or doing a 100-mile bicycle race. When your muscles oxidize free fatty acid as part of the energy production process, another substance—called **carnitine**—plays an important role.

Supplement manufacturers have capitalized on this by distributing carnitine pills, touted to increase endurance. Taking the pills is supposed to increase the amount of carnitine available within muscle cells. This, supposedly increases fatty acid oxidation, and thus, endurance.

Does carnitine supplementation in fact increase endurance? In a recent study, members of a group of healthy, untrained subjects were given two-gram oral doses of either L-carnitine or a neutral substance (placebo). Supplementation continued daily for fourteen days. Then, during the next fourteen days, the subjects who had been getting the L-carnitine were given the placebo, and those who had been getting the placebo, the L-carnitine.

Three times during the study—before the supplementation began, after fourteen days (when the switch was made from one substance to the other), and after twenty-eight days—the subjects were tested at different exercise intensity levels for amount of carbon dioxide in their exhalations (a measure of how hard their aerobic systems were working) and heart rate. Researchers also determined the subjects' maximum heart rates and maximum aerobic capacities.

The entire procedure was then repeated with another group of subjects, with the supplementation period for each substance increased to twenty-eight days. The subjects showed no significant differences in either maximum heart rate or maximum aerobic capacity for placebo versus L-carnitine supplementation.

The bottom line? The authors conclude that "...carnitine supplementation may be of little benefit to exercise performance." ❏

The Effect of Oral Supplementation with
L-Carnitine on Maximum and Submaximum
Exercise Capacity
C. Greig et al.
European Journal of Applied Physiology
V 56 # 4: 457-460, July 1987

EFFECTS OF CHOLINE INGESTION ON ENDURANCE

Choline is a commonly advertised supplement, often touted as a "fat burner."

By "fat burner" the advertisers are claiming that choline mobilizes fat from fat stores into the bloodstream, where the fat is utilized for fuel. There are substances, such as caffeine, that promote mobilization of fat from fat stores. These substances can improve endurance, because they cause more energy to be drawn from fat stores and prolong limited muscle glycogen stores.

If supplemental choline is indeed a "fat burner," it might be expected to improve performance in endurance exercise just as other fat-mobilizing substances do.

Does choline improve endurance?

Researchers from the Human Performance Lab at Ball State University in Muncie, Indiana gave athletes supplemental choline to find out. Endurance-trained cyclists received either 1.1 grams of choline, 1.8 grams of choline, or a choline-free placebo. They were then tested on several prolonged strenuous stationary bike rides. Diet was controlled for choline intake.

The cyclists showed significantly higher blood choline after supplementation. However, they showed no improvement in performance.

This suggests that, while choline from supplements does get into the bloodstream, it does not have enough of a fat-mobilizing effect to make a difference in endurance performance.

These findings call into question the "fat burning" properties of supplemental choline. ❏

Effects of Choline Ingestion on Endurance Performance
J. Burns et al.
Medicine and Science in Sports and Exercise
V. 20 # 2: S25, April 1988

SPIRULINA

Spirulina is a blue-green algae grown in ponds, from which it is harvested, dried, and sold as a supplement. Ads aimed at athletes call spirulina a "superfood," stating that its nutrients increase energy and endurance, build muscle mass, stimulate the immune system, and help make "strong, clean cells."

What are the nutrients in spirulina? Like most food, it contains *some* protein, carbohydrate, fat, vitamins, and minerals. But does it contain enough of any of them to make any difference?

It doesn't look like it. The U.S. Nutrition Co. Inc. of Farmingdale, N.Y. was selling spirulina tablets in bottles whose labels stated the tablets were a dietary and nutritional supplement. The FDA ruled that this was "false and misleading labeling," since "no nutrients were present in sufficient amounts to significantly supplement the diet."

It's hard to justify calling something that has no nutrients present in sufficient amounts a superfood. And incidentally, none of the athletic claims for spirulina has been adequately supported by scientific evidence. ❑

FDA Consumer
V 22 # 9: 37, November 1988

BAKING SODA AS AN ERGOGENIC AID

One of the limiting factors of short, high-intensity exercise is the accumulation of lactic acid. Lactic acid, a by-product of anaerobic energy production, builds up in muscle tissue and blood and causes fatigue. When it builds up to a certain point, fatigue becomes so overwhelming that the athlete has to stop.

In your body there is a substance, **bicarbonate**, that helps neutralize lactic acid. The more bicarbonate in your bicarbonate reserves, the more lactic acid can be neutralized, and the more fatigue can be delayed. In your kitchen there is a related substance, *sodium* **bicarbonate**, commonly known as baking soda, that also has the potential to neutralize lactic acid. Ingesting baking soda has been shown to increase the body's bicarbonate reserves.

This suggests that ingesting baking soda may improve performance. However, studies investigating whether baking soda does in fact improve performance have yielded mixed results—some showing improvement, some not. Often, the studies showing no improvement used doses of baking soda which were too low to increase body bicarbonate reserves. To clarify the role of dose, these researchers experimented with higher doses of baking soda.

Six trained runners ran three 400 meter races a week apart. The first week they ran to establish a baseline time. The second and third weeks, they again ran 400 meters, but an hour before the race they drank a sports drink solution to which either baking soda or a placebo (calcium carbonate) had been added. Baking soda was added in the amount of 400 mg/kg, or about 30 grams (8-3/4 teaspoons, the equivalent of 15 Alka Seltzers) for these roughly 165-pound athletes.

Times for the 400 meter run improved significantly, decreasing by an average of 1.52 seconds (from 58.46 to 56.94 seconds). A 1.52 second improvement represents over a ten-meter lead at the finish line.

Lactic acid build-up plays a greater role in limiting short, high-intensity exercise (such as the 400 meter run) than in limiting prolonged, submaximal exercise (such as a 10 K). Consequently, the ergogenic effects of baking soda are probably more pronounced in short, high-intensity exercise. However, baking soda has been shown to cause improvements in more prolonged exercise as well, such as 15 minute runs and stationary bicycling to exhaustion. Very short events, such as the 100-yard dash, are not likely to show improvement, since lactic acid does not have sufficient time to build up.

Lest it appear that baking soda is the ideal ergogenic aid, be warned that it has at least one significant side effect. In a similar experiment, half the runners experienced "urgent diarrhea" about an hour after taking the baking soda. Since many athletes who compete in track events participate in more than one event in a day, or in more than one heat, and since starting times often change, timing baking soda ingestion to avoid untimely episodes of urgent diarrhea might be tricky. For athletes who don't experience urgent diarrhea, this ought not be a problem.

Aside from urgent diarrhea, no other side effects from a single large dose of baking soda have been reported. Long-term effects are as yet unknown.

[Ed. note: "If a little is good, a lot must be better" definitely does not apply here. Although no side effects other than diarrhea have been reported for single doses at these amounts, safety at still higher doses or with repeated high doses has not been established. Doses higher than those used here have the potential to cause significant electrolyte abnormalities, abnormalities that can be potentially life threatening, especially to people with kidney problems. (Electrolytes are blood components, such as sodium and potassium, that are responsible for maintaining proper salt-and-water balance.) In addition, sodium bicarbonate is over 25% pure sodium by weight, which can be a problem to those who need to cut down on their sodium intake. Anyone who considers using baking soda as an ergogenic aid should do so only under a doctor's supervision.] ❑

Induced Metabolic Alkalosis and its Effects on 400-M Racing Time
J. Goldfinch, et al.
European Journal of Applied Physiology
V 57: 45-8, Jan 1988

Bicarbonate Ingestion and Anaerobic Performance
N. Glenhill
Sports Medicine
V 1: 177-80, 1984

EQUIPMENT

In most sports today, athletes are faced with many decisions about equipment and accessories. Often the athlete's safety is at issue. This chapter looks at the effectiveness of a variety of training and protective gear.

RELIABILITY OF HEART RATE MONITORS

Heart rate is a convenient and reliable indicator of exercise stress. The usual exercise recommendation for aerobic exercise, in fact, is based on heart rate: raise your heart rate to 60 to 80% of its maximum (roughly 220 minus your age) for at least 15 minutes at least three times a week.

Many athletes rely on commercial heart rate monitors to keep track of their pulses, thereby better targeting their workout. But according to a recent study, these devices can be unacceptably inaccurate.

Researchers tested three commercially-available heart rate monitors designed for exercise use. They found all to be accurate for resting heart rate, giving readings within about 2 to 3 beats per minute (bpm) of standard EKG (electrocardiogram, or heart tracing) readings. However, for subjects walking or running on a treadmill, they found anywhere from 20 to 70% of the readings were off by more than 20 bpm, and at times over 50% of readings were off by over 50 bpm.

The authors conclude that "none of the machines examined can be described as either accurate or reliable." They attribute the inaccuracy to an inability of the monitors to detect pulse without "picking up interference due to movement and giving grossly erroneous readings." For the athlete trying to get an edge on his or her training, the sedentary American trying to improve cardiovascular health, or the heart attack victim doing some cardiac rehabilitation, heart rate monitors giving "grossly erroneous readings" are unhelpful at best and dangerous at worst.

[Ed. note: Unfortunately, the authors did not reveal which brands were tested, nor how these brands were selected. This makes it difficult to determine whether the inaccuracies encountered with the three monitors tested are likely to be found in other brands as well. Nonetheless, that three were tested and none found to be accurate or reliable calls the accuracy and reliability of all exercise heart rate monitors into question.] ❑

The Accuracy and Reliability of Commercial Heart Rate Monitors
M. J. Burke, MSc and M. V. Whelan, PhD
British J. of Sports Medicine
V 21 # 1: 29-32, March 1987

MINI-TRAMPOLINES FOR AEROBIC EXERCISE

Minitrampolines are one of the more recent arrivals on the home exercise equipment scene. They are promoted as providing the cardiovascular (aerobic) benefits of running, without the risk of shin splints or foot and ankle injuries that running or aerobics can bring on. Do minitrampolines really measure up to the claims?

Four studies have investigated the benefits of training with minitrampolines. All used similar durations of exercise (30 to 40 minute bouncing sessions, 3 to 5 sessions per week, for 8 to 10 weeks) but used different measures of exercise intensity. Improvements in aerobic capacity were, depending on the study, "minimal improvement," 4.5% improvement, 9.0% improvement, and 11.5% improvement.

The 4.5% to 11.5% figures indicate that minitrampolines improve aerobic capacity about as much as aerobic dance, cycling, walking, or jogging. The studies also found that, depending on how vigorously you bounce, energy expenditure on minitrampolines can vary from approximately that of a brisk walk to rivalling that of an eight-minute mile run. On average, though, minitrampolining probably meets the American College of Sports Medicine recommendations for an exercise that improves cardiovascular health.

The variance from study to study probably stems from the difficulty in standardizing bouncing intensity. Intensity can vary considerably, depending on the number of bounces per minute, how high the feet are lifted, and whether bouncing is done by lifting knees up in front or by keeping knees stationary and kicking feet straight back. When done with a high number of bounces per minute, with knees lifted high on each bounce, minitrampolining can be quite a good aerobic exercise. An additional increase in aerobic intensity (of 26% to 60%) can be gained by pumping hand-held weights while rebounding.

Minitrampolining can be a convenient, relatively inexpensive, and relatively injury-free way to exercise. These studies suggest that, if done properly, it can be good for your heart as well. ❑

Rebounding Exercise: Are the Training Effects Sufficient for Cardiorespiratory Fitness?
J. F. Smith and P. A. Bishop
Sports Medicine
V 5 # 1: 6-10, Jan 1988

EYEGUARDS FOR RACQUET SPORTS

A racquetball or squash ball can travel at speeds in excess of 100 mph and can carry more energy than a .22 caliber bullet. The most vulnerable site for injury from these high-speed missiles is the eye. Small wonder that eye injuries are a major concern for participants of racket sports.

But many brands of protective eyewear available on the market are less-than-adequate, and may give the wearer a false sense of safety and security. In fact, there are only seven models that currently meet the standards of safety set by the Canadian Standards Association and/or the American Society for Testing and Materials.

Since the late 1970's, the Canadian Standards Association has overseen experiments using high-speed film to assess adequacy of eyeguards.

They have found that:

- Lensless eyeguards provide *no* protection against ball-in-the-eye injuries (which cause 95% of eye injuries in racquetball). They do not prevent racquetball and squash balls from hitting the eye.

- Eyeguards with lenses, while adequate to prevent direct injury, may still have their frames shatter under impact.

- Ordinary prescription lenses, glass or plastic, can shatter, and therefore offer inadequate protection.

Nor does experience protect a racquet sport player; in fact, experienced players may be more likely to suffer a serious injury, since they rarely take their eyes off the ball.

The United States Squash Racquets Association, for its part, has made eyeguards mandatory for all USSRA-sanctioned tournaments. The military services, and many private clubs, YMCA's, and universities have mandated eyeguards for all indoor racquet sports as well.

Eyeguard models that meet Canadian and/or American Standards:

- Action Eyes (Viking Sports, San Jose CA)
- Albany (LST Leader Sports Products Inc., Essex NY)
- CRS 300 (CRS Sports Int'l, Edmonton, AB, Canada)
- Defender 600 (Peepers Int'l, New York NY)
- New Yorker (LST Leader Sports Products Inc., Essex NY)

- Safe-T Eye-Guard (Embassy Creations, Holmes PA)
- Sports Scanner (American Optical, Southbridge MA)
- ❏

Eye Protection in Racket Sports: An Update
The Physician and Sportsmedicine
V 15 # 6: 180-192, June 1987

COMPARING ROWING MACHINES TO CYCLING MACHINES

For years, the cycling machine was the primary piece of home equipment available for indoor aerobic exercise. Recently, however, sales of rowing machines have challenged those of cycling machines. Sales literature on rowing machines touts their workout as aerobically superior, citing the fact that rowing machines work both upper and lower body. But do rowing machines really provide a better aerobic workout than cycling machines?

Researchers from Dartmouth Medical School recently compared maximal aerobic output on rowing and cycling machines in both collegiate women rowers and untrained women. Importantly, they used a *variable resistance* rowing machine. Not all rowing machines provide variable resistance. Variable resistance is important in achieving maximal aerobic output, because good rowing technique (and thus maximal aerobic output) is compromised with a stroke rate exceeding twenty-eight to thirty-two strokes per minute. A variable-resistance rowing machine can provide appropriate resistance at ideal stroke rates.

A total of twenty-nine women participated in this study. For both the rowing and cycling machines, the resistance was increased every minute until the subjects reached exhaustion.

Maximum ventilatory rate and maximum carbon dioxide production are two measures that reflect maximum aerobic output. Both the trained rowers and the untrained subjects showed greater maximum ventilatory rate and greater carbon dioxide production on the cycling machines than on the rowing machines. Peak power production was significantly greater on the cycling machine for both groups.

This suggests that cycling machines provide a better aerobic workout than rowing machines. However, this study does not evaluate the anaerobic component of either exercise. Because many athletes use rowing machines for both the aerobic and anaerobic benefits, the question of which provides a better overall workout depends on the goals of the individual athlete. From a purely aerobic standpoint, cycling machines appear to be better. ❏

Comparison of Exercise Performance on Rowing and Cycle Ergometers
D. A. Mahler et al.
Research Quarterly for Exercise and Sport
V 58 # 1: 41-46, March 1987

MARGINAL BENEFITS OF RUNNING WITH HAND WEIGHTS

Many runners and walkers have begun carrying small hand weights during their aerobic training to increase the aerobic demand and promote upper body strength. They may not be getting the benefits they're looking for.

Twenty healthy male runners between the ages of 25 and 45 were tested for aerobic capacity and for peak strength in certain upper body muscles: elbow flexors and extensors (the muscles that bend and straighten the arm) and shoulder flexors and extensors (the muscles that raise the arm forward and up, and pull the arm back and down).

The runners were then randomly assigned to either the experimental or control group.

Over the next eight weeks, all subjects maintained their normal running routine. The experimental group ran with light hand weights, carrying 1.0 pounds in each hand during weeks one and two; 2.0 pounds in each hand during weeks three through five; and 3.0 pounds in each hand during weeks six through eight.

At the end of the eight week period, researchers measured the subjects' aerobic capacity and upper body strength again.

Results showed no significant strength gains or increase in maximum aerobic capacity for the runners using the hand weights.

The authors conclude that "the lack of significant strength gains and the possibility that the extra weight may add additional impact stress on the lower extremities indicates that light hand weights are of marginal value as an adjunct for long distance running in relatively well-trained individuals."

[Ed. note: Other studies have indicated that running or walking while carrying light hand weights does require slightly more energy and does increase oxygen consumption slightly. This current study, however, suggests that these small increases probably fail to translate into measurable increases in strength or aerobic capacity.] ❏

Effects of Exercise With Light Hand Weights on Strength
Allison Ewing et al.
Journal of Orthopaedic and Sports Physical
Therapy
V 8 # 11: 533-536, May 1987

The running shoe has two primary purposes: absorbing shock and providing foot stability. How well it performs these tasks depends on shoe design, shoe materials, age, and wear.

The most important part of the shoe is the **midsole.** The midsole is primarily responsible for cushioning the runner against the high impact forces of running. While shoe manufacturers have made substantial improvements in midsole design and construction during the past ten years, the midsole remains the part of the shoe most vulnerable to change over time, deteriorating long before the rest of the shoe.

Most high-quality running shoes have midsoles constructed of ethylvinyl acetate (EVA), compression molded EVA, or polyurethane, all materials that deteriorate with age and wear. Some shoes have pockets of gel or air, or mechanical coils, but the primary midsole material remains EVA or polyurethane.

What happens to running shoes as miles go by? To find out, researchers gave new pairs of running shoes to each of six experienced runners. Before beginning training and every two weeks thereafter, the runners (and their shoes) were put through a battery of tests, over a total of six weeks and more than 300 miles.

Result: at the end of the six weeks, several measures pointed to a significant decrease in the shoes' shock-absorbing ability. Other changes suggested a breakdown and hardening of midsole materials.

However, while shock-absorbing ability seemed to worsen over the course of the experiment, foot stability—the other primary function of running shoes—seemed to *improve.* It appears that, as the midsole hardens, it provides more side-to-side (medial-lateral) stability for the foot, resulting in greater foot control. Foot control accounts for at least half of running-shoe related injuries. Thus, changes seen in running shoes with age and wear are not necessarily all bad.

However, once once the midsole hardens to the point of no longer acting as an effective shock absorber, the shoe loses much of its ability to prevent impact injuries—despite imparting greater foot control.

In other words, there is a trade-off. As the shoe ages, it loses shock-absorbing ability, increasing risk of impact injuries, but gains in foot stability, decreasing risk of foot control injuries.

RUNNING SHOES

An important implication of this study is that a shoe may not be at its best when brand-new. A few minutes spent walking around the shoe store in a new pair of shoes may not be the best way to judge their eventual performance, because the initial "feel" of a new pair of shoes may not be the best criteria for judging. Certain changes, some of which may improve the function of the shoe, occur during the first several hundred miles of wear. ❑

A Kinetic Evaluation of the Effects of In Vivo Loading on Running Shoes
J. Hamill PhD, B. Bates PhD
Journal of Orthopaedic and Sports Physical Therapy
V 10 # 2: 47-53, August 1988

BICYCLE HELMETS

About 75% of the more than 1,000 bicycling fatalities occurring every year in the U.S. are caused by head injuries. In an attempt to lower this grim statistic, new attention is being focused on the potential for bicycle helmets to prevent head injuries.

The purpose of a bicycle helmet is to provide maximal protection while causing minimal impairment for the rider. This is necessarily a trade-off. A thick, heavy, cumbersome helmet might protect but might not be worn; a thin, light, minimally-bothersome helmet might be worn but might not protect.

In fact, the first helmets were more like the latter. They were made of leather and soft foam, but provided little protection. New approaches, borrowing proven techniques from hockey helmet and mountain climbing helmet design, resulted in the development of the current generation of bicycle helmets.

Helmet Components

A bicycle helmet should have four components: **shell**, **liner**, **comfort pads**, and a **retention system**.

The Shell

The shell is the outermost part of the helmet, the "first line of defense" in any accident. In contrast to earlier shells, which used soft leather, most current shells use a hard plastic, usually polycarbonate (Lexan) or fiberglass.

The shell should be rigid, to distribute an impact over as wide an area as possible; have a relatively low degree of friction, to slide over rough areas (such as asphalt) without "catching"; and be strong, to protect against penetration by rocks or car door handles.

Some approved helmets do not have a hard plastic shell. In general, these models do not stand up as well as do models with hard shells.

The Liner

While it is the responsibility of the shell to distribute the impact over as wide an area as possible, it is the responsibility of the liner to absorb the impact. The liner is usually made of some kind of "crushable" foam, such as Styrofoam, that permanently deforms as it absorbs the impact. Resiliant foams, such as foam rubber, do not absorb the impact as well,

▌

BICYCLE HELMETS APPROVED BY THE AMERICAN NATIONAL STANDARDS INSTITUTE AND/OR THE SNELL MEMORIAL FOUNDATION

ACI Century	Brancale SP-4	Maxon
ACI Targa	Brancale XP-5	Monarch Super
Avenier	Cycle Products	Tour
Avenier Advantage	Etto	Monarch Trackstar
Axent	Giro	MSRNava
Bailen BH-1	Hanna Pro HP-1	Pro-Tec Breeze
Bailen BH-2	Hanna Pro Model	Pro-Tec Mirage
Bell L'il Bell Shell	500	Vetta Corsa
Bell Stratos	Kiwi K25/K35	Vetta Super Corsa
Bell Tourlite	Kiwi KB/K15	Vetta Touring II
Bell V1-PRO	Lazer EM	
Bell Windjammer	Lazer LZ1	

and transfer more of the impact to the head. Consequently, resiliant foams do not protect as well.

Comfort Pads

Comfort pads are pieces of foam and cloth placed to position the helmet snugly and comfortably on the head. Comfort pads do more than simply ensure comfort; they also position the helmet on the head so that the shell and liner can protect most effectively.

Retention System

The retention system consists of those parts concerned with keeping the helmet on—the chin strap, chin strap buckle, and devices for attaching the chin strap to the helmet. The retention system must ensure that the helmet stays in place during normal cycling and in the event of an accident.

Two groups, the American National Standards Institute (ANSI) and the Snell Memorial Foundation, are the most widely recognized bicycle helmet-evaluation agencies. They put commercially available helmets through a variety of tests, including impact tests. The helmets that meet or exceed the standards of either testing agency are listed (see box).

The most important standard for a helmet to meet is that of impact-absorption. For ANSI approval, a helmet must withstand an impact of 300 g's (a deceleration force equal to 300 times the force of gravity). The Snell standard is even higher.

Some controversy surrounds the choice of foam for the liner. A denser foam affords better protection for accidents involving higher impact, but doesn't protect as well for accidents involving lower impact because it does not deform enough. Conversely, a less-dense foam affords better protection for accidents involving lower impact, but doesn't protect as well for accidents involving higher impact because it deforms completely before all the impact has been absorbed. Ongoing research may resolve this controversy soon.

What about comfort? Cyclists are concerned about how much they may be trading comfort for safety. And any decrease in comfort, whether from loss of coolness, ventilation, sweat control, or increased weight from the helmet, can compromise performance.

As it happens, most of the helmets that have the ANSI or Snell stamp of approval do not interfere with cooling, ventilation, or sweating. Furthermore, hard-shell helmets weigh only 16 to 20 ounces; cyclists generally adjust quickly to this amount of weight.

It should be noted that, since crushable foams *permanently* deform, a helmet that has survived an accident will probably be at least partially damaged. A damaged helmet is not safe, and the damage is not always readily apparent. A helmet that has survived an accident should be replaced or returned to the manufacturer for evaluation. Also, the materials used in helmet manufacture have finite lifespans. A helmet that has been frequently used for five years or so should be replaced.

Interest in the use of bicycle helmets is growing. The U.S. Cycling Federation requires wearing of approved helmets for all U.S.C.F.-sanctioned events. California has recently passed legislation requiring ANSI-approved helmets for all children aged four and under on bicycles, whether as riders or passengers. A school program emphasizing bicycle safety in Seattle resulted in increased helmet use. Using an approved bicycle helmet is probably the best way for a cyclist to keep from becoming a "grim statistic."

[Ed. note: *While empirically it makes sense that bicycle helmets might decrease incidence and severity of head injuries, to date there is little strong evidence supporting this position. Nevertheless, until there is concrete evidence to the contrary, wearing bicycle helmets seems to be a prudent thing to do.]* ❑

Safety Standards for Bicycle Helmets
Edmund R. Burke, PhD
Physician and Sportsmedicine
V 16 # 1:148-153, Jan 1988

SPORTS BRAS

Proper protective gear is essential for reducing risk of injury and allowing pain-free sports performance. Unfortunately, few styles of sports bras, the piece of protective gear most needed by women, have been designed to reflect findings on the biomechanics of breast motion.

In general, existing research supports the recommendation that all female athletes employ some sort of breast support while exercising, to reduce the risk of breast injury and the incidence of soreness. The primary goal of the sports bra is to minimize vertical displacement of the breasts during exercise.

This current study examined eight sports bras for effectiveness in this regard.

Four of the eight bras tested performed well in terms of limiting vertical displacement. In order, starting with the most effective, they are:

- **Exercise Sports Top.** Manufactured by Creative Sport Systems, 147 Hearthstone, Irvine, CA 92714. (714) 733-1425.

- **Lady Duke.** Manufactured by Royal Textile Mills, Box 250, Firetower Rd., Yancyeville, NY 27379. (800) 334-9361.

- **Freedom Frontrunner.** Manufactured by Olga, 7900 Haskell Ave., Van Nuys, CA 94109. (818) 782-7568.

- **Sports Bra.** Manufactured by Lily of France, 136 Madison Ave., New York, NY 10016. (212) 696-1110.

General guidelines cited by the authors for best choice are as follows:

Cup Size

Large-breasted women should choose a more-rigidly constructed bra, with less elasticity in fabric and straps. Small-breasted women have a greater range of options, and may find a stretchy bra to be more comfortable while still providing adequate support.

Sport of Choice

Women engaged in sports requiring much overhead reaching, such as basketball and volleyball, should use a sports bra with elastic straps to prevent the bra from riding up over the breasts. Women engaged in sports requiring running, jumping, or kicking but little overhead reaching are better served by a bra with inelastic straps that attach directly or almost directly to a non-elastic cup.

Protection Needs

Women who participate in contact sports should consider using a **breast protector** (a pad that can be inserted into the sports bra cup) to provide additional protection.

Design and Construction

Best choice is a bra with non-slip straps and no potentially irritating seams or fasteners next to the skin. Also important: A silhouette that holds the breasts in a rounded—as opposed to pointed—shape, close to the body. A rounded shape results in less breast motion. ❑

Selected Sports Bras: A Biomechanical Analysis of Breast Motion While Jogging
Deana Lorentzen PhD and LaJean Lawson MS
Physician and Sports Medicine
V 14 #11: 128-139, May 1987

SIDE EFFECTS OF KNEE BRACES

Knee injuries are the most common injury in college foot-ball. They threaten not only the performance of the team but the injured player's immediate and long-term physical functioning. A number of knee braces have been designed in attempts to protect the player from injury, especially ligament tears from impact against the side of the knee. But two separate studies indicate that those wearing prophylactic (protective) knee bracing may actually *increase* their risk of knee injury.

One study looked at a single major college football team, and compared the rates of knee injuries when all players were required to wear knee bracing to rates of knee injuries when no players were required to wear knee bracing. All athletes in this study wore the Anderson Knee Stabler.

The second study examined data from seventy-one NCAA Division 1 schools. Many different makes of braces were worn in this study.

Both found rates of knee injury significantly higher when braces were worn than when braces were not worn. The two studies disagreed on the severity of the injuries: the multi-school study found no difference in the severity, while the one-school study found a substantial increase in severity. (This increase in severity was partially reflected in the fact that during the braced period almost twice as many knee operations were required.)

Controlling for factors such as player positions, playing surfaces, mechanisms of injury, skill levels, and type of brace did not change the fact that braced players sustained more injuries.

The increased incidence of injuries while wearing knee braces designed to *prevent* injuries may be due to decreased agility caused by the braces, carelessness on the part of players who believed themselves to be protected from injury, or from differences in knee load distribution adversely affecting knee stress.

The braces also resulted in complaints of thigh muscle cramping, required frequent attention to ensure proper positioning and state of repair, and were expensive—averaging about $400.00 per player per season.

These two studies indicate that prophylactic knee braces do not prevent injury and may in fact put the player at greater risk. ❑

Prophylactic Knee Bracing in College Football
G. D. Rovere, MD et al.
American Journal of Sports Medicine
V 15 # 2: 111-116, 1987

Evaluation of the Use of Braces to Prevent Injury to the Knee in
Collegiate Football Players
C. C. Teitz MD et al.
Journal of Bone and Joint Surgery
V 69-A # 1: 2-9, January 1987

Nautilus weight machines have become common fixtures in gyms across the country. Their claim to fame is a specially designed eccentric cam, which delivers resistance that varies across the range of motion of the exercise. The purpose is to provide resistance that is better matched to the strength curve of a given muscle—more resistance where the muscle is stronger, less resistance where the muscle is weaker—resulting in a better, more uniform workout.

Great in theory, but does it work? Five Nautilus machines were studied (arm curl, chest fly, leg extension, leg flexion, pullover) to see how closely they matched the human torque (human strength at every angle throughout the motion) to the machine resistive torque (machine's resistance at every angle throughout the motion).

Result? "There was little correspondence between machine resistive torque patterns and human torque capability curves for the muscle groups examined."

As an example, with both chest fly and knee flexion machines, machine resistive torque *increased* continuously throughout most of the movement while human torque *decreased* by 80%.

The author concludes, "...cam shapes would require considerable modification to achieve closer correspondence between machine resistive torque and human torque capability patterns."

[Ed. note: Although Nautilus is the best-known brand of eccentric cam-based machines on the market, it is not the only one. Others, such as Icarian, Eagle, and Polaris, are available. This study only dealt with Nautilus, and then only with five machines from the Nautilus line. It would be valuable to see a more complete assessment of this segment of the weight training market, to see if other machines share the same flaws in cam design as these five.] ❑

Resistive Torque Analysis of Five Nautilus Exercise Machines
Everett Harman
Medicine and Science in Sports and Exercise
V 15 # 2: 113, 1983

CAM-BASED RESISTANCE MACHINES DON'T PROVIDE APPROPRIATE VARIABLE RESISTANCE

BREAKAWAY BASES

Some 40 million Americans, from teenagers to seniors, play softball. Though a reasonably safe game, injuries do still occur. Surprisingly, 71% of recreational softball injuries occur from one aspect of the sport: base sliding.

Base sliding injuries include abrasions, sprains, ligament strains, and fractures of the legs and arms. The medical costs of these injuries can be considerable: a knee sprain evaluated and treated in a hospital emergency room can easily come to $200 to $400, and if surgery is required, costs can top $10,000.

Several approaches have been tried in attempts to decrease base sliding injuries. One approach, outlawing base sliding altogether, has met with a predictably cool response from devotees of the game. A second approach, holding instructional seminars on safe sliding, is appealing but probably impractical: since one out of six Americans plays softball, the numbers are too vast to deal with effectively. Furthermore, since many players participate only occasionally, seminars requiring learning a new set of motor skills would be of limited benefit over time.

A promising new approach is the use of the "breakaway base." Unlike the conventional base, which is firmly rooted in the field, the breakaway base is made to release on impact. It has two parts: a rubber mat and the base itself. The rubber mat is flush with the ground and anchored as would be a conventional base. The mat has rubber nipple-like projections that engage with the overlying base, holding the base firmly until it is acted upon by a strong lateral force such as a base slide. When acted upon by such a force, the mat and base separate.

Many of the sliding injuries are caused by the sudden deceleration of sliding into an unyielding base. This sudden deceleration is substantially lessened with breakaway bases, suggesting that breakaway bases should make a difference in injury statistics.

To see whether they really do make a difference, researchers tabulated the incidence of base sliding injuries from over 1,250 softball games. About half of these games were played on fields with stationary bases, and half on fields with breakaway bases. Otherwise the fields underwent identical maintenance and were exposed to identical weather conditions.

There were forty-five sliding injuries on the stationary base fields, but only two sliding injuries on the breakaway base fields, a significant difference. Total medical costs for the stationary base injuries were $55,050; for the breakaway base injuries, $700.

The breakaway bases did not detach except during base slides, did not significantly delay the games, and (according to the referees) did not interfere with referees' judgment calls.

Breakaway bases appear to lower significantly the risk of base sliding injuries. Certainly base sliding injuries will continue to occur, as other predisposing factors—such as poor sliding technique, poor timing, poor physical conditioning, and alcohol consumption—continue. However, breakaway bases can make America's favorite pastime safer for everyone. ❑

Softball Sliding Injuries: A Prospective Study Comparing
Standard and Modified Bases
D. Janda MD et al.
Journal of the American Medical Association
V 259 # 12:1848-1850, March 25 1988

INDEX

Index

growth hormone, 211
Hydrostatic weighing, 135

I

Injuries
    cold therapy for sprains, 197
    compartment syndrome from
        cross-country skiing, 185
    consequences of triathlons, 189
    effect of ultrasound on tendons, 198
    emotional responses to injury, 176
    foot nerve damage in runners, 188
    from aerobic dance, 178
    from breakaway bases, 300
    from overuse, 174
    low back pain in retired athletes, 177
    martial arts, 190
    NCAA injury survey, 193
    nerve damage from push-ups, 196
    overtraining, 14
    prevention with indomethicin, 221
    reduction of injuries through
        fitness, 172
    risk factors for football, 194
    shin splints, 180
    taekwondo, 192
    tendon deterioration from
        steroid use, 203
    variation among runners, 187
    weight training and muscle repair,
        104
Isometric training
    response to angular specificity, 47
    versus isotonic exercise, 45

J

Jumping
    effect of motivational jumping on, 29
    plyometric training for, 41

K

Keto acid dehydrogenase
    role in energy production, 238

L

Lactic acid
    effects of baking soda on, 280

warming down after exercise, 13
Learning
    its effect on performance, 52
Long distance running
    See running

M

Magnesium, 261
Martial arts injuries, 190, 192
Maximal oxygen uptake (VO2 max)
    as measure of aerobic fitness, 4
    effect of weight training, 116
Metabolic rate variation and
    exercise, 31
Minerals, 257
    average intakes, 251
    chromium, 258
    copper, 259
    dietary requirements, 257
    effects of exercise on blood levels,
        257
    magnesium deficiency, 261
    See also nutrition
    supplementation, 248
Mini-trampolines, 284
Motivation and competition, 63
Muscle
    anatomy, 86
    and the nervous system, 93
    angular specificity in isometrics, 47
    breakdown and rebuilding, 99
    effect of growth hormone, 211
    electrical activity and fatigue, 107
    fatigue, 105
    fatigue and injury, 174
    fiber recruitment, 120
    fiber types, 88
    injury prevention, 221
    isometric versus isotonic training, 45
    mass and performance limiting
        factors, 109
    neurological activity and load
        intensity, 112
    training and the rate of repair, 104
    training the rotator cuff, 43
    using anti-inflammatory drugs to
prevent soreness, 218
Muscle tissue protein
    effect of exercise on, 99
Muscle-boundedness, 35

N

Nervous system
    and muscular reponse, 93
    and muscular response to weight
        load intensity, 112
    reaction and mental focus, 65
Neuromuscular Electrical Muscle
Stimulation
    See electrical muscle stimulation
Nutrition
    average vitamin and mineral
        intakes, 251
    combining caffeine and car-
bohydrates, 245
    demands of athletic training on, 226
    fasting and physical activity, 246
    healthy levels of vitamin B-6, 253
    possible side effects of carbo
        loading, 241
    problems of using hair analysis, 263
    vitamin and mineral supple-
        mentation, 248

O

Overtraining, 14

P

Pain management during exercise,
    33
Performance
    consequences of passive smoke
        inhalation, 170
    effect of cocaine, 216
    effect of learning, 52
    effect of lowering body
        temperature, 67
    influence of motivational states, 63
    response of weightlifting to aerobic
        exercise, 118
    role of genetics in, 129
    specificity of training, 97
    task-specific training, 29
    weightloss for competition and
        dehydration, 168
Periodization
    See weight training
Physiology
    muscle anatomy, 86
Plyometrics, 41, 60

SynerShape: A Scientific Weight Loss Guide

We're surrounded by weight loss myths. Crash diets. Spot reducing. Exotic herbs. Still, most plans fail, and most people who lose weight gain it back again. Is there really an honest, effective solution? **Yes!** **SynerShape** represents the next generation in awareness of how the body gains and metabolizes fat. It synthesizes the most recent findings on nutrition, exercise, and psychology into a TOTAL program, offering you the tools you need to shape the body you want. **SynerShape** works. Let it work for *you! A 24 p. illustrated manual.*

The Psychology of Weight Loss

This special program-on-tape picks up where **SynerShape** leaves off. Noted psychologist Carol Landesman explores eating problems and *solutions* based on the latest research into human behavior and metabolism. Then, through a series of exercises, she helps you begin to heal the emotional conflicts behind your weight problem. **The Psychology of Weight Loss** is a unique program that brings the power of the therapy process into the privacy of your home. *A 90-minute guided introspection. On audio cassette.*

SynerStretch: For Total Body Flexibility...FAST!

Two programs in one: Both deliver lower and upper body flexibility in less than 8 minutes a day! **Syner-Stretch A** is for you if you need to maintain your flexibility. Originally designed for martial artists—who depend on extreme flexibility— **SynerStretch A** will also help bodybuilders, dancers, and other athletes stay flexible in less than *5 minutes per workout.* A great way to end a training session of any kind! **Syner-Stretch B** is for you if you need to increase your flexibility. Not only does it take less than 8 minutes, but because it makes use of a new, relatively unknown technique (Isometric Agonist Contraction/Relaxation), it eliminates most of the pain usually associated with stretching. It works! When you order **SynerStretch**, you get both programs in one manual. Get loose, and stay loose with **SynerStretch**. *A 28 p. illustrated manual.*

Power ForeArms!

Here at last is a program that specifically targets the hard-to-develop forearm muscles. Like all Health For Life programs, **Power ForeArms!** is based on the Synergism principle, and yields maximum results in minimum time. Designed for serious bodybuilders and martial artists, **Power ForeArms!** will help you build strong, solid, massive forearms in just 7 to 12 minutes, twice a week. Give **Power ForeArms!** a try. *A 32 p. illustrated manual.*

Maximum Calves

Imagine reducing calf workout time to just fifteen minutes, twice a week! That's exactly what **Maximum Calves** does. For the serious bodybuilder, **Maximum Calves** is the secret to piling on mass. For the martial artist, gymnast, or tennis player, it's the key to supercharged footwork and incredible ankle stability. The course also includes a full calf flexibility program to keep you loose as you gain strength and mass. Fast and secure footwork is the foundation for superior athletic technique; symmetry and mass are essential elements of a winning bodybuilder's physique. Whatever your training goal, **Maximum Calves** will help you achieve it! *60 pp. Over 100 illustrations.*

For price and order information, call **1-800-874-5339**
(in California, call **1-800-523-9983**), or write us at...

Health For Life
8033 Sunset Blvd., Suite 483
Los Angeles, CA 90046